Oral Histories of Older Gay Men in Hong Kong

Queer Asia

The Queer Asia series opens a space for monographs and anthologies in all disciplines focusing on non-normative sexuality and gender cultures, identities and practices across all regions of Asia. Queer Studies, Queer Theory, and Transgender Studies originated in, and remain dominated by, North American and European academic circles. Yet, the separation between sexual orientation and gender identity, while relevant in the West, does not neatly apply to all Asian contexts, which are themselves complex and diverse. Growing numbers of scholars inside and beyond Asia are producing exciting and challenging work that studies Asian histories and cultures of trans and queer phenomena. The Queer Asia series—first of its kind in publishing—provides a valuable opportunity for developing and sustaining these initiatives.

Selected titles in the series:

As Normal as Possible: Negotiating Sexuality and Gender in Mainland China and Hong Kong
Edited by Yau Ching

Boys' Love, Cosplay, and Androgynous Idols: Queer Fan Cultures in Mainland China, Hong Kong, and Taiwan
Edited by Maud Lavin, Ling Yang, and Jing Jamie Zhao

Conditional Spaces: Hong Kong Lesbian Desires and Everyday Life
Denise Tse-Shang Tang

Contact Moments: The Politics of Intercultural Desire in Japanese Male-Queer Cultures
Katsuhiko Suganuma

Falling into the Lesbi World: Desire and Difference in Indonesia
Evelyn Blackwood

First Queer Voices from Thailand: Uncle Go's Advice Columns for Gays, Lesbians and Kathoeys
Peter A. Jackson

Gender on the Edge: Transgender, Gay, and Other Pacific Islanders
Edited by Niko Besnier and Kalissa Alexeyeff

Obsession: Male Same-Sex Relations in China, 1900–1950
Wenqing Kang

Queer Bangkok: 21st Century Markets, Media, and Rights
Edited by Peter A. Jackson

Queer Politics and Sexual Modernity in Taiwan
Hans Tao-Ming Huang

Queer Singapore: Illiberal Citizenship and Mediated Cultures
Edited by Audrey Yue and Jun Zubillaga-Pow

Shanghai Lalas: Female Tongzhi Communities and Politics in Urban China
Lucetta Yip Lo Kam

Undercurrents: Queer Culture and Postcolonial Hong Kong
Helen Hok-Sze Leung

Editorial Collective

Chris Berry (King's College London, UK), John Nguyet Erni (Hong Kong Baptist University, Hong Kong), Peter Jackson (Australian National University, Australia), and Helen Hok-Sze Leung (Simon Fraser University, Canada)

International Editorial Board

Dennis Altman (La Trobe University, Australia)
Evelyn Blackwood (Purdue University, USA)
Tom Boellstorff (University of California, Irvine, USA)
Pimpawan Boonmongkon (Mahidol University, Thailand)
Judith Butler (University of California, Berkeley, USA)
Ding Naifei (National Central University, Taiwan)
David Eng (University of Pennsylvania, USA)
Neil Garcia (University of the Philippines, Diliman, The Philippines)
David Halperin (University of Michigan, Ann Arbor, USA)
Josephine Chuen-juei Ho (National Central University, Taiwan)
Annamarie Jagose (University of Sydney, Australia)
Yinhe Li (Chinese Academy of Social Sciences, China)
Song Hwee Lim (The Chinese University of Hong Kong, Hong Kong)
Kam Louie (UNSW, Australia)

Lenore Manderson (Monash University, Australia)
Fran Martin (University of Melbourne, Australia)
Mark McLelland (University of Wollongong, Australia)
Meaghan Morris (University of Sydney, Australia)
Dede Oetomo (University of Surabaya, Indonesia)
Cindy Patton (Simon Fraser University, Canada)
Ken Plummer (University of Essex, UK)
Elspeth Probyn (University of Sydney, Australia)
Lisa Rofel (University of California, Santa Cruz, USA)
Megan Sinnott (Georgia State University, USA)
John Treat (Yale University, USA)
Carol Vance (Columbia University, USA)
Audrey Yue (National University of Singapore, Singapore)

Oral Histories of Older Gay Men in Hong Kong

Unspoken but Unforgotten

Travis S. K. Kong

Hong Kong University Press
The University of Hong Kong
Pokfulam Road
Hong Kong
https://hkupress.hku.hk

© 2019 Hong Kong University Press

ISBN 978-988-8528-06-6 (*Paperback*)

All rights reserved. No portion of this publication may be reproduced or transmitted in any form or by any means, electronic or mechanical, including photocopying, recording, or any information storage or retrieval system, without prior permission in writing from the publisher.

British Library Cataloguing-in-Publication Data
A catalogue record for this book is available from the British Library.

10 9 8 7 6 5 4 3 2 1

Printed and bound by Ocean Printing Co., Ltd. in Hong Kong, China

To All Older Male *Tongzhi*

Contents

Preface and Acknowledgements viii
Note on Romanization x

Introduction 1
1. Old Chan: Brokeback below the Lion Rock (1924–2013) 21
2. Brother Ming: Who Says There Are No Communist *Tongzhi*? (1935–2010) 29
3. Shmily: A Butterfly with 1,500 Male Lovers (1949–) 40
4. David: A Charming Liar (1946–) 53
5. Robert: A Banished Expatriate Officer in the Royal Hong Kong Police (1947–) 65
6. Jonathan: A Gay Gambler Who Turned over a New Leaf (1948–) 76
Letters Provided by Interviewees 91
Photo Exhibition of *An Oral History of Older Gay Men in Hong Kong* (2014) 95
7. Uncle Lee: A Sunset *Tongzhi* (1940–2016) 101
8. May Wu: A Divine Woman's Poisons of Ignorance, Attachment, and Aversion (1940–) 109
9. Brother Shing: Only Men Understand Me (1944–) 121
10. Uncle Leung: A Lifelong Libertine Who 'Queered' around Hong Kong, Macao, and Canton (1945–) 130
11. Tommy: A Bisexual Butterfly (1949–) 138
12. Tony: The Bear Chaser (1950–) 149
13. Nigel Collett: A History Boy, a Military Man, a Writer, and an Activist (1952–) 161
Conclusion: Transformation of an Academic Project into Participatory Action Research 171

Glossary 179
Maps 182
References 183

Preface and Acknowledgements

Sexuality, as a distinct area of specialization within sociology, emerged internationally in the 1960s. Its development in Hong Kong and China came much later, in the late 1980s. I have been working in this neglected and taboo area since the mid-1990s, and homosexuality has become my principal area of research (Kong 2000, 2002, 2004, 2005, 2009). In 2011, I published my first monograph, *Chinese Male Homosexualities: Memba, Tongzhi and Golden Boy*, which is the culmination of over ten years of ethnographic study of the identities, intimacy, and sexual citizenship of post-war Chinese gay men in three major locales—Hong Kong, London, and China. In the course of completing this book, I found older gay men aged 60 or above are a missing piece of the puzzle of Chinese *tongzhi*—a Chinese synonym for lesbian, gay, bisexual, transgendered, and queer—history. They are marginalized in ageing studies, sexuality studies, and social history studies in Hong Kong. Starting in 2009, I began to address this gap, using the oral history method. This effort led to the publication of a Chinese book entitled *Oral History of Older Gay Men in Hong Kong* (2014), which documents twelve older gay men's life stories. Using their own voices, the book captures how the complexity of their lives is interwoven with Hong Kong history, as well as the difficulties and hardships they have encountered, especially due to their sexual orientation, from colonial to contemporary times. The book has a long and theoretical introduction, followed by the twelve life stories with short commentaries and academic remarks. It mixes academic analysis with autobiography. With the success of the Chinese book, now in its fourth reprint, I would like to share their stories with English-speaking readers who are interested in ageing, Hong Kong history, gay and lesbian studies, or Chinese sexuality. This English book is the translation of the Chinese book. I have revised the introduction, updated their stories, added one more story, and included a new conclusion that discusses new developments after the publication of the Chinese edition. I am very happy to see how this oral history project has eventually transformed into participatory action research through various community activities and public events such as book talks, seminars, media interviews, school sharing sessions and photo exhibitions with the outcome of setting up the first social self-help group for older gay men in Hong Kong called *Gay & Grey*.

Preface and Acknowledgements

I would not have been able to finish this book without the help of the following individuals, whom I would like to thank: Wilson Chiu for helping me translate the first draft of the book, Chris Berry for proofreading the whole manuscript and giving me invaluable advice, the two anonymous reviewers for giving me constructive comments, the editors of the Queer Asia Series for appreciating my work, Eric Mok and Clara Ho from Hong Kong University Press for their meticulous help and support, and Eva Li and Karen Laidler for their generous help in the final stage of proofreading. Moreover, this book would not be made possible without the initial publication of the Chinese book. I would like to thank Carol Lai Pui Yee and Kong King Chu, editor and publisher of the Chinese book respectively, for their generous help, and the University of Hong Kong's Knowledge Exchange Office for funding the publication of the Chinese book.

Hong Kong
March 2018

Note on Romanization

This book uses Cantonese romanization for Chinese words, names and phrases except in instances in which a preferred alternative spelling in the Hanyu Pinyin system is widely used (for example, *tongzhi* rather than *tungzi*). The book does not use English plural markers (e.g., *tongzhi* is used instead of *tongzhis*). All Chinese titles appear in the Glossary.

Introduction*

> To be gay . . . is not to identify with the psychological traits and the visible masks of the homosexual, but to try to define and develop a way of life.
> —Michel Foucault, 'Friendship as a Way of Life', 1996

There are many defining moments of *tongzhi*[1] history in Hong Kong: the criminalization of 'buggery' in 1842 when the British took over Hong Kong; the MacLennan incident in 1980, which triggered the subsequent ten years of public and legal debate over whether male homosexual conduct should be decriminalized; the arrival of AIDS in 1984 and its alleged association with gay men; the decriminalization of male homosexual conduct in 1991; the mushrooming of *tongzhi* organizations and the emergence of a substantial *tongzhi* consumption infrastructure, including bars, clubs, saunas, massage parlours, cafes, and bookshops beginning in the 1990s; the equalization of the age of consent from 21 to 16 between homosexuals and heterosexuals in 2005; the International Day against Homophobia (IDAHO) marches since 2005; pride parades since 2008, the inclusion of same-sex partners in a domestic violence ordinance in 2009; the public 'coming out' of pop stars Anthony Wong Yiu-ming and Denise Ho

---

* Some of the material in this introduction appeared in an earlier version in a different form as Kong (2012) and Kong, Lau, and Li (2015).

1. *Tong* (meaning 'same') and *zhi* (meaning 'ideal' or 'aspiration') exist in classical Chinese literature but the combination of the two words *tongzhi* was first used in 1911 to signify a revolutionary and political subjectivity "comrade" by Sun Yixian (or Sun Yat-sen), father of the modern Chinese nation, who encouraged Chinese people to fight against the Qing imperialist regime in the early twentieth century. His saying, 'the revolution has not been successful; comrades should fight for it until the end', became a famous slogan for the revolution in both the Republican and People's Republic of China eras. After the First Gay and Lesbian Film Festival, held in 1989, was referred to as the Tongzhi Film Festival by local gay writer Edward Lam, *tongzhi* suddenly became an umbrella term for people with non-normative genders and sexualities and a synonym for LGBTQ (lesbian, gay, bisexual, transgendered, and queer). The queer appropriation of the term became very popular in both the LGBTQ and straight communities in Hong Kong and then in Taiwan, and finally in the LGBTQ community in China. Its popularity may be due to its erasure of sexual connotation, unlike the clinical term 'homosexual' or the Western term 'gay', and its affirmation of a 'positive' rather than 'negative' (e.g., 'queer') identity (Leung 2008, 1–6; Kong 2011, 14–15; Bao 2018, 65–91; Kong, Lau and Hui 2019).

Wan-see, also known as HOCC, as well as legislative council member Raymond Chan Chi-chuen, in 2012; and Pink Dot Hong Kong since 2014, with the latest one in 2017 reported by the organizers to have attracted 11,000 people—straight and *tongzhi*—to celebrate inclusiveness, diversity, and the freedom to love.

Parallel with this social-historical transformation of homosexuality is the study of homosexuality, which started in the late 1980s but has focused overwhelmingly on post-war (i.e., second Sino-Japanese War [1937–1945]) *tongzhi* generations in Hong Kong. These studies have documented how *tongzhi* realize their same-sex desires; struggle with their sexual identity and thus their coming out stories; seek same-sex encounters; form intimate relationships; live in the stratified *tongzhi* worlds; challenge heterosexist assumptions in virtually all social institutions; fight for equality; and advocate activism and *tongzhi* movements (e.g., Ho 1997; Chou 2000; Ho and Tsang 2000, 2004, 2007; Kong 2002, 2004, 2005, 2011; Wong 2004, 2007; Yau 2005, 2006, 2010; Leung 2008; Tang 2011).

What is missing from this oversimplified history and the studies of homosexuality is the history of the early generations who were born before the 1950s and how they live their present lives. We know very little about the past of older *tongzhi*, from their problems of identity formation and issues with coming out to their struggles in creating a social and sexual space for community networking during the era when homosexuality was still a crime. We also know nothing about their present lives, and what problems they face in their private and social lives, both in the straight and the *tongzhi* worlds.

International research also shows that there is an acute research gap in our understanding of older gay men and lesbians (as well as other sexual minorities). They are under-researched in academic scholarship, under-represented in mainstream and queer popular cultures, invisible in social policy and social services, and marginalized even within the LGBTQ community. In short, they are an 'unseen minority' (Berger 1982) or 'a minority within a minority' (Jones and Pugh 2005). While the issue of sexuality is under-researched in the sociology of ageing, the issues of age and generation have also been relatively neglected in the sociology of sexuality (Plummer 2010). Only recently has research recognized the intersections between the two, attempting to capture the complexity and diversity of how ageing is experienced and negotiated (e.g., Heaphy, Yip, and Thompson 2004; Heaphy 2007; Cronin and King 2010; Cruz 2011; Suen 2015).

Older gay men and lesbians definitely constitute a missing piece of the puzzle of Chinese *tongzhi* history and also a marginalized area in ageing studies, sexuality studies, and social history studies in Hong Kong. As stated before, local (homo-)sexuality studies focus overwhelmingly on gay men (and lesbians) born in the 1950s or after. This is also the case in local *tongzhi* stories and novels (e.g., Chou, Mak, and Kong 1995; Chou 1996; Mak and King 2000; Kam 2001; Yip 2003, 2004). Moreover, local ageing studies assume their older participants to be heterosexual, failing to consider the specific experiences of older gay men (e.g., Yip, Chi, Chiu, Kwan, Conwell, and Cane 2003; Chou, Chow and Chi 2004; Cheng and Chan 2006; Yeung and Fung 2007; Phillips, Siu, Yeh, and Cheng 2008). Finally, the stories of older gay men are also absent from the social history of Hong Kong, which focuses overwhelmingly on heterosexual men and women in discussions of the emergence of an indigenous Hong Kong identity (e.g., Pun and Yee 2003; Mathews, Ma, and Lui 2008; Lui, Ng, and Ma 2011).

Oral Histories of Older Gay Men in Hong Kong aims to fill the gap by using an oral history approach to document and examine the lives of older gay men who were born before the 1950s, capturing how the complexity—the flux, ambiguity, and contradiction—of their lives is interwoven with Hong Kong's history. It seeks to understand how:

(1) they narrate and retell their past, especially how they managed same sex desires when they were young in the period when male homosexuality was defined and treated as a medical, legal, and moral aberration; how they realized their gayness; how they hung out, and where they went for social and sexual liaisons; how they related to the underground gay subculture or 'scene'; how they formed intimate relationships or families; how those who got married managed their double lives; and how they managed their closeted life at work.

(2) their earlier life experiences may inform their present life of being gay, male, and older, and especially how they negotiate ageing and sexuality: how they handle the ageing process and possible internalized homophobia; how they deal with their family, including parents, siblings, wives, children, and grandchildren (if any); how they cope with social isolation and ageism from the straight and the *tongzhi* worlds; and how they survive despite limited access to *tongzhi*-friendly health care and other social services.

Since 2010, I have been interviewing gay men aged 60 or above who have been living in Hong Kong for at least 30 years of their lives. Since 2012, I have held regular monthly *yum cha* ('drinking tea') gatherings at a local restaurant, followed by visits to a volunteer's home for a focus group discussion loosely on four themes: work, family, social services, and the gay community. These interviewees were mainly recruited through *tongzhi* and AIDS non-governmental organizations (NGO) using the snowball technique. As of 2015, I had formally interviewed fifteen such men. They were aged from 63 to 89. Eleven were born into the working class whilst four were from middle-class families. Seven had primary education, four had secondary education, and four had university education. All are Chinese except two, who are British and came to Hong Kong in the late 1970s and early 1980s respectively. All interviewees were born before the 1950s except one, who was born in 1952 but is over 60 years of age. Thirteen of these men's stories are presented in this book. Two were excluded as their deteriorating health precluded obtaining a complete portrait of their life histories. Consent was sought before recording. All names are pseudonyms and minor alterations to the biographies of the interviewees have been made for anonymity and confidentiality. The only exception is Nigel Collett, who preferred to use his real name. No alterations to his biographic details have been made.

Older Gay Men and Hong Kong *Tongzhi* History

First tongzhi *generation, colonial Hong Kong and familial heteronormativity*

It is evident that traditional Chinese society had a strong homosocial culture (Louie 2003), which tolerated men who had same-sex desires (Van Gulik 1961, 62–63; Ruan and Tsai 1987; Hinsch 1990; Samshasha 1997) and even men who possessed feminine beauty (Song 2004). The tales of *yutao* ('the peach remainder', pinyin), *duanxiu* ('the cut sleeve', pinyin), and Lord Long Yang are commonly cited euphemisms among the literati for male homosexuality in Chinese history. The social morality of male sexuality primarily concerned conformity to power hierarchies, within which men had to fulfil social expectations, including marriage and family, and secondarily the containment of excessive sexuality, as manifested in masturbation, prostitution, and so on (Louie 2003, 6–7). Although male same-sex relations were not seen as a threat to masculinity, they were always in a marginal position, subsumed under the Confucian patriarchal family and the institution of marriage. In other words, heteronormativity in ancient China, with the effect of marginalizing male same-sex relations, was not so much based around exclusive sexual orientation (same-sex desire) or sexual identity (the homosexual), but around the *normalcy* of being a son who must fulfil familial roles and social expectations.

Heteronormativity changed its form when Hong Kong became a British colony (1842–1997). Consistent with the colonial government's overarching ideology of 'law and order', buggery first became a crime in Hong Kong in 1842, when the colony was founded. In English law, buggery is a generic term which could mean anal intercourse between two men or between a man and a woman and between a man or a woman and an animal (Lethbridge 1976, 300–306). The criminalization of homosexual acts meant that buggery, whether private or public, consenting or coerced, involving persons of any age, as a pair or in larger groups—was a punishable offence. Other gay male practices such as 'gross indecency' (including fellatio, mutual masturbation) and 'soliciting' (any public indication of interest in sex) were also criminalized. It should be noted that male rather than female homosexual conduct was the main concern in legal cases then.

As a colony, Hong Kong followed English law closely. The death penalty for buggery, for example, was abolished in 1861 in England and in 1865 in Hong Kong; and the Criminal Law Amendment Act of 1885, dealing with acts of 'gross indecency' between males, was made into law in Hong Kong in 1901. The colonial government, however, did not follow suit with the UK's Sexual Offences Act of 1967, which decriminalized male homosexual conduct in private. It is believed that homosexuality was not even perceived as a social problem by the population before the 1980s, and thus the government had no intention of changing the law as such a move would have been considered too 'liberal' and 'radical'. This can be seen from the average of less than five arrests reported per year between 1842 and 1975, in strong contrast with the UK (Miller 1995, 280–81) or the US (Chauncey 1994, 9). Chinese homosexuals were highly discreet under British rule, and the few more 'visible' and 'outrageous' homosexuals were mainly Europeans who were usually sent back home, with their contracts un-renewed, or encouraged to resign. Both the colonial government and the population seemed to tolerate homosexuality as a 'necessary evil' (Lethbridge 1976, 306–10).

This tolerance of homosexuality can be explained by looking at the relationship between colonial governance and society especially since the post-war period when the population increased due to the civil war in China. There are two possible explanations. Under the minimally integrated-social-political system, Lau (1982) argues that the colonial government had no intention to interfere with the population and Chinese inhabitants relied on family rather than making demands on the government. The colonial government constructed colonial subjects with minimal civil, political, and social rights (So 2002; Ku and Pun 2004), and treated social welfare as a residual concept, with the underlying principle of charity and benevolence. Hong Kong Chinese thus sought help from their families, voluntary agencies, or the market, rather than from the government, to satisfy their welfare needs (Ho 2004). Under British rule, with the conditions of laissez-faire capitalism, Hong Kong Chinese families developed extraordinary discipline for hard work, fierce competition, and tight control over family members to improve family livelihood and wealth, a condition famously characterized by Lau (1982) as 'utilitarianistic familism'. This 'boundary politics' (Lau 1982, 163–72) was carefully played up by both parties, serving to differentiate the public space of the British colony and colonial polity from the private space of Chinese society. The tolerance of homosexuality could be viewed as an example of this functional explanation.

However, scholars increasingly view 'utilitarianistic familism' not as the 'inherent nature' of Chinese culture but as a strategy used by the colonial government to manage the refugee and immigrant families of post-war Hong Kong (Ong 1993; Law 1998; Ho 2004). These strategies, which Ong (1993, 753–62) calls 'family biopower' and Law (1998) calls 'colonial managerialism', shifted the site of governance from the state to the family. 'Family biopower' encoded a series of family practices and ideologies—symbolic, emotional, and utilitarian contractual obligations and mutual support—that regulated economic, productive, and hardworking Chinese bodies.

Whether one adopts a functional ('boundary politics') or a Foucauldian ('family biopower') explanation, the result is the same: the production of healthy, reproductive, and heterosexual bodies—the disciplined father, the sacrificing mother, the filial son, and the dutiful daughter—in post-war Hong Kong. A child's—especially a son's—sense of moral worth requires him to comply with parental wishes to marry, to continue the family bloodline, and to do nothing to harm family status and reputation (Kong 2011, 95–98). This largely explains why most Hong Kong *tongzhi*, especially the first *tongzhi* generation, were highly discreet and always worked within the parameters of the family institution. So how did men who had same-sex desires manage themselves when they were young, in the 1940s to 1960s?

Yatkayan, 'all in the family'

The Hong Kong population has always been over 90 per cent Chinese. After the end of the Japanese occupation in 1945, the Hong Kong population consisted overwhelmingly of returned immigrants and refugees from mainland China. It more than doubled in size from 625,166 in 1921 to 1,639,337 in 1941 and reached 2,360,000 in 1950 (Hong Kong Government 1952, 23; Faure 1997, 149). Government revenue relied heavily on land sales and taxes, as land development played a central role in Hong Kong's economic development. The colonial government adopted a policy of high land prices, resulting in half of the population living in crowded public housing (Cuthbert 1995, 298).

Most of my interviewees were working class, settling in Chinese tenement-type buildings, squatter homes built on hillsides or rooftops, or alleys (Rooney 2003, 18). In tenement buildings, floors were usually sub-divided into small rooms or cubicles (averaging 5.57 square metres), each floor accommodating three or four households, who shared a communal kitchen, latrines, and bathrooms (Hong Kong Government 1947, 54). Family members—immediate family as well as relatives and fictive kin—and neighbours formed a fluid collective mode of living under the same roof. This led to an 'all in the family' (Lau 1982, 74) notion being adopted by working-class families in the 1940s and 1950s, where mutual assistance and economic exchange, family ownership of property, and utilitarian cooperation became defining norms of 'utilitarianistic familism'.

'Home' has many meanings—'shelter', 'hearth', 'heart', 'privacy', 'root', 'abode', and 'paradise' (Somerville 1992; see also Gorman-Murray 2007). For the interviewees in this study, cramped, badly ventilated, unhygienic spaces, and quasi-kin communal familial living was their first experience of 'home'—a site of physical security and emotional and psychological comfort and support. The family home was where they learned to be filial sons and to work hard to contribute to the family economy in close relationships with other family members. Their parents taught them frugality, hard work, and compliance with the group—crucial components of the socialization process in the self-sufficient family system (Salaff 1981, 35).

The family home was also where heteronormative culture was fostered. Family members usually did not talk about sexuality, or did so mainly in heterosexual terms. No one mentioned homosexuality. The home, under the gaze of other household members, did not permit privacy or cater to the needs of men with same-sex desires. Heteronormativity was thus materialized in this site of territorialized power and regulatory practices, not so much from government intervention, but more under surveillance by family and other household members who silenced these young men's same-sex desires.

Most interviewees had no idea how to name their same-sex desires when they were young. They did not know the word 'homosexuality', or had not heard the traditional Chinese euphemisms *yutao*, *duanxiu*, and Lord Long Yang. This was long before the queer re-appropriation of the term *tongzhi* (see Footnote 1). They discovered their interest in men through playing with their relatives or neighbours (for example, Shmily, Tommy, and David). However, these homosexual encounters were usually fleeting and had to be carried out secretly. The boys who played together were usually not gay, just adolescents seeking sexual release. As rightly pointed out by Connell (1995, 149), young men's sexuality is a field of possibilities, not a deterministic system. This familial environment shaped how these young men discovered their same-sex desires, some through writing to pen pals (for example, Brother Shing), some reading scant published discussions, usually negative media reports about homosexuality (for example, Shmily, Brother Shing, and Brother Ming), but most through going to public spaces to find other gay men.

After their interactions with other gay men, or even the development of same-sex desire-based identities following participation in the gay 'scene' elsewhere, the family home often became a difficult place to inhabit. Hiding their same-sex desire and emerging identity became a pressing issue. They developed argots to communicate. As I learnt from them, especially through Uncle Leung, 'playing *mahjong*' came to mean 'having sex', and '*mahjong* tile' referred to the male organ. Public toilets were called *fayuen* ('gardens'; later, *yuetong*, 'fishponds'). *Yaufayuen* ('wandering around the garden'; later *potong*, 'wandering around the fishpond') or *diuyu* ('fishing') meant 'cruising' (US) or 'cottaging' (UK). As de Certeau's (1984) discussion of the tactics of introducing alternative meanings within a dominant cultural system indicates, these young gay men did not openly resist domestic heteronormativity; rather, they used covert tactics, such as argots and the cover of the homosocial overcoat,[2] to realize same-sex erotic experiences. As these men got older, however, parents urged them to marry. Marriage usually led to a double life, although some interviewees stayed single and lied to their family throughout their lives. In any case, all had to work within the parameters of familial heteronormativity.

The secret garden: The emergence of the early gay 'scene'

The colonial government's strict control and discrimination policies concerning the use of public space mainly focused on public hygiene (such as hawker control) and social problems like gambling (Too 2007, 31–36). In this situation, Hong Kong gay men found the space to develop a 'fishing' subculture. Before the 1980s, when public debate over homosexuality began in Hong Kong, the interviewees had not heard of the law governing homosexuality and had no idea that homosexual conduct was a criminal offence. They only believed it was a moral issue that would bring shame to the family. Family networks were crucial, and they mainly found work through family members, relatives, or neighbours. There were no exclusive spaces for homosexuals, only one or two Shanghai-style saunas for presumably heterosexual men (the most popular one was Yuk Tak Chee which was closed in 2006), a few hotel cafes, and secret parties or boat cruises catering for mainly the gay and lesbian middle-class, celebrities, and expatriates. We can grasp some of these scenes through the stories told by Jonathon, David, and Robert. For most gay men, public space became the major site for finding sex, love, and friendship. They sought privacy in public, as they had little freedom to express their sexuality in the 'privacy' of their homes. As Chauncey (1994) puts it succinctly in his description of pre-Stonewall gay subculture in New York, 'privacy could only be had in public' (179–206). The cruising ground was thus the site for the redefinition of public and private, where there was no freedom to be 'out' and no possibility of subscription to any identity or community (Bell 1995, 308).

My interviewees 'found' other gay men virtually everywhere—walking down streets, on ferries (Brother Ming), at street performances (Old Chan, Uncle Leung), in railway stations (Tommy, Jonathan), or in cinemas (Tommy and Jonathan). De Certeau (1984, 97) discusses walking as 'a process of *appropriation* of the topographical system on the part of the pedestrian' (emphasis original); 'queering the street' can thus be seen as a way to form queer consciousness through wandering, walking, looking, and being looked at. Such 'acts of operating' are moments of transgression that destabilize 'the assumed heteronormativity of urban public space with theatrical displays of queer affection desire

---

2. The homosocial overcoat relates to the idea of homosociality (e.g., Sedgwick 1990), which refers to a same-sex relationship that is not of a romantic or sexual nature but signifies friendship or mentorship. The latest colloquial term is 'bromance'.

and rage.' (Bell and Binnie 1998, 131) The public toilet was the most common site for 'fishing'. 'Fishing', like walking down a street, became almost a routine. Some would fish for immediate quick sex, but most went to public toilets to meet friends or catch up on gossip, which subsequently led to knowing more men with same-sex desires or even joining small gay subcultures. The public toilet was like Starbucks nowadays. This concept of 'fishing', a form of non-normative intimacy, redrew the public and private distinction and challenged normative intimacy. It was public in terms of location but private in terms of the intimate moment the participants shared. It was criminal intimacy, not just if sex occurred, but also because showing interest in sex publicly was considered 'soliciting'. But this eroticism outside of the conventional couple form gave these men tremendous pleasure, especially when there was no material gay space for them to go to. Affections formed with strangers and acquaintances could even develop into lifelong friendships or partnerships. We can read some beautiful (but mostly sad) love stories from Brother Ming.

This non-normative, even criminal, intimacy bears 'no necessary relation to domestic space, to kinship, to the couple form, to property, or to the nation' (Berlant and Warner 1998, 558), but it does bear a necessary relation to a 'counter-public': 'an indefinitely accessible world conscious of its subordinate relation' (ibid.). It was this network of erotic and non-erotic friends—acquaintances, friends, sex partners, lovers, and life partners—that provided a loose sense of 'gay community', a counter-public, or a heterotopia (Foucault 1986) that nurtured a local gay identity and facilitated sexual and social liaisons.

Decriminalization of Homosexuality and the Rise of the *Tongzhi* Identities and Movement

Public debate about homosexuality came to the surface when the Scottish police inspector John MacLennan, who was employed by the colonial police force then, was charged with acts of gross indecency and later committed suicide in his apartment in 1980. Some observers suggested that his death was a murder as he had access to a file that contained names of government officials who were suspected to be homosexuals. His death was thus seen as a result of a police cover-up, which raised media attention and brought into question the justice and integrity of the colonial government. The colonial government responded by appointing a judicial committee (Commission of Inquiry) to investigate the case and another committee (Law Reform Committee of Hong Kong) to review laws governing homosexual conduct. The Commission of Inquiry concluded in 1981 that the case was a suicide, with the Law Reform Committee publishing a report in 1983 recommending that male homosexual conduct be decriminalized (Ho 1997, 7–21; Chan 2007, 38–45). If the Stonewall Riot in New York in 1969 signified the formal beginning of the LGBTQ movement in the US, the MacLennan

Incident in Hong Kong in 1980 similarly paved the way for the *tongzhi* movement in Hong Kong. It was an opportunity for different social sectors to examine the prevalence of homosexuality and evaluate the appropriateness of pre-existing laws governing homosexual conduct (Wong 2004, 200).

The debate on the decriminalization of male homosexual conduct involved three main issues: whether homosexuality was scientifically proved to be normal; whether it was a 'Western' disease not found in traditional Chinese (family) culture; and whether homosexual activity was a human rights issue. The debate involved many parties. Among the most visible was the Joint Committee on Homosexual Law, an anti-decriminalization alliance formed in 1983 by Choi Yuen-wan, an evangelical medical doctor, and made up of thirty-one pressure groups consisting mainly of social workers, teachers, and church leaders. A loosely structured alliance arguing for decriminalization was also formed, consisting of a pool of academics, journalists, progressive thinkers, the Hong Kong Human Rights Commission, and a few gay men (Ho 1997, 61–93). Religion (particularly Protestantism and Catholicism) and Chinese tradition (in the name of the Chinese family) were two major weapons used by members of the anti-decriminalization coalition to present their arguments, while the pro-decriminalization alliance used the language of democracy and human rights to advance their own arguments. After a decade-long debate, a law decriminalizing male homosexual conduct was passed in 1991. Decriminalization, however, did not mean legalization. The colonial government only agreed to decriminalize male homosexual acts under certain conditions—two men aged 21 or above who engaged in consensual sex 'in private'. The colonial government had no interest in endorsing gay rights or even in recognizing a gay lifestyle. Sir David Ford, then Chief Secretary, summarized the debate in the Legislative Council as follows:

> A vote in favour simply signifies recognition that personal moral codes may differ and can co-exist in a society. Nor does a vote in favour signify a state of approval, it signifies only recognition of an individual's rights to personal choice in his private sexual matters. A vote in favour does not signify personal acceptance of the rightness or wrongness of such acts, but only suggests whether such acts committed between consenting adults and in private merit mobilisation of the full machinery of law enforcement. (quoted in Ho 1997, 84)

The final move to decriminalization was believed to have been a response to the newly introduced Bill of Rights and the urgent need to speed up legal and democratic reforms in the aftermath of the 1989 Democratic Movement in China (or known as the June Fourth Incident in Hong Kong), rather than an endorsement of gay rights or recognition of gay lifestyles by the government (Ho 1997, 75–80; Chan 2007, 39).

The 1980s thus marked the first wave of the Hong Kong *tongzhi* movement. It should be noted that very few gay men came out and fought for their own rights during the debate. The coming-out of *tongzhi* identity was almost absent and the right for gay men to engage in consensual sex in private was the primary concern. The first wave of the Hong Kong *tongzhi* movement was therefore a movement without *tongzhi* identity; it symbolized the politics of privatization that confined *tongzhi* rights to the sphere of 'private individual rights' rather than conceiving of them as 'human rights' (Kong 2011, 50).

Once the long debate over the decriminalization of male homosexuality (or, rather, male homosexual conduct) was over, the original legal debate was transformed into arguments about various social and moral disputes. Different parties, including the government, church people, social workers, teachers, lawyers, doctors, cultural workers, journalists, and more, whether pro- or anti-gay, contributed to policing a range of binary divisions: normality versus abnormality; heterosexuality versus homosexuality; masculinity versus femininity; Chinese tradition versus Western culture; and so on. The result was a separation between the straight-dominant culture and the *tongzhi* subculture, in the context of which a distinctive social type of 'homosexual' was subsequently generated. It is this 'homosexual' type that led to the development of homosexual identities in Hong Kong, including: *kei* ('gay'); *keilo* ('gay man'); *memba*;[3] *les* ('lesbian'); TB ('tomboy'); TBG ('tomboy girl'); pure; no label; *tungzi/tongzhi*; and others (Ho 1997; Kong 2011; Tang 2011).

Decriminalization had numerous effects in the 1990s. It not only protected gay men who engaged in private sexual acts, but also triggered the emergence of a range of '*tongzhi*-scapes' (c.f. Parker 1999, 218–21 on the notion of the 'homoscape') in Hong Kong. These included the emergence of *tongzhi* groups such as Hong Kong Ten Percent Club (formed in 1986 but officially registered in 1992), the Association for the Welfare of Gays and Lesbians (1989), Horizons (1991), 97 Tongzhi Forum (1992), Satsanga (1993), Isvara (1994), XX Gathering (1994), Queer Sisters (1995), the Blessed Minority Christian Fellowship (1995), Lui Tung Yuen (1996), Freeman (1996), Joint Universities Queer Union (1997) (later named as Joint College Queer Union), and the Hong Kong Tongzhi Conference (1996, 1997, 1998). The rise of a pink economy was also enabled and 'scenes' such as bars, discos, saunas, fitness centres, shops, and guest houses proliferated. Among them, the gay bar Dateline and the dance club Disco Disco (D.D.), both opened in the mid-1980s and closed in the early 1990s, were frequently mentioned by interviewees.

The colonial government took a guarded approach to political development, and the *tongzhi* movement was no exception. As a result, the movement has largely been framed around economic development (e.g., the burgeoning of commercial and consumption *tongzhi* venues such as bars, clubs, and saunas) and cultural expression (Kong 2011, 47–72). Before the 1980s, homosexuality was

---

3. 'Memba' is local parlance used exclusively by Hong Kong gay men for self-identification. It is a Cantonese derivative of the English term 'member'.

Cover of Ten Percent Club newsletter. Source: Interviewee.

only hinted at, or was pathologized, in popular culture and mainstream media (Kong 2005). In the 1990s, there was an increase in the visibility of representations of *tongzhi* in mainstream media, including in films featuring gay stories such as *Oh! My Three Guys* (dir. Derek Chiu, 1994), *Boy's?* (dir. Hau Wing-Choi, 1996), *A Queer Story* (dir. Shu Kei, 1997), *Happy Together* (dir. Wong Kar-wai, 1997) and *Bishônen* (dir. Yonfan, 1998). Specific *tongzhi* media also spread, such as the Hong Kong Lesbian and Gay Film Festival (1989–); *tongzhi* magazines and newsletters such as *Tongzhi New Wave* (1988) and *Contact Magazine* (1992); gay plays directed by Edward Lam; books and novels written by gay writers Edward Lam, Michael Lam, Julian Lee, and Jimmy Ngai; and more academic texts including writings by Samshasha, Chou Wah-shan, Anson Mak, Yau Ching, and Ho Sik-ying. Last but not the least, *tongzhi* cyberspace such as websites and chatrooms (e.g., http://www.gaystation.com.hk and http://www.gayhk.com) emerged, which provided an important means for *tongzhi* to identify one another through sexuality, language, and values.

The *tongzhi* movement in Hong Kong began to be more progressive in the 1990s with the building of the *tongzhi* identity as the major concern. *Tongzhi* groups in the 1990s were mainly self-help, service oriented, and community based in nature, with the aim of developing a positive self-identity. They tried hard to dissociate homosexuality from pathology, to downplay the 'sexual' aspect of the *tongzhi* identity, and to stress the similarities between heterosexuals and homosexuals (Kong 2011, 52–53).

Post-colonial Hong Kong and Older Gay Men

Hong Kong was handed over to China in 1997 and the new HKSAR (Special Administrative Region) government has actively promoted the heterosexual nuclear family as a core value, emphasizing close and mutually supportive relationships between the married couple and their parents and siblings as an essential part of 'Chinese culture' in its policy addresses in 2001, 2006 and 2011 (http://www.policyaddress.gov.hk). The government set up the Family Council in late 2007 to consolidate core family values and harmonious relationships among family members, thereby further institutionalizing familial heteronormativity.

This harmonious family model has the monogamous heterosexual nuclear family as its prototype, which is not so much the continuation of traditional Chinese culture (as polygyny was the norm) but more of a Christian (especially evangelical) ideal. As a continuation of the anti-decriminalization alliance of the 1980s, a new generation of evangelical Christians has taken up the mission to revive a strong Christian presence and monitor social and moral development through the establishment of organizations such as The Society of Truth and Light (1997), Hong Kong Sex Culture Society (2001), Hong Kong Alliance for Family (2003), New Creation Association (2003), and Family Value Foundation of Hong Kong Limited (2007). These groups, which Wong (2013) claims engage in 'evangelical activism', have a strong resemblance to the American Christian Right movement. They focus on sexuality as the central issue to advance their political agenda and emphasize the necessity to protect the dominance of the monogamous heterosexual nuclear family to restore social order and public morality. About ten per cent of the population is Protestant Christian (480,000) and Catholic (353,000) in Hong Kong, but they have significant presence in education, medical, and social services, as well as inside the government bureaucracy. Seventy-five per cent of the top administrative positions in the government are held by Christians (Wong 2013, 344). Hence, it can be argued that Protestantism and Catholicism have a certain influence over Hong Kong policy making.

It is in this context that we are witnessing a few battles between evangelical activism and the *tongzhi* movement. For example, the government planned to propose a Sexual Orientation Discrimination Ordinance (SODO) in 2004, but discussion was dropped due to strong opposition from the Hong Kong Alliance for Family as they gathered 10,000 signatures to show their worries that the law would promote an 'unhealthy' lifestyle and erode 'family values'. This incident also triggered the first IDAHO event in 2005. The second Chief Executive Donald Tsang, himself a Catholic, publicly opposed the court's decision for the equalization of the age of consent between homosexuals and heterosexuals and made an appeal in 2006. However, the Court of Appeal confirmed the High Court's decision in 2006. In 2009, the original 'Domestic Violence Ordinance' was changed to the 'Domestic and Cohabitation Relationship Violence Ordinance' following strong lobbying from evangelical groups to make the distinction that cohabitation does not equal marriage. In this way, they indirectly disqualified same-sex couples and relationships as valid family forms and valid intimate relationships.

New *tongzhi* groups have been formed such as Rainbow of Hong Kong (1998), Rainbow Action (1998), Civil Rights for Sexual Diversities (1999), F' Union (1999), *Tongzhi* Community Joint Meeting (1999) (later called Pink Alliance), Women's Coalition of HKSAR (2003), Fruits in Suits (2004), Nutong Xueshe (2005), Midnight Blue (2005), For My Colours (2008), Queer Straight Alliance (2008), Gay Harmony (2009), Big Love Alliance (2012), Hong Kong Scholars Alliance for Gender and Sexual Diversity (2013), Q action (2014), and many more. They have been more vocal and proactive in fighting for various *tongzhi* sexual citizenship rights. *Tongzhi* identity has become even more political and the movement has advocated a full notion of sexual citizenship, which ranges from conduct-based claims ('rights to various forms of sexual practices in personal relationships') to identity-based claims ('rights through self-definition and the development of individual identities') and to relationship claims ('rights within social institutions: public validation of various forms of sexual relations') (Richardson 2000, 107–8). They have sought the right to disclose sexual identity without being penalized, the right not to have to hide their sexual identity, the right to same-sex marriage or domestic relationship, and the right to accessing social and legal benefits (Wong 2004, 201–2). The pink economy has even further expanded. Local free gay magazine *Dim Sum*, for example, publishes a long list of venues and places (http://dimsum-hk.com/). The visibility of *tongzhi* in popular culture is increasing, including in gay-specific films such as Scud's trilogy *City without Baseball* (2008), *Permanent Residence* (2009) and *Amphetamine* (2010); gay plays such as *Queer Show* by Wong Chi-lung and Leung Cho-yiu; gay works by novelists such as Yip Chi-Wai; and various community online television channels such as G-spot TV, internet radio programmes and *tongzhi* websites (http://www.tt1069.com, http://blur-f.freebbs.tw/index.php) (Kong 2011, 64–66; Tang 2011).

Perhaps the most visible events are the IDAHO (Hong Kong Parade), the Hong Kong Pride Parade, and Pink Dot Hong Kong. Started in 2005, IDAHO (Hong Kong Parade), later renamed IDAHOT, International Day against Homophobia and Transphobia in 2012, aims to eliminate discrimination based on sexual orientation. Pride Parade started in 2008. It aims to celebrate *tongzhi* identity and pride, seek inclusion and justice, and challenge heteronormativity. Pink Dot Hong Kong, which started in 2014, includes many *tongzhi*-friendly straight participants. Participants range from few to tens of thousands. All these events tend to focus less on identity politics but more on the politics of difference to celebrate diversity and draw a wider audience in society.

Under such different social, political, and cultural circumstances, how do my interviewees live as older gay men in post-colonial Hong Kong?

The home of one's own

With the population of the small territory (1095 square kilometres) growing from three million in 1960 to seven million in 2010, housing has always been a big and thorny problem for the government. Since the 1960s, the government has taken an active role in developing public housing estates (including resettlement estates and low-cost public estates), establishing an infrastructure of new towns, and providing home ownership schemes and loans to the emerging lower middle class. The 1997 Asian financial crisis led to a collapse in property prices and prevented the first Chief Executive of the new HKSAR government from carrying out his pledge of 85,000 new flats a year. The government's public housing and high land-price policies have restricted the living space of most Hong Kong residents. By 31 March 2010, about 2.06 million people, or 30 per cent of the population, were living in public rental housing estates (http://www.censtatd.gov.hk). Although Hong Kong people have changed from homeless immigrants to public housing tenants or home-owning citizens, most are still subject to limited choices and conditions in choosing living environments and the financial burden of securing permanent homes.

Compared with the past, the living conditions of most interviewees are much improved. My working-class informants have moved from tenement buildings or squatter homes to public estates. Few could afford private flats, even with government assistance. They were manual workers or low-skilled clerks and all are now retired, some receiving social security allowances (such as from the Comprehensive Social Security Assistance Scheme). Their family homes are now more spacious and possess basic facilities such as a bedroom, living room with basic furniture, private toilet, bathroom, and kitchen. The communal living space has gone and family life has permitted more privacy. This new familial environment serves as both a site of resistance and surveillance.

Half of my interviewees are now living alone due to widowhood, separation, or divorce from their wives, or having never married. The other half live with their family members—wives, children, and/or siblings. For those who are living alone, their homes tend to be a place of security, free from surveillance, where they may resist heterosexual norms. However, they feel quite lonely and isolated after retirement and some may hang out with friends, do *tongzhi* volunteer work, and watch television. They are still closeted and do not participate in any open *tongzhi* events. The only exceptions are Shmily and May Wu, who have both gone to the Pride Parade. In 2011, they were holding banners, which made older gay men visible for the first time: 'Our hard lives have been full of discrimination. Can you see us, the older *tongzhi*?' and 'Set up a residential care home for elderly *tongzhi*, let us live our lives with dignity.' (See photos below.)

Hong Kong Pride Parade 2011. Source: Author.

For those who live with family members, the private family home is a challenge. On the one hand, living without their wives is easier. For example, Brother Ming, who died in 2010, at age 75, separated from his wife and lived with his boyfriend and his son for four years. He never made explicit his relationship with his boyfriend to his son and his son never asked. On the other hand, living with their wives is more difficult. Couple intimacy is avoided as much as possible, by making excuses such as exhaustion from work, coming home late, or swapping rooms with the children and leaving their wives with their daughters. Uncle Lee and Old Chan both maintained a good relationship with their wives and children. For them, to have a good wife was important for the family, and they had had only fleeting sexual encounters with men. It was at the age of 60, having fulfilled their family duties—conjugal duty to their wives, fatherly duty to their children—that they decided to explore gay romance. Salaff (1981) has aptly described the dutiful 'working daughter' of the 1970s, who sacrificed her own self-development, gave up secondary education, and worked in a factory to contribute to the family economy. Likewise, these men sacrificed their own self-development by suppressing their same-sex desire and marrying to contribute to the heterosexual family economy. Like the working daughters, they did not really regret their decisions, beginning to explore the gay world later in life. Uncle Lee's 'puppy love', sounding like he was a 16-year-old boy, happened when he met his first boyfriend at the age of 60! However, he refused to leave his family, and chose familial intimacy over gay romance.

Coming out is always a difficult and lifelong process. The notion of individuality, as well as the implicit economic and material affluence of 'moving out' to live on one's own or with one's same-sex partner, sometimes clashes with the notion of the relational self in the biopolitics of Hong Kong Chinese families (Kong 2011, 94–119). Whether single or married, my interviewees negotiated their gay identities in the closet under the parameters of familial heteronormativity. The real opposition is sometimes not so much between homosexuality and heterosexuality, but 'between those who are willing and able to play traditional family roles and those who are not' (Berry 2001, 219).

The new **tongzhi** *space and homonormativity*

Most public toilets in Hong Kong have been renovated in accordance with urban renewal and redevelopment, which was stepped up after the SARS crisis in 2003. A traditional public toilet usually consisted of two parts: the 'open' part with several urinals or a urinal wall and trough; and the more 'private' part, which consisted of squat toilets in two parallel rows over long gutters, partitioned into five or six cubicles with metal doors. If someone stood up, his head would be above the partition. Public toilets are now equipped with individually partitioned urinals and fully partitioned cubicles with walls from floor to ceiling. Most have attendants who clean them. The 'garden', or the 'fishpond' (for cruising) has disappeared. Most of my interviewees occasionally go to public toilets, but they now run a higher risk of being arrested by the police or blackmailed by male sex workers.

After the decriminalization of homosexuality in 1991, sites exclusively for *tongzhi* consumption have burgeoned in Hong Kong. This apparently successful 'territorialization' of *tongzhi* spaces and the pink economy have nurtured the new *tongzhi* image of the 'good consumer citizen', in contrast with the older image of the 'citizen-pervert', and this has provided a significant and positive cultural sense of belonging for *tongzhi* (Kong 2011, 73–93). This new *tongzhi* identity, closely associated with consumption, is cosmopolitan in outlook, commercially driven, and conspicuously consumed on the body—it might be considered derivative of a 'global queer identity' (Altman 1997). However, rather than promoting solidarity and identification, it also divides those who can access this ideal from those who cannot. The emerging gay world discriminates along the lines of class, age, gender, sexuality, race, and body type. Most interviewees have had extreme difficulty accessing this exclusive gay space, and complain about its high prices and obsession with youthfulness. If bars and clubs marginalize gay men in terms of class and age, gay saunas discriminate in terms of age and body shape. Shmily, May Wu, and Brother Shing have all experienced ageism inside the gay community.

If heteronormativity functions to create a hierarchy of 'good' and 'bad' citizens by privileging heterosexuals and stigmatizing homosexuals, the new homonormativity not only endorses a depoliticized gay culture anchored in privatized domesticity and consumption (Duggan 2002, 179), but also creates a hierarchy of queer identities and places. In Hong Kong, this hierarchy of identities and bodies has transnational middle-class Chinese gay men and gay Caucasian expatriates at the top; local-born Hong Kong gay male denizens in the middle; and new mainland Chinese migrants, male sex workers, and other gay subordinates at the bottom, defined according to age, class, gender performance, ethnicity, and body type. *Tongzhi* space is thus stratified—bars and clubs in Central Hong Kong attract predominately middle-class, hip, cool, and 'in' young male professionals, whilst Kowloon caters more to working-class gays. Most gay saunas privilege muscular athletic and/or youthful bodies; very few welcome the elderly. Very few *tongzhi* NGOs have put older gay men on their service agendas except Hong Kong Rainbow and Midnight Blue. Within this new homonormative logic, 'fishing' is regarded as cheap, irresponsible, unrespectable, and undesirable, and older gay men are alleged to be self-loathing, closeted, and sad creatures who only 'fish' in a seedy underworld. A few of them 'quit' the gay scene and only socialize with close friends (e.g., David, Brother Shing). Most still hang out in saunas that tolerate them, and pursue sex tourism in mainland China or other Asian countries, such as Taiwan, Thailand, and Malaysia (e.g., Shmily, May Wu,

Tommy, Tony). Some of them participate in *tongzhi* volunteer work (e.g., Shmily, May Wu).

Conclusion

I have traced a brief *tongzhi* history in Hong Kong and have highlighted certain key sites governing homosexuality in Hong Kong: the government, family, and religion. Homosexuality was first made a crime when Britain took over Hong Kong in 1842. The colonial government and the HKSAR government both confine Hong Kong people with limited civil, political, and social rights. *Tongzhi* or not, Hong Kong people have only been able to attain partial citizenship. For *tongzhi*, the situation is even worse. Hong Kong's anti-discrimination laws do not cover sexual orientation. There is no same-sex marriage. Discrimination cases against *tongzhi* have been widely reported (Chung, Pang, and Lee 2012; Suen, Wong, Barrow, Wong, Mak, Choi, Lam, and Lau 2016). In contrast with the welfare state in Britain, the colonial government treated social welfare as a residual concept. The family became a self-regulating self-reliance mechanism which turned people away from the government for welfare needs. The family could be seen as a tool of state governance and served as a powerful site enforcing heteronormativity. This was especially true in the past. The close-knit family network defined people's social roles, provided career possibilities, arranged marriage for them, and gave them social belonging. This encompassing network was safe and comforting but at the same time suppressed people's self-expression and individual development. Religion (especially Protestantism and Catholicism) has been providing education, medical, and social services and thus has been significant in shaping sexual morality in Hong Kong since early colonial days. The rise of evangelical activism in the late 1990s took a particularly conservative stand and saw homosexuality as a deviant and sinful act, and an unhealthy lifestyle. The substantial presence of Christians in the top administrative positions in the government, including two Chief Executives, should be noted. These three sites of governance sometimes establish an implicit alliance, and have produced a heteronormative culture of intimacy in Hong Kong that constrains and confines (homo-)sexual identities, desires, and practices.

However, the site of governance is also the site of resistance. It is evident that the emergence of the *tongzhi* movement since the 1990s—the mushrooming of *tongzhi* social and political groups, the burgeoning of *tongzhi* commercial and consumption venues, the emergence of *tongzhi* representation and other cultural productions in mainstream and alternative media, and the rise of annual *tongzhi* public events such as IDAHO/IDAHOT, Pride Parade, Pink Dot, and the Hong Kong Lesbian and Gay Film Festival, has helped identity and community building among *tongzhi*, bolstered the fight for *tongzhi* rights, and increased *tongzhi* visibility and public recognition under the government's surveillance, family control and religious backlash.

It is under this context that we can understand, through the stories of the older gay men, the micro forms of struggling (or sometimes even resistance) of Hong Kong *tongzhi*. These older gay men are part of the first generation of Hong Kong people and they have succeeded in surviving, living through the various major transformations of Hong Kong. They lived in the period when homosexuality was a criminal offence, homosexual identity had yet to develop, and the only possible identity available was a heterosexual male identity in which one had to fulfil the roles of being a hardworking labourer, a filial son, a dutiful husband, or a stern father. They struggled for a suitable male role without a clear heterosexual/homosexual identity binary, created secretive pleasures in the communal family, negotiated with familial heteronormativity by using different tactics (e.g., getting married, being single, postponing same-sex desires, or having heterosexual marriage with a secretive homosexual romance), and radically challenged the rigid distinction between private and public by developing a cruising or 'fish pond (public toilet)' subculture.

Since the 1990s, they have slowly developed a "gay" identity but have found it difficult to come out as there is a great contradiction between their social roles and their sexuality. Jonathon's only wish is to come out to his two sons before his death, and David insists that his family members will not know even after his death. Apart from their coming out difficulties with their close family members and relatives, they still long for stable, long-term, and intimate same-sex relationships, they still feel frustrated that the gay community is youth-oriented and consumption-based, and they still hope that the government would care about them and offer any social services for older *tongzhi*. Health is a major problem for these men. They all have different degrees of illness, and frequent the hospital. It is unfortunate that I have a few interviewees who have passed away (Old Chan, Brother Ming, and Uncle Lee) and others' health have gone downhill rapidly in these few years (Jonathan, May Wu, Brother Shing).

The stories of these older gay men demonstrate how they realize same-sex desires and negotiate same-sex intimacy in everyday lives over time. Their narratives help us rethink what is meant by being gay, the significance of coming out, the intricate relationship between individuals and the family, the government and other social institutions, and the changing meaning of (homo-)sexuality from colonial to post-colonial Hong Kong. These men are marginalized individuals who live under a complex web of dominations—hetero/homo-normativities—embedded in the social, cultural, economic, and political transformations of Hong Kong. They create a *tongzhi* heterotopia, a counter-public that is 'represented, contested, and inverted' (Foucault 1986, 24)—no matter how fleeting and ephemeral—for love, sex, and intimacy.

1
Old Chan

Brokeback below the Lion Rock (1924–2013)

Born in mainland China in 1924, Old Chan was 86 when we first interviewed him in 2010 at his apartment in Shatin. He lives on his own in a public housing estate. He came to Hong Kong when he was six and he vividly remembers what Hong Kong was like during the Second Sino-Japanese War (1937–1945). Society was rather poor then, and he could only enter a *szesuk*, a kind of private village school which was usually run by one or two teachers who covered classic Chinese literature, mathematics, and English. He was therefore never properly educated. When he was a teen, the movie industry took off. However, there were not enough release prints and it was common for two movie theatres to share the same copy of a film. Therefore, runners were hired to deliver prints between theatres. Old Chan made a living by delivering reels for Gala Theatre and Yau Ma Tei Theatre in Kowloon. He remembered the movies *King Kong* and *Tarzan* very well.

> They were such blockbusters and people queued up for a long time for their tickets. We had to rush between theatres; otherwise the film would have to stop if we were late.

Living under Gunfire during the Japanese Occupation

Old Chan delivered film reels until the end of 1941. When the Japanese Army invaded Hong Kong, a difficult life of three years and eight months began for everyone, and he had to find another living.

> It was tough. You had to live it to believe it. When the Japs came, food was gold. My mum was still alive then. My brothers and I were all single, except my eldest brother. We went outside looking for food, but we didn't know how expensive it had become. The prices went crazy. We bought whatever food we saw on the streets. Stores were robbed all the time. The Japs were coming, so what choice did we have? We bought soy beans, peanuts and whatever food we saw. When things got a bit quiet, the Japs started giving out some kind of identification. We called it the certificate of good conduct

then. You had to carry it to go on the streets. We had some I.D. card holders, which looked like those plastic holders we have nowadays. My eldest brother worked in a movie theatre. He had to pick up film reels every morning at a studio for screenings, so he knew a guy at the studio who was supposed to be in the movie industry. There were no screenings when the Japs were here, but they had a lot of film reels in the studio, and I mean a lot. They had to sell them all, so my brother bought the film reels, which were sold by weight. He got as many reels as he could for just a little bit of money. However, there were a lot of black parts in the frames. The film was transparent, but he had to clean all the frames with water. Then he could use the frames to make card holders. Those card holders were very much needed then. People from all over Hong Kong came and bought from us. That's how we made our living.

Those certificates of good conduct were seen as our identity documents. If you passed by a guard post without saluting to the Japanese soldiers, they would ask you to come over and slap you in the face.

Apprenticing in an Optician's Shop after the Liberation of Hong Kong

All in all, we had to watch our every step on the street. We had no food then. To be frank, people might even have eaten other people. I saw someone in an alley behind a theatre in Yau Ma Tei carving the flesh off a dead person's thigh. That person must have starved to death, so he was eaten by others. In 1945, atomic bombs were dropped on Japan and the war was finally over. There was chaos in Hong Kong after the war. The Republic of China soldiers came, but nobody knew who was going to take over Hong Kong, and order wasn't restored. Churchill, the Prime Minister of the United Kingdom, Roosevelt, and Chiang Kai-shek all got together to negotiate. It wasn't decided who was going to take over Hong Kong then. They were still negotiating. The Chinese government said after the war that they'd take everything back, but the foreigners said treaties had been signed, so nothing could be returned. That's the reason why China took back everything gradually in the end. You wouldn't know the process unless you were there.

Although what Old Chan described might not be entirely accurate, he witnessed how order was restored among the ruins when Britain took Hong Kong back. The first issue the government had to address was rubbish collection.

When the British Army took over Hong Kong, the streets were covered in litter. After the army reacquired Hong Kong, they came up with an idea. Since food was much needed then, they offered people a dollar a day to clean the streets. Many people took up this task. They had no job, so of course they'd do it. But they didn't exactly give you a dollar. They might give you 5 catties of rice, which was about a dollar. That's how they paid you.

Old Chan's mother and eldest brother were given Fixed-Pitch Hawker Licences after the war and started running small businesses, while Old Chan became an apprentice.

> I started working for an optician, as an apprentice of some sort. The owner taught me how to sell eyeglasses until I could . . . He taught me how to fill prescriptions, and how to use the machines . . . Then I bought my own machines one by one and started running my small business, but I only rented half a shop. And, of course, I sold eyeglasses.
>
> We provided the full service as opticians, and that included eye-testing, gathering all the information from our customers, registering and filling their prescriptions. There were all kinds of lenses, such as clear lenses or rose-tinted lenses. After getting their prescriptions, we had to confirm the prices and when they would come back for their glasses. As for us, after getting their prescriptions, we ordered the kind of frames our customers chose. Then we had to draw the shapes of the lenses and put them into the frames ourselves. We cut the lenses into the correct shapes and then we started grinding.

Old Chan was a shop owner for twelve years, until he had to give up his shop because of a huge rent increase.

> The rent kept rising, so I closed the shop down when I couldn't afford the rent anymore. I gave it up, but now my children have grown up. They have their jobs and they have been good to me. They asked me to retire and they give me money every month, so I don't have to work at all. We are all doing fine. Life is good.

However, being only in his sixties, it was too early for Old Chan to live idly. A friend referred him to work as a security guard, and he worked there for a few years.

> I worked in a computer company . . . I just watched people go in and out. The staff had their own cards, so I could just ignore them. All I needed to do was to register the people who visited the staff.

Getting Married at 24 after Love at First Sight

Old Chan got married at 24 after falling in love with his wife at first sight.

> My wife was no more than 20 before the war. She went back to her hometown in mainland China with her mother after meeting me . . . We fell in love with each other when we first met . . . When Hong Kong was finally liberated, her mother came back to Hong Kong with her.

Mrs. Chan gave birth to five children. Society was generally poor then, so life was even more difficult for them.

> I was lucky to have a great wife. She did whatever it took to find work. She sewed shoes and gloves. She had to ask someone to teach her because she didn't know how. So, the wife is most important in a family. Besides helping you, she brings up your children . . . I was very stern. How stern was I? If you did not behave, or when you did something wrong . . . I'd be very hard on you. But I only did that once. My children have been great since then.

They manage themselves very well now. They are all doing great. Now that they've grown up, they make money and they have been good to me.

Old Chan treats all his children equally. He does not give his sons preferential treatment. He even put his daughter through tertiary education.

My god-sister said girls do not need to be highly educated. A daughter has to get married some day and she wouldn't even care about you. But I don't agree. She'll care about you if you treat her nicely and help her every way you can.

Old Chan is not highly educated, but he understands parenting.

You shouldn't do anything wrong if you are a parent. You have to set a good example to your children. . . . now that my children are all happy and they are good to me, it's all because of the good deeds that I've done in my life.

An Undercurrent of Ambiguous Sexuality

If it were not for his same-sex desires, Old Chan would have lived his life quietly like any other seniors in Hong Kong. Ever since his adolescence, he has had a vague attraction towards the same sex, bringing a kind of undercurrent to his life. He has kept this secret ever since.

When I was young, part of it was just curiosity, an attraction towards the same sex. It was strange. When I was about 15 or 16, people came and harassed me, or teased me. There were lots of martial artists performing on the streets, with an audience watching. Someone would come and stand by me, touch me with his hand or something. But I was kind of shy, so I panicked. I was so panicked that I'd just leave. But we all become curious sometimes. So, one day it happened to me again somewhere. But I'd got married by then and now I was curious, so I touched him back. It all started from there.

Old Chan realized that he had same-sex desire, but he had to repress his needs when he was young due to family and social pressure. When he saw someone he fancied, he would be sexually aroused, but he had to restrain himself.

I held myself back. To be honest, I got married when I was 24, but people flirted with me when I was 16. I had a high sex drive. I had to hold myself down when I was wearing shorts. I had to hold my rod down because it sprung up all the time. I had to hold it down whether I was wearing trousers or shorts. I had a high sex drive. I was born that way.

People approached me when I was around 20. But I had a normal husband-and-wife relationship after we got married, so all I knew was sex between a man and a woman. After all my children started working, I tried seeking other thrills out of curiosity. I kept it secret, especially from my family.

Unleashing His Homosexual Desire after the Death of His Wife

> I started doing it after my wife died (over a decade ago). I had tried it a little bit when my wife was alive, but only a few times.
>
> It usually happened on the streets then. We exchanged numbers. Then we went out to have tea. We had to take some time to get acquainted with each other first, so that we could find out if we could trust each other, that we wouldn't be blackmailed. The government was oppressive then. It wasn't as tolerant as it is now. Now there are saunas where you can play. We didn't have that, but we followed our hearts and our beliefs.

Old Chan usually went to public toilets, commonly known as 'gardens' or, later, 'fishponds' within the community, to look for peers. To him, same-sex sexual encounters in public toilets opened a new world for him.

> It was all about curiosity, and the thrills. At the toilets, you would look at people and people would look at you. It was a kind of sexual arousal. People'd look at you and it'd turn you on. You'd get a hard on. And they'd touch you. I had that kind of feeling too. The feelings started to build up and it became your sexual orientation. Before I was exposed to this kind of idea, I was a normal man. I was married and I had children. In the end, I found it very different so I fooled around. I did it out of the excitement of doing something new, and out of curiosity.

Besides going to 'gardens', Old Chan sometimes found acquaintances in a cinema in San Po Kong.

> It wasn't an all-porno theatre, so there were some great films as well. But the film ticket didn't cost a lot. It cost very little money. The reason people went there was to meet friends.
>
> When you walked down the aisle, they'd flirt with you even if you didn't. It was very strange. They'd touch you if they had the hots for you. Some people stood at the back, and there were lots of them. They didn't sit in the front. They stood at the back while they watched the movie. So, they weren't watching at all. They just wanted to fool around with you. They wanted to look for trade.
>
> If they liked you, they'd use their cock to touch you. They'd touch your hand asking you to touch it back.
>
> Then they'd take you outside to get to know you. They'd ask about your job. They'd inquire about you, try to find out if you were telling the truth.

Whether people were in a 'garden' or a cinema, if two people liked each other, they would go to a love hotel. Old Chan still remembers how he felt when he got a room with another guy.

> That kind of place . . . I was very embarrassed. I was afraid. When I got there . . .
>
> Sure, they rented out rooms for two people. Sure, even for two guys . . . As long as you paid the rent, they'd register your I.D. card.

> Of course, I was afraid. But it was fine if we knew each other well. We'd give them our I.D. cards. It was okay. We just borrowed a place to do it, that's all. That's how it happened.

Getting Hit on in His Eighties as a Huge and Tall Old Man

However, cinemas are public after all. No matter how smart gay men are when they look for trade there, there is always the risk of hitting on the wrong guy.

> Some people yelled at you when you felt them up. They might not be one of us, but you'd hit on them. It happened in Taiwan too. I checked in at that Orient Hotel and I stayed there. I looked outside the window and saw a theatre. People told me about that theatre . . . Yes, the Red House. There were screenings 24 hours a day. You could go in and out whenever you wanted. You could even go back inside after exiting. I went there because I was curious too. I went in and sat down. As soon as I sat down, four guys sat down around me. I caught their eyes, but then I didn't know if I could trust them. So, I went into the toilet, and they followed me in. I was so scared. I really was, so I just left.

Old Chan was tall and muscular when he was young. Both men and women were attracted to him; even people of different ages were fond of him. He still gets hit on now that he is in his eighties.

> Now that I'm older, I'm not that active. Some might ask if I still get hit on. I still do. I was on the street one day and someone in his twenties came over and asked me, 'do you still play about, old geezer?' So I asked him, 'play with what?' I didn't know him; I had just met him on the street. He saw how old I was and asked me if I still do it. I said 'no'. Then he said I was smart. I told him it's a phase of life. Some old people still have sexual desire, but not me for now. I try to avoid it. I'm much older now, so I have to take care of my health. I don't pay that much attention to sex, not anymore.

Old Chan was probably most active in the gay circle when he was 50 or 60.

> I was already 50 or 60, but I had the figure of a 40 or 50-year-old. It was strange. They'd follow me for blocks, even though we didn't know each other's roles— 'top' or 'bottom', or, 'giver' or 'receiver'.

'I Do Both. I'm Versatile.'

> I'm not embarrassed to say it now: I do both. I'm versatile. Versatility means you can be either the 'man' or the 'woman'. Front or back, I can do it both ways, except if you don't like that person at all. If you like someone, your erogenous parts become extremely sensitive. It's strange. If you like someone, you want to stay with him all day, and you want to do it with him every day. It's like that, that's what you want. I had a high sex drive. When I liked someone, my rod got hard so I wanted to be with him to let off some steam. That's what happened. It's kind of strange. This is very personal and private, but I've told you everything.

Old Chan cheated on his wife with other men, but he never laid eyes on another woman besides his wife.

> It's strange. I never liked any other woman except my wife.

Old Chan could be a bisexual, but he does not like feminine men.

> I like only masculine men. I never got close to feminine guys. I couldn't. We don't speak the same language.
>
> There were times when I had one or two regular partners. We got together all the time. We hung out when we had a day off. I did it with one or both of them. Then I started to like him, and he liked me as well. It's the only way that would work. The feelings had to be mutual. It wouldn't work if the feelings were one-directional. It was about the sexual encounter, sensitivity, and pleasure. That's all. That's how it happened.

Old Chan does not disagree with the idea that a man can live happily ever after with another man, like a man can with a woman, but he is adamant that that fairytale will not happen for him.

> It has never occurred to me, because I have a family of my own so I don't think about it. That's all. It's because of my family, and I don't like it, either. I don't. When I go out with someone, I keep it very casual. We go our separate ways after getting off. It might become regular if it feels really great. Otherwise, it'll just be a one-night stand.

Breaking away from His Sexual Desire and Living in One Big Happy Family

Old Chan is now in his eighties and it seems that he has broken free from his sexual desires.

> Now I'm more independent. I take care of everything myself. I've totally given up on sex. People might still be interested in me, but I turn all of them down. I'm not interested. All that stuff is the past. You can say that I've retired from it. I've given it all up. I don't even want to make contacts with most of them. I value my family a lot, as well as my children, my wife. I respect my family. So I've given up on all those distractions.

However, Old Chan's health has worsened in recent years. He was even admitted to the hospital a few times in 2009.

> I'm getting old. The air quality wasn't too good outside, so I didn't even know I was infected. I felt dizzy one day when I came home and I had to be admitted. Luckily my eldest son was home, so he called an ambulance right away. I was taken to the hospital, but I waited for a whole night for a bed. It took so long. I had to be isolated the first time I was there. They didn't know what I had. It was last year.

Partly because of his health, Old Chan became a Christian a few years ago.

Old Chan did not have time at first when we did the interview that day before Chinese New Year.

> If I hadn't agreed to your interview, I would have gone to the bank to get some paper money. I have to get some banknotes in advance so that I can put them in red packets. I have a big family, dozens of family members, young and old. Almost 30 people come visit me during Chinese New Year. I have to give them red packets.

With a big family and lots of grandchildren, Old Chan said it happily and contentedly.

As the oldest interviewee in this book, Old Chan was tall and huge. He spoke loudly and clearly. Moreover, he laughed aloud all the time. He was such a kind and affable old man. Every time I saw him, he would extend his hand to hold mine. His big hands felt warm, firm, and dependable.

Old Chan reminds me of Janet Salaff, a Canadian sociologist who passed away in 2010. Salaff (1981) explained that in the 1960s and 1970s when the economy of Hong Kong started to take off, young women had to give up their studies to work in factories. They gave up their life to contribute to their families, because of patriarchal Chinese traditions. It was the same for Old Chan, who got married and had children to fulfil the expectations and social norms in the traditional Chinese community. He could only start satisfying his sexual needs in the later part of his life. He represents a typical example of a gay son who fulfils the moral economy of the Chinese family by getting married and suppressing his same-sex desires. He exemplifies an interesting example of the closeted—created not just by the hetero/homo distinction but the family/individual dualism. The only part he shared with his family and society was the struggles he had early in life—typical among Hong Kong people living below the Lion Rock,[1]—but not the later quest he experienced in the gay circle. While the former seems to be obvious and straightforward, the latter is almost like a skeleton in the closet. I still remember how blunt and honest he was when he talked about his love and lust during our interview that day.

Old Chan passed away in 2013.

---

1. Lion Rock is a hill on the Kowloon peninsula. It is seen as a symbol of the Hong Kong spirit, especially in the 1970s or early 1980s, because Radio Television Hong Kong broadcast a TV series called *Below the Lion Rock* to depict the real life and hard struggles of Hong Kong people then. The theme song, bearing the same title, has become an anthem for that generation.

2
Brother Ming

Who Says There Are No Communist Tongzhi?
(1935–2010)

Born in 1935 in Shantou, Brother Ming was brought up by his grandmother in his hometown, and did not come to Hong Kong with his parents and siblings. Country life was difficult, but what really bothers Brother Ming is that he did not have a chance to receive a proper education.

> I entered junior 1 when I was over ten years old. Actually, I skipped junior 1. I started at junior 2. Life was tough in my hometown. I had to pay a few catties of rice as my tuition fee every semester, but my family couldn't even afford that. I had to work to put myself through school by picking up dog pooh, so that I could pay a few catties of rice.

In 1949, when Brother Ming was 14, he finally came to Hong Kong to join his family. He took a boat from Shantou to Hong Kong, boarding at seven in the evening and arriving at seven the next morning—a total of twelve hours.

> My dad was a sailor, so he had some foreign friends. My mum asked a friend of hers to tell me to contact somebody's son. He was a relative of a sailor, so I didn't have to pay him. In Chaozhou, it was regarded as *tauto* [illegal immigration].

Brother Ming's father had already died when he arrived in Hong Kong, so he lived with his mother, his elder brother, and his sister-in-law. However, he did not receive a proper education, even in Hong Kong.

> After coming to Hong Kong, I told mum that I could work during the day and go to school at night. Do you know what she told me? She said so and so got rich without going to school, and so and so got rich without going to school as well. So what's the point of studying at all? I didn't have a chance until I entered a spinning mill.

The trade union offered culture classes then, with a volunteer teacher teaching the workers, so, finally, Brother Ming could study after work. 'It was very hard taking those culture classes, though. I went to class at the Labour Department two or three years later. That's how I received my education.'

Learning Chinese Words by Listening to Cantonese Operas

> You couldn't even get a driving license without an education. You had to study the Road Users' Code on your own if you wanted to apply for a driving license.

Besides taking classes, Brother Ming seized every opportunity to learn in life.

> I was willing to learn. I used to work in a spinning mill. I listened to the radio when they played Cantonese operas. The *Overseas Chinese Daily News* used to print lyrics of Cantonese operas, so I learnt Chinese characters from the lyrics in the newspaper. Whenever I saw words that I didn't know, I wasn't embarrassed at all to ask somebody at the dim sum restaurant. That's how I learnt Chinese characters, or else I'd still be illiterate.

His hometown was 'liberated' by the Communists six months after he came to Hong Kong.

> One of my uncles died back home. They called me that morning and asked me to go back, but then they later told me not to. They said Shantou was already 'liberated' and I shouldn't go back, so I remembered it very well.

Since Brother Ming could not go back, he was determined to work hard in Hong Kong.

> There weren't many jobs then (early 1950s). You had to know somebody to get a job even as a labourer . . . You got $1.5 a month and you didn't get paid every month. I cut hair and sold clogs. Do you know how durable those clogs were? I sold clogs and cut hair, but I didn't get paid.
>
> Then I worked in a herbal tea shop and got $15 a month. I was only in my teens when I came to Hong Kong, but I started working already. After a few years, I entered a spinning mill and eventually I opened a food stall. When China was liberated, people came to Hong Kong to invest. There were lots of spinning and weaving mills (mid-1950s). You could get a job easily. So, I worked there for more than twenty years.
>
> Then I went and got a driving license (1970s). After getting my license, I drove a *pakpai* [an illegal minibus with nine seats]. It hadn't been legalized then. I was a driver's assistant in the beginning. There were 20 or even 30 passengers on a minibus then. Traffic wasn't that bad. And the assistant held a few passengers in at the door to keep them safe. The traffic was okay . . . I worked on the Kowloon side. When I finally got my license, I started driving, and I still do now.

He started working as a driver in 1967. The business was great at first, but it has been difficult since the MTR was built.

Brother Ming should have retired, now that he is 75 years old. However, he is not used to a life without work, so he still works as a part-time driver.

> Life is hard without a job. I work occasionally. I don't do it all the time, just two to three days a week. Sometimes I work only one day as a substitute. It's a hobby for me. But driving doesn't make a lot of money nowadays. You even

have to pay some costs and work on holidays. After all, we drive students to school or drive people to work. Sometimes you don't even earn enough money to rent a minibus for a day.

When he is not working, his favourite pastimes include hiking and watching television. He lives in a rooftop apartment in an old building with his son. There are no elevators, but it is not a problem at all for Brother Ming.

It's fine when you're used to it. It's not a problem. You might hurt yourself if you take two or three steps at a time, but one at a time would be fine. The point is not to climb the stairs in a rush. You run out of breath easily. Even my son can't climb the stairs as quickly as I can.

His Wife Became Mentally Ill after the 1967 Riots[1]

Brother Ming got married in his thirties. It was considered late.

I was quite late, because I didn't know how to meet girls. There were lots of girls at my spinning mill. I went on a trip with a dozen colleagues, but we were kind of naive. We didn't know how to date guys or girls.

He met his wife when they were both young. They even lived together in the same tenement apartment in their teens.

We all lived together. Her family sublet a flat to us, so we were her family's tenants. Life was difficult then in those subdivided flats. I know there were eight people living in my wife's room, including her five brothers and her parents . . . I still remember that some of them slept under the bed, while her parents and the two smallest children slept on the bed. They didn't have a bunk bed. They got one later, but they didn't have one at first. There was no place to sit, so they ran outside like dogs. That's how people lived.

His wife gave birth to three sons and a daughter after they got married. Brother Ming had to support his whole family on his own. Unfortunately, his wife was traumatized by the 1967 riots and became mentally ill.

My two sons were born before the riot. My wife was frightened out of her wits. The mill I was working in was right behind a police station. We lived in a public housing apartment . . . I didn't go out a lot then. I behaved very well. I came home as soon as I left work and played with my sons in the neighbourhood, while my wife stayed home. When she heard a bang, she rushed over to the opposite flat to find the matronly woman who lived there. The woman asked her what she wanted. She said she was looking for her sons. I had a car accident soon after that. The double blow finally drove her mad.

---

1. In 1967, a minor labour dispute escalated into large-scale strikes and pro-Communist demonstrations against British colonial rule in Hong Kong, staged in sympathy with the Cultural Revolution in mainland China. These events are commonly known as the 1967 riots.

Brother Ming supported leftism then. He was a union member and supported the riot.

> Most of the workers in the mills were union members. Then I became a driver and joined the Transport Workers Union, later known as the Motor Transport Workers General Union. I'm a lifetime member. It doesn't matter if the Communist Party or the Democratic Alliance for the Betterment and Progress of Hong Kong [a pro-Beijing political group] is right or wrong, we support them no matter what.

However, the 1989 Democratic Movement gave him mixed feelings about the Communist Party. It still brings him to tears of indignation when he talks about it.

> China will never progress without the Democratic Movement. In my opinion, you shouldn't have too much freedom in a society, or it'll become a total mess like the Soviet Union. If China didn't repress them, there might have been a warlord in Guangdong and another in Hunan. The country would fall apart. We heard about the news and it was a bit cruel. I was furious at the time. I was furious when I watched the news. You didn't know if it was real when you heard about it. We are all Chinese after all.

Getting Felt up from behind on a Ferry

Brother Ming started having same-sex experiences before he married.

> I remember I was seduced by someone when I took the ferry across the harbour, but I didn't know what was going on. The guy behind me put his hand . . . I stood in front and he stood behind me. He touched me, but I didn't respond. I thought he . . . He did it a few times. He followed me when we got off the ferry. Then he asked me to go up a flight of stairs with him. He touched me and kissed me. That's how it all began. I was curious and it felt kind of good. Books and newspapers then . . . I remember *Kam Yeh Pao* or that kind of tabloid, there was a small paragraph talking about it. And *Reader's Digest* said something. I was so obsessed and I bought them all the time, just for those small paragraphs.

Brother Ming and the guy then saw each other quite often after that.

> We kept in touch by phone. It wasn't so convenient then, especially when he was working, but he'd call me and ask me out.

That man was already in his forties, so he was twice Brother Ming's age, and he already had children. When they went out, they usually strolled around and listened to music. 'I was happy enough when we saw each other . . . We went to the movies too. I was rather passive. He felt me up all the time.'

> People were more innocent back then. That's why I think people's relationships were stronger. It was difficult for us to meet people. We weren't as casual as people are now. When we met someone, we'd be friends for years.

> Even if there was nothing between us, it felt great when we just talked to each other.

They kept in contact for over a decade, until one day, Brother Ming heard from another friend that this man had killed himself, and it was because of a relationship with another man that went wrong.

> He knew a chicken seller in Central, and he found out that the man had met someone else. So he killed himself . . . He took his own life for that. That's what I heard, but I don't know if it was true.
>
> I made some calls. His company said he didn't come to work, and his family said he was dead.

Brother Ming was not married then. Like most gay men then, he finally married because he understood little about his own sexual orientation and felt increasing pressure from his family and society.

> I didn't know a lot about it. I had only a vague idea. I wouldn't have got married if I was the man I am now . . . My mum tried to pressure me into marriage all the time, but I didn't date any girls. So, my mum set me up with my wife.

Two Married Men Falling Deeply in Love

After getting married, Brother Ming had another male lover, Mr. Shum, whom he met outside a public toilet.

> I went into the toilet as he was going out. When I got inside, I didn't stay long. He was waiting for me right outside. He asked me if we could be friends in the beginning. I thought he looked alright when he was young, so I gave him my numbers. I only had a home number and a work number. There weren't mobile phones back then. I called him at home and we went out all the time. He told me his last name openly. It was Shum and it was his real name. We even came from the same hometown, so we felt even closer. We were friends for thirty or forty years.
>
> When he first met me, he was crazy about me. I worked in Kwun Tong, but he came to see me just for a while. He went to his factory after seeing me and asked me to have dim sum when he left. It was easy for us to find parking spots. We had our own cars, so we could have dim sum wherever we found parking spots. He didn't see anyone else, but he came all the way to have lunch with me and waited for me to leave work. After I finished work, we went and had tea, then we walked. He worked in a plastics company in Tsim Sha Tsui. I went over and waited for him to leave the office in the evening. He would go home, and I returned to mine.

Brother Ming had a friend who was single and lived alone. He would find an excuse to borrow the keys from his friend. When his friend was not home, he would meet Shum at his friend's place.

Shum was also married with children. He had to go to the Mainland a few years later because of his job.

> China was opening up. He said, 'it's no good, Ming. I've done less business since I met you. I have to go to the Mainland to make money.' He was gone for eight years. I was very sad, and I cried all the time.

Brother Ming was angry with him at first. However, time healed all wounds. After Brother Ming had calmed down, he finally understood Shum.

> He swore that he never met anyone else, and that he had to work. You can't get in the way when somebody has to work . . . He said it was his chance, so I couldn't blame him. I gave him the cold shoulder when he first came back, so eventually he left for eight years. His life was more stable after eight years. Then he came back and contacted me. However, the passion was gone. Now we are great friends and he cares a lot about me. He said he never met anyone else, but for all I know he actually might have . . . However, he didn't treat them like he treated me. Their relationships were casual and those men were not as important as I am in his life.

Brother Ming and Shum loved each other. However, they never thought about living together because it was unrealistic.

> It's impossible. We both have our own family after all. We've always had our family and relatives, and we can't leave our children.

After Shum went to the Mainland, Brother Ming met another close friend, Mr. B, who was much younger than Brother Ming.

> I met him at a toilet, too. It happened the same way. One of us went in as the other was going out. I probably looked quite decent when I was young. I wasn't this ugly . . . We took some time to get to know each other. Then I started my own food stall. He came to help every night after work, staying till two or three in the morning. He didn't want to go home. He waited until I closed my food stall to see me home. And he didn't let me go straight home. He kissed me and held me on the staircase. He didn't want me to go. He had to work in the morning, so he got up at 8 a.m., but he was infatuated with me and clingy. We stayed friends for many years. He was a great person. He was good to his friends and he was always willing to help people. He was great, so I spoiled him a lot.
>
> I knew him for over a decade. He died three years ago. He was the same age as my eldest son and he came from my hometown as well. I treated him almost like my own son, and I was heart-broken when he died.

Making a New Buddy and Shacking up with Him

Besides Shum and Mr. B, Brother Ming had another friend, Mr. C, and they even lived together. Meeting Mr. C was very different from his other close friends. They met in a video arcade, but they did not know each other's sexual orientation at first.

> We were playing arcade games. He had spent all his tokens and I had won some, so I gave him some tokens. That's how we met. I didn't know he was that kind of man right away. He asked me where I was from. I said I came from Chaozhou. He said, 'Me, too.' Then we talked more and found that we had the same family name. So I went to his place all the time. His parents were great to me, and his siblings were nice. He was the eldest in his family, but I was older than him.

Brother Ming called Mr. C his little brother. After separating from his wife (see below), Brother Ming and his eldest son lived in a two-bedroom flat owned by his friend who had moved abroad. They had a room each. Mr. C moved in with Brother Ming and slept in his bedroom, but Brother Ming's son did not suspect a thing.

> We lived together for a few years, about three or four. After I opened my own food stall, I didn't have time for my little brother while I was running my business. He met someone else about my age, he moved in with that man, and they have been together since.

Brother Ming has always kept his sexuality a secret. His friends, family, and even his wife have never suspected.

> What's the point of talking about it? It doesn't do anyone any good. Some people might disapprove and have the impression that . . . we are 'camp', that we are queer. What's the point of telling people? I never told anyone. I never revealed it at home, and I never told them what kind of person I really am. I'm married after all, so people thought I'm normal. Nobody would call me gay.
>
> When I hung out with my friends, they never suspected my real sexuality.

Brother Ming has been able to keep this secret because he has been very discreet about it. Besides, neither he nor his friends are effeminate at all.

> I don't like men who are camp. I just don't fancy them. I don't have many friends who are like that. Maybe a few, but most of my friends are very masculine.
>
> I don't really like them. It's very risky . . . At first, I was afraid of them—those men who think that they are women.

Brother Ming has not lived with his family for many years. He separated from his wife, who suffers from mental illness, for almost twenty years.

> I moved out more than ten years ago. Why? First, when my three children were at home, they would fight sometimes. Some were meaner than the others, and whoever was gentler would get bullied, which I didn't like. So, I moved out and asked one of my sons to live with me, because he listens to me and I like him better . . . Ever since my wife became mentally ill, I couldn't stand her. I was a driver. But whenever I got home, she wouldn't care about me. She would turn on the radio, television, or put on music. I told her all the time to turn them off, I had to work in the morning, and I had to concentrate. But she didn't care about me at all. So, I couldn't stand her anymore.

It was fortunate for him to have the friend who emigrated and leave a vacant apartment for him. So, Brother Ming moved out with his eldest son. Then another friend was offered a public housing apartment by the government, leaving his rooftop apartment for Brother Ming. He has rented it for HK$3,000 and lived there with his other son since then.

> I'm doing alright now that I have more free time. I don't have a job now. Usually when I have a lot of time, I go and visit my hometown. I do that most of the time.

Brother Ming would not dare go to gay places in the past. Now he goes to a gay sauna whenever he has time.

> I seldom go to gay bars. I didn't dare go to saunas before. I asked my godson, the one who died a few years ago, to take me to a sauna, but he refused. He said it wasn't the kind of place for me. I told him I'd go to a sauna myself if he didn't take me. In the end, another friend took me. Now I usually go to XX [the gay sauna]. It's convenient. Why? You can get there by MTR. It's also cleaner, and the place isn't so dangerous.
>
> I go to XX whenever I have time.

Getting More Open-minded in the Latter Part of His Life

As Brother Ming gets older, he has become more open than he was before.

> I probably have heard more about it, so I don't think it's really a big deal anymore. Now I have the courage to be more open about it. I used to be so discreet, but now I don't have so many hang-ups. People are more open. It's mainly because of the openness. It's not that big of a secret anymore . . . We are all the same kind of people in a gay sauna, so it's better than going to a toilet on your own, where it could be dangerous. It's not that easy to meet people outside, because you have a lot to worry about. But you don't have so many hang-ups in a gay sauna. You have to be very careful in a toilet or other public places. You have to worry about the cops, the bad guys, or blackmailers. I dare not go to a toilet, unless I have a friend with me.

Brother Ming does not go to the sauna for the same reason he used to when he was young.

> Many of the customers sing Cantonese operas very well. I listen to them in the Cantonese opera room. I go there for the Cantonese opera room as well as the movie room. I spend most of my time in these two rooms.[2]
>
> I only chat with them. I did it once or twice when I first went there. I'd rather keep them as friends if there's something I don't like about them. I don't need it if they get too clingy. When I see someone who throws himself at everyone he sees, I'd rather for us to be just friends. I met a few of those people over there . . . But it doesn't feel like they're there for you after all, so what's the

---

2. This sauna has a few karaoke rooms and movie rooms and also serves meals.

point? It's fine if you're not very fond of them, because you can't take it if you really like them.

It doesn't matter for us if we really get lucky or not. I'm not that young anymore. Sometimes I just feel people up. I go into the dark room to touch them. Now that I look like this, some people might be scared when they see me. I still get it sometimes . . . But most of the time, I might not like someone when he shows an interest in me.

With more people available now, we can meet someone new almost every day. But it wasn't like that before. It wasn't so easy to meet people, unless you knew where to look for friends. For you to just go out there to meet someone, it didn't happen a lot. It might happen, but people in the past were more serious about their friendships. They weren't as casual as people are nowadays. Now people might pretend not to know you once you leave the place. People kept in touch for a while in the past, perhaps one or two years. Some people might be friends for eight or even ten years, but not now. It's too easy. There are too many people. You can meet them anywhere. If you look good, you can literally meet people everywhere. But we are too old, so it's not that easy.

Homosexual Taboo as a Thing of the Past

As for his views on homosexuality, Brother Ming used to see it as taboo. However, as society progressed, Brother Ming changed his mind.

> Chinese people think that it's immoral after all . . . Most people think this way. It's probably because we are quite conservative. I might have picked it up from other gay men so I'm more open now. I used to have a lot of inhibitions.

> I used to feel guilty about it, but not anymore. It's not such a big deal. You can find them in all walks of society. It's probably a Western influence. It exists in Chinese culture as well . . . It's called 'passion of the cut sleeve': when someone likes you, he cuts his sleeve off so that he doesn't wake you when you're sleeping on his arm.

Brother Ming has slowly changed his mind about homosexuality since he started going to saunas over ten years ago. Now it does not bother him anymore.

> I'm not so stubborn now. It's tricky, these kinds of thoughts. You don't think about it when you are busy. But you can't stop thinking about it when you have nothing to do. It's like heroin, you're hooked. It was okay for me not to go to XX for a few months. But I'm doomed when I have too much time on my hands. It's so convenient now. You pay no more than HK$100 to get in, and it's conveniently located. That's the biggest reason. Besides, you can eat there.

Now in his twilight years, Brother Ming sometimes goes back to his hometown to visit his relatives and be with his sister's family. He volunteers occasionally to help gay men in need. That's how I met him through an AIDS NGO.

> I take patients to see their doctors. Old people have to go to doctors. But I haven't done that a lot lately. I had a car accident in April. I can't even take care of myself, so I passed my cases on to other people.
>
> I'm glad. It's wonderful to help people. That's the only reason I do it. We're not doing it for the money! I take them to see their doctors. Sometimes I take them to have dim sum afterwards. Sometimes I pay for their taxis. I don't want them to pay. For an old person living in a nursing home, it's quite a lot of money for them even though it costs no more than HK$100. We know each other, after all, so it's nothing for me. That's what I believe. I don't ask for anything in return.

His health has not been so good lately.

> I don't worry about anything much now. Why should I worry? Anyway, I don't think it's going to be so easy to get rid of me. I should have died a few times already, but I'm still here. It was mostly because of anaemia. It happened to me a few times before. I didn't feel dizzy, but my blood pressure was very low and that was it. My doctors always say that I don't have enough blood, and I am scrawny. But I have enough nourishment every time when I come back from my hometown. I eat well there, because I have regular meals, but I probably don't eat regularly and properly in Hong Kong. I mean, I'm on my own. When my son is not there, I only eat when I want to; otherwise I don't eat.

Difficult Relationships, Mostly with a Miserable Ending

Brother Ming is not opposed to the idea of same-sex marriage, but he is not optimistic about it either.

> It's fine, as long as it's between two consenting people, as long as they like it. Just don't get married one day and get divorced the next. Keep up the marriage. But I think it's difficult in this circle. Most couples end miserably. They don't last till the end. It's a great thing if they can be together for eight or ten years. But they often end miserably. You either get dumped or you break up. It happens most of the time.

Brother Ming might have experienced a lot of 'miserable endings'. However, he never forgets the joy of being loved.

> When you meet a guy who is your type, and you like him and he loves you too, it's bliss. It's like seeing my godson. I knew him for over ten years. I was so happy. I was happy knowing Shum for a few decades as well. He was so nice to me, but I didn't do a lot of nice things to him. He was mostly the one being nice. I was really happy. It was great to be loved.

I saw Brother Ming only once, because he passed away soon after our interview in 2010. I played the recording over and over again, listening to his heavily-accented Cantonese, telling his own tale in his own words. He was one of those Chinese immigrants of the older generation, who received little education and had many different kinds of labouring work. He worked in a spinning mill, opened his own food stall, and drove a mini-bus. He joined the union and became a leftist. However, the 1989 Democratic Movement in China had a huge impact on him. The thing about him that really stuck with me was not his heart-breaking stories of love that faded away, but the tears he shed because of his mixed feelings towards the Communist Party when he talked about the 1989 Democratic Movement. Can anyone really say there is no **tongzhi** in the Communist Party? This project has triggered a similar project in Guangdong and I would love to hear stories from older gay men living in mainland China who have experienced traumatic political turmoil in their early lives.

There are lots of people who play around in the gay community. Apart from monogamy, there are many different forms of relationships tried by gay men (e.g., Adam 2006; Kong 2011, 107–17). Only a few stay monogamous, but Brother Ming was certainly a great example. He lived in a rooftop apartment before he died, and he said he planted a lot of flowers on his rooftop. I told him I like flowers and asked if I could visit him sometime. He gladly said yes, but he was shy at the same time, saying his house was a dump and there was not much to look at. He said in the end, 'It's okay, if you don't mind.' I always feel bad that I did not find time to go see his flowers on the rooftop.

3
Shmily

A Butterfly with 1,500 Male Lovers (1949–)

Shmily, which stands for 'see how much I love you', is the pseudonym of my interviewee. He was born in 1944 in Hong Kong during the Second Sino-Japanese War, so his mother registered his birth date a year later. Because of this mix-up, he got his Senior Citizen Card a year late. He had to wait a year to receive the social welfare offered to senior citizens over 65 years old, but he did not bother to correct his age. He is so carefree that he said it was fine, as long as his age is correct on his gravestone. After all, he said he was only 55 years old at heart.

He does not know when his sexual orientation started. Like many other gay men, he had crushes on his male teachers, especially his form teacher, when he was little. However, he did not know then that people of the same sex could be in love with each other. He felt the homoerotic impact for the first time when he saw his male cousin naked. The first real same-sex sexual experience he had was with a neighbour.

Making out in the Attic with a Young Man

Shmily was 15 or 16 years old when it happened while he was living on Wellington Street in Central on Hong Kong Island. With a few households living in an old tenement building, it was exactly like the classic comedy, *The House of 72 Tenants* (dir. Chor Yuen, 1973), the Cantonese blockbuster depicting a group of tenants living in poverty in the 1970s in Hong Kong. The young male neighbour sometimes fooled around with him. He found it exciting, but he did not feel the same way about girls.

> When I danced with girls, I didn't feel anything even when we were so close dancing the foxtrot. But when I held a guy, I would get so turned on and get really hard. That's how I found out.

There was a young single man living in their attic, and that is where they started having sexual contact.

> I didn't know what we were doing, but I liked it a lot. I thought it was fun. When he was free, or when he didn't have to study, he would ask me to go up. His attic was my dungeon. I really thought this young man was my first love. So, it has now become a 'thing' for me. I like looking for attics to spend the night, to relive that sexual fantasy.

They ran into each other years later and greeted each other politely. His first love was already married. Shmily said he did not ask for a photo or ask about his wife and children. However, he would not have declined had he made a move on him.

> It was okay. He was my first after all, so it was hard getting over him.

There were no private toilets or showers in most public housing estates in the 1950s and 1960s. So people had to go to public toilets and showers, which became the venue for some people to satisfy their sexual needs. However, not only gay men hit on each other in these places; all kinds of sexual experimentation went on there.

> Gay men or even straight men had a lot of opportunities to seduce or be seduced. So, if you were sexually adventurous, or not monogamous, people would touch you, grab you, and feel you up, until you got a hard on. Really. It wasn't such a surprise. That's why I think us gay men are all bad seeds. We are such flirts.

In the 1960s when people were not familiar with the issue of homosexuality, few gay men were open about their orientation. Gay men did not have a lot of space. According to Shmily, same-sex sexual activities were all carried out behind closed doors. There were several gay men living around him, including his landlord. Public showers and toilets were convenient places for same-sex sexual activities, and even straight guys took part sometimes.

Being Gay Unrelated to the Absent Father

Shmily was born into a single-parent family. He lived with his mother. His father had several women and children, so they did not see each other too often. He is not sure if his sexuality is a result of his broken family, either directly or indirectly.

> It was probably because I didn't have any male role models. I never experienced fatherly or brotherly love, so that might be a problem. However, I heard from the post-90s generation that not only do they have fathers, but they can also lean on their dads' shoulders while they talk. Their fathers are present, but it seems these young men are gay—and are bottoms!

He went to a Catholic school. His family was poor. His mother wanted him to be baptized. She thought it would be an advantage because churches gave food to the poor all the time. Shmily was given 60 cents every day by his father. He spent 30 cents on bus fare, and 10 cents each on fried egg noodles, fried rice noodles, and sweet potato soup for lunch. He did not have money for breakfast, so he went to mass early each morning to get a meal ticket at the church.

> It was like *Oliver Twist*: you got a bowl of oatmeal porridge and a piece of bread with that ticket.

He only went to secondary school for a year before he left school, but he speaks English quite well.

> I went to a Catholic school after all, so I learnt the basics at least. It was a shame that I didn't have more opportunities.

His dissolute father could not pay his school fees, and free education was not provided then. There were no social workers who helped people to apply for financial assistance either, so he left school and started working. His first job was as an office assistant in his uncle's company. Then he worked in various big enterprises. You can sense his pride about his work through his words. The areas he mentioned were all parts of the central business district in Hong Kong.

> It was my destiny to work in all those big firms. I never worked in small companies. I told people that I worked only in Central, or maybe Wan Chai or Causeway Bay. As for Kowloon, I would go to Tsim Sha Tsui but nowhere else. I wouldn't go to Kwun Tong. It was below me. How could I go there? That would be crazy.

A Butterfly over the Course of His Love Life

He is proud and confident about his love life as well.

> People want to have a relationship with me, but I don't want that. It is a nuisance. If you are with someone, he may ask you all the time: Where are you? What are you doing? Are you having sex with someone else? What kind of noise do you make?

Shmily believes in sexual liberty and he is a typical social butterfly. He does not want a stable boyfriend and he does not like the feeling of being constrained. 'When it comes to relationships, I like doing retail, but not wholesale.' He explains that 'doing retail' means dating around, and seeing one man after another, while 'wholesale' means sticking to the same man.

He might be a social butterfly, but he does not like going to gay clubs. Besides the expense and noise, he has another reason.

> If we have to go on dates, we have to talk and spend time together. We have to go out, hang out, and maybe go shopping. We'd only have sex after dating for a few months. It might be too late if I only find out he has body odour then. So, don't you think it's better to get things done quickly? My principle is putting sex before love. Let's do it quickly. Fuck first.

Gay saunas are a frequent outlet for sex.

After having fun, we leave the room and you take your shower, I take mine. Then I play with another man. What's the point of getting so obsessed with someone? Save the I'll-call-you bullshit. They never call. I tell people not to get others' numbers. Don't be so happy even if you've got their numbers, because you might not reach them anyway. We know it after everything we've been through. But young people nowadays don't know that. They are filled with romantic ideals.

However, his go-as-you-please attitude is a result of his disappointment over the years. He used to be serious about his relationships. He was once madly in love, and he still vividly remembers the pain he suffered in the name of love.

Crying Like a Baby When His Boyfriend Got Married

The love of Shmily's life, 'Glue', was only 18 and a university student. Glue was the 'leftover'—a back-up boyfriend—of a friend. The friend's real boyfriend got jealous, so the friend set Glue up with Shmily, who was 28 then. He tried to be the best boyfriend. They chatted for one hour every night and he thought they got along well.

However, Shmily could not reach him after a while. So, he went to Glue's home and waited for him outside, but there was no sign of Glue all day. He eventually plucked up courage and asked Glue to meet him outside a department store. He even brought a present for Glue. However, there was a girl with Glue when he arrived. Shmily believed Glue was telling him something.

> He was trying to say that he was fed up with this kind of life, that he was getting married.

Shmily was not only going up against a woman but also against the morality and norms of society. Getting married was a must for everyone, and the only option was to marry someone of the opposite sex.

> I couldn't help it. I never cried so hard in my entire life. Once he turned around, tears kept rolling down my face. I was so numb when I got home. I was living in an old house in Wan Chai. I didn't have the nerve to tell my mum. I couldn't even eat, and I couldn't reach him over the phone. I wasn't myself for months. If he had told me he was tired of me, so he was looking for someone new, I'd have given him my blessing. But he shouldn't have kept me hanging and made it so difficult for me. I was doing my laundry one day, I fell on the floor, and it was a wake-up call. I told myself, 'I've been so stupid. I really have.' From then on, I never took it seriously with another guy again. It hurt too much.

Shmily ran into Glue a few years later at the airport in Thailand. Glue was taking a vacation alone. That made Shmily think that Glue had never got married; it was just an excuse.

> He was just looking for an excuse, so he said he was with a woman. It was a perfect excuse, because you can't force somebody to be gay. That's why I tell all the young people, if a guy tells you that he has a wife, you have to wise up. He's actually not that into you.

Glue is now in his fifties. They run into each other sometimes, but they do not keep in touch. Shmily still remembers his birthday, but he says, 'I still remember it, but so what?'

Hung up on a Man for a Decade after a Glimpse at a Public Toilet

There was another story between Shmily and a man that lasted for years. Shmily lived in a temporary wooden house in the 1980s. It was not convenient for him to take showers at home, so he went to public showers all the time after work. When he was washing, he had his eyes on another man. That man surprisingly hooked up with Shmily for years.

> He followed me. He walked only when I walked. So, I just stood there. I didn't move. After standing there for a while, I asked him for his number.

They saw each other on and off for a decade. Shmily never asked if he was with other men, and they never got mixed up with money. When they had sexual needs, the man went straight to Shmily's place for a hook up. They had

Young Shmily. Source: Interviewee.

sex about once a month. However, Shmily thought he was only 'doing retail' with the man instead of 'wholesale'. They seldom see each other anymore. The man had clearly lost interest in Shmily's body the last time they met.

> He was terrible. I didn't mind serving him, but he should have at least given me a little response. He shouldn't have acted like that. What did he think I was? We'd known each other for ten years. It wasn't a joke.

Shmily has not seen the man for a while. He never called him either.

> Why bother? I prefer it to be easy come, easy go. Why do people have to be so clingy?

Shmily does not believe that two people can be together forever. At least in this aspect, homosexuals and heterosexuals seem to be very similar.

> Keep steady, but what for? It's all a lie. It's fine as long as someone knows when to return home, and as long as he remembers to change his underpants after hooking up with someone else. It's all just an illusion. A couple may seem very happy together for decades, but in fact, one of them might go out looking for hook-ups, and the other might go and hire a masseur. Everyone screws around. You just keep someone at home waiting for you. Couples nowadays get bored easily after a while.

Fearing Sting Operations When 'Fishing' in Fishponds

In the 1960s and 1970s, gay men in Hong Kong looked for sexual partners in public toilets. Such a public toilet was called a 'fishpond' or 'garden' and the act was called 'fishing' in the gay community. Society was rather conservative, so most gay men looked for acquaintances to satisfy their sexual needs in 'fishponds'. However, there were not only 'fish' [gay men] in the 'fishponds'. Heterosexuals had to go to toilets as well. Moreover, there were plain clothes cops who targeted gay men. They posed as gay men to entrap gay men in their sting operations, especially in the 1980s. There were even homophobes entrapping and beating gay men up for no reason.

> There were cops and fake cops. It was best not to do anything without seeing a hard-on first. They might open their [toilet stall] doors, but they were phonies. I was smart enough. I told people, if he didn't open his door and do it 'by hand', I wouldn't go over. Someone did try but got kicked. He didn't even get a chance to put his trousers on when he ran away. I still remember that. So, I thought, what have we done to deserve that? That's how I found out about those bigots. There's nothing wrong with being a homosexual. People only looked down on us because of our behaviour. So why did we do it anyway? The problem was we had no space. We didn't have [gay] saunas like we do now.

Most gay men do not go 'fishing' in 'fishponds' nowadays, because there are so many gay venues. At the same time, public toilets have changed radically.

> There are attendants now, so it doesn't happen a lot. They are probably there as lookouts. You should go to the famous 'fishpond' in Mong Kok. The toilet attendant, he was a bastard. That dickhead is such a pain in the ass. He makes his rounds all the time, watching what you're doing and asking us why we don't close our doors. I don't like closing it. What's wrong with that? Is it against the rule or something?

However, gay men were sometimes violent with each other as well.

> Yes, it did happen, that asshole. It was a guy in Rome Club [a gay sauna, now closed]. I only touched him, but he punched me, and I fell to the ground. I asked him afterwards, 'Did you have to punch me?' Most people just told others, 'Sorry, you're not my cup of tea!'

Before gay saunas were opened, a Shanghainese bathhouse called Yuk Tak Chee became an alternative venue for gay men. However, it was very different from today's gay saunas. Since most of its customers were not gay, it was still risky for gay men to look for sex there. 'A friend told me that a "sister" hit on a guy, who rejected him. However, he thought the guy was playing hard to get, so he kept going. In the end, he was handcuffed and taken away by the police.'

Handwritten Letters Establishing Sincere Communication

Besides 'fishponds', some tabloids used to print personal ads, which became another way for gay men to look for each other.

> There were personal ads in tabloids like *Kam Yeh Pao* and *Sing Yeh Pao*. You could send letters to those people. They usually said their life was dull, so they wanted to meet new friends. Then they exchanged letters. That's how I met one of my friends and we've known each other for decades. The letters were handwritten. Now we use computers to send mail and we can't see people's handwriting. It wasn't like that. Handwriting reflected trust and honesty.

In traditional Chinese culture, you can form a first impression of a person by looking at their handwriting. Now we communicate with each other through email in standardized fonts. It is not just superficial, but also somewhat insincere. It is like people wearing the same mask even though they look different underneath.

Those tabloids are long gone, and personal ads have disappeared for years as well. Meeting people online is now the most common way to make new friends in the gay community. Online dating is easy, but it can also be a sham.

> Everything is virtual on the internet. I heard there are many frauds. When you meet someone for real, he might look 25 from behind. But when you see his face, he actually looks 52. They are all frauds.

Without the approval of society, gay men have to be more cautious when they meet others. Shmily rarely brought new acquaintances home.

> First of all, my mother was always home. Besides, you didn't really know him. He might come and stalk you or ask for money. I was quite cautious. I didn't give people my phone number easily. I only gave them my pager at most. I had to really trust someone before giving him my home number.

Normally, he would only let his guard down towards someone referred by a trusted friend in the gay circle.

Human Touch and Heart-warming Soup in a Gay Sauna

At the age of 65, Shmily has to deal with another problem—ageism. Some gay saunas may turn away senior customers who are worn out with age. But of course, they would not say outright that 'people over 60 are not welcome.' Instead, customers are screened at the entrance.

> They would see me in their CCTV monitor, and tell me through the door phone. They said, 'I'm sorry, we are "members only".' So, I'd ask them, 'Since when have you become "members only"?' They'd say, 'Since today.' I'd tell them I could apply for membership, but they'd say they are already full.

However, not every sauna is prejudiced like this. Some old venues with long histories still cater to the senior crowd. The older gay men are treated nicely so they still have a place to go.

> Just look at XX [a gay sauna]. They know how to do business. People of all ages are welcome. It's fine even if nobody wants me, because the entrance fee is cheaper. It only costs $58, even after the fee was raised. There's also soup on weekends. You should try their soup sometimes. It tastes great! You can have two bowls of soup filled with meat. You have big chunks of bone for you to suck the marrow out of. For an extra HK$10 to 20, you can have your meal there. It's like a nursing home, with three karaoke rooms for customers to sing in. Sometimes it's so busy that all the lockers are taken; customers will have to wait in line. I don't care if other saunas charge more than HK$100. I heard there were only four customers once in another sauna, so there was nothing they could do. You could only watch TV if you didn't like the rest of them. But why the heck would you watch TV in a sauna? That's not [what saunas are for]. [Sauna owners] should know better. Why do they have to be so discriminatory?

Few gay men would come out voluntarily in the past. Shmily did not come out either although he tried to stay true to himself.

> I can't hide some of my feminine little gestures, especially with my fingers. I believe gay men have to be somewhat feminine. It's natural. Acting straight is just too much work. Why should we pretend [to be someone we are not]? Why can't we be ourselves? If you are gay, just accept it and enjoy your life.

A Loving Mother and a Difficult Father

Shmily never told his mother about his orientation, because he understood that no mother would want her son to be gay. His mother might have guessed it, but she never said anything. The only thing she told people was 'my son is perfect, except that he never got married.' However, Shmily believes his sexuality is 'a beautiful flaw'.

His mother told him when he was 12 that she could not support him anymore because she did not have enough money, so he was asked to go to his father. However, he had never met his father before. There was not a family portrait at home with both his parents in it. He did not even know what his father looked like. So, his uncle arranged a meeting for him with his father. His father bought him some clothing 'out of duty' for the meeting, but his mother did not get anything. He was caught in the middle. 'That's why I thought I was miserable during my childhood.'

Shmily and his mother took care of each other. 'She moved to a nursing home. I secretly visited her every other day during office hours. I never missed a visit in eight years, unless I went on vacations, at which time I'd tell her I couldn't visit her for a few days. Otherwise, I visited her every other day.'

Shmily did that until she passed away. However, it was totally different with his father.

> [One day] my stepmother called me and said my father had been admitted to hospital. She asked me to visit him if I could at St. Paul's Hospital. But that dickhead yelled at me. He sat on his bed and asked me, 'What do you want?' I said he was my father after all, so I was visiting him. I thought I might have to help him taking showers one day. 'You don't have to,' he said. 'Fine,' I said, 'if you say so.' Okay, it was him who said I didn't have to see him. I wasn't the one who refused to go, so don't say that I was an ungrateful son. He died three days later, so it was somewhat fortunate for him.

Many gay men cannot accept their own orientation for various reasons. Claiming to be a Catholic, Shmily struggled and was scared at first because of his faith. However, after his breakup with Glue, he let go of all inhibitions and moved on. He started playing around. He cut loose and accepted his sexuality.

> Why is it a sin? Why don't you ask God why I was born gay? I have no idea why I become such a slut whenever I see a guy, but I wouldn't take a second look at a woman. Let me tell you, you can fool the world but not yourself. What would happen during the Last Judgement? God wouldn't ask you what great things you've done. He'd only ask you how many people you've loved. I'd tell him I've loved 1,500 men. We'll all go to hell anyway, so what? There'll be plenty of us. We'll be in the lowest hell, where we'll have enough *mahjong* buddies.

Shmily is now taking part in a lot of gay-related events. He even joined the pride parade. His gay identity has become a calling for him.

I am a *memba*, so I have to help even more. Besides, it's not a problem at all for me to be seen in public. Dressing as a woman is nothing. I'm an extra in movies. I'm acting, so what do you care? Everyone is afraid, afraid of going public and admitting that they are gay. But you won't look the same with your make-up on. You can put a paper bag on your head if you want. Nobody says that gay men aren't allowed on the street. Look at Mardi Gras. They do it so well in Australia with thousands of people attending. It's big. Hong Kong is no comparison. There were 1,800 people in Hong Kong this year. I hope there'll be 2,800 people next year, with more and more people joining our parade. It was very popular in Taiwan. There were 60,000 people.

A Great Listener at the Gay Hotline

Shmily started volunteering at a gay hotline in 2000, answering questions for other gay men who might have questions about their sexual orientation.

He saw a guy at a beach writing something with a stick in the sand once, 'no one is like me, unless there are two of me.'

> I thought that was deep, so I kept it in my heart. And it's true. Nobody will be exactly like you. Everyone thinks differently. How can you expect someone to be like you?

Shmily thinks that every individual's situation is different, and he thinks gay men should take up some social or family responsibilities.

> I encourage them. If you are the only heir in your whole family with a long family history, you should get married if you can still get your dick up. It's really sad though.

He saw many gay men trying to fulfil their family duties even when they were cheating. Some who looked for sex in a sauna would suddenly tell him, 'I can't. Time's up. I have to go home to take care of my grandchild.'

Those people never came out. They played their parts as husbands, fathers or even grandfathers because of social norms. They hid their primal desire quietly, and played roles foreign to their nature by separating love from lust.

Shmily believes homosexuals should play their part for family and society. However, when it comes to sex, he cannot accept any of them having sex with women.

> What? I cut all ties with anyone who had a wife. I disliked married men. No way [I would be in a relationship with a married man]! I couldn't do anything if he [kept the marriage from me]. But if I ever found out, I couldn't be with him anymore. We couldn't even stay friends. It'd feel kind of dirty, like I was wrecking a happy family.

Shmily would not want to come between any couple, not even a gay couple.

> There was no way I'd be a home-wrecker. I'd stay with you if you would break up with your other partner. Otherwise, I'd rather end things with you.

You should go back to him. That's what I'd do. I'd hold on tight to you if you were the only one left in the world. But there are so many gay men in Hong Kong. Even if just one-tenth of the population is homosexual, there are 700,000 [gay men], so why should I be bothered [with one]?

Sexuality was never a problem for Shmily at work. He believes it was because of his sense of responsibility. Some people have asked him directly about his orientation, but he neither admitted nor denied it. He told people, 'I am if you think I am. I'm not if you don't think so.'

> It was simple. I didn't have to tell them anything.

As a typical gay man, he was very popular among his female colleagues. He has his own explanation for this phenomenon where gay men and women make best friends:

> Because we understand them. We have the mind-set and the sensitivity of a woman, as well as the masculinity of a man. We make decisions quickly, so it's different. I think gay people have higher IQ, and a higher pitch when we speak.

His Epitaph: 'This Man Died a "Virgo"'

Shmily is quite proud of his rather essentialist notion of gay identity, and he is satisfied with his career. When asked about regrets of his life, he said he certainly had some. First of all, he did not go to university. Second, he did not even want to acknowledge his father. His last regret was that he never lost his virginity. Shmily met someone when he was young, one of the men he never got over.

> He was really great in bed. He licked me, and he just blew my mind. People say that gay men don't just fuck someone else, but they can be fucked as well. He totally loosened me up and I was completely relaxed, but he couldn't get inside. I didn't know how to work with him either. So, I regret that I never lost my virginity. I was never fucked. So, I can write on my tombstone that 'this man died a "Virgo"'.

The definition of virginity seems to be more complicated in the gay community. Now that Shmily is retired, he sometimes works as an extra or a volunteer when he has time.

> I get up at 5 a.m. Then I go jogging. I have to jog. I take a shower, then I go home and take a nap after my morning jog. Nobody calls me in the morning. Nobody wakes me up. This morning nap is bliss. I wake up and cook after that. I volunteer in the afternoon, go to Midnight Blue [an NGO for male and transgender sex workers], go to a sauna or go to Shenzhen. I stay home in the evening watching TV or taking phone calls.

He even goes on vacation sometimes with financial help from his rich friends.

> I told my mum, 'Don't worry about me. You know how thrifty I am. Besides, I have so many friends. They always help me and take care of me. So, relax!'

He borrowed an office from Rainbow of Hong Kong (a *tongzhi* group) to hold his birthday party a few years ago, and all his friends, old and new, attended.

> I saw all my friends there, everybody that I knew. I told them not to bring me gifts. I had everything I needed. But Rainbow of Hong Kong didn't have any money, so I put a box there. [People] could donate as much as they wanted. The group got over HK$3,000 at the end. That slut I know said, 'This old queen's raised a lot of money.' Ken [cofounder of rainbow of Hong Kong] was surprised as well that I had such generous friends.

Not Alone in the Gay Circle If Everybody Stands Out

Shmily has so many friends who sometimes give him headaches, but he still thinks that 'you can't isolate yourself if you are gay. I have some friends who are cocooning themselves. They are not cocooned teenagers, but cocooned old folks. There are so many of them. I'm one of them, so I have to come out.'

He stays true to himself, and he supports people who have the courage to stand out and be themselves.

> There's a line in a Chinese opera: 'Deny all you want, but you have to admit it eventually.' So, why pretend? That's why I think Ken has guts. He admits that he is HIV positive, so everything's out in the open. It's the reason why I'm willing to help him, to distribute leaflets and set up information booths on the street for him. I want to support him.

A recent picture of Shmily. Source: K.

Looking back on his life, he concluded sentimentally:

> Being gay is my biggest failure, but it's also my greatest achievement. I wouldn't have led such an eventful life if I weren't gay.

Shmily is a famed icon. Being one of the very few older gay men who have come out in Hong Kong, he is frequently interviewed by the media. He was also the first chairperson of Gay & Grey and has done a lot of talks and interviews to educate the public about the challenges of being an old gay man living in Hong Kong. He is, of course, empowered by the whole process. I remember after he attended the book launch, he told me how frightened he had felt initially when he stepped into the room with hundreds of people looking at him: 'They seemed nice, and so I could relax and tell them who I was. The experience was wonderful.' However, his story was reported in the mainstream newspaper **Ming Pao**. *Then one day when he went to church, a priest handed him the newspaper without saying a word. He said the book officially outed him.*

Shmily likes dressing in colourful clothes, and he loves being 'a slut and a flirt'. He spent HK$300 once on a bottle of Dior fragrance when he was young. I joked with him, 'After this book is published, some directors might be interested in your story and adapt it into a movie. You will no longer be an extra. You'll get a leading role instead.' He took it seriously and thought about it carefully. 'I'll have to dress up as a woman, and I want Eddie Peng Yu-Yen [a Taiwanese young actor] to play my younger self.'

Back in his own 'ordinary' life, Shmily usually plays a nobody as an extra. He is not well-off, but he is very generous. He brings gifts for everyone at our monthly gatherings. The things I have received include a large pile of newspaper clippings on gay issues, tableware redeemed through collecting supermarket stamps, fake silk pyjamas embroidered with dragons and phoenixes that usually appeal to Westerners, and a large pile of gay DVDs, porno, and otherwise. I have no idea why he gave me those gifts, and most of them are not too useful for me, but I accepted them, because he is such a passionate soul. No wonder he has so many friends. He is a common, very straightforward man with a great sense of humour. I genuinely see it in him the primary meaning of the word 'gay', which is 'happy, joyful'.

He has begun to write his autobiography and is currently seeking a publisher.

4
David

A Charming Liar (1946–)

Born into a large family in Hong Kong in 1946, David is the youngest of many siblings. Some were killed during the war. His father died when he was very young. After graduating from college, he worked as a social welfare professional for over thirty years before retiring. He realized his sexual attraction towards men in secondary school. When he watched movies, he was attracted to the male lead. He realized his orientation after an ambiguous same-sex experience he had in his teens.

> I tried it with a friend. His father was a friend of my dad's. We hung out at his place. We were just playing and then we started wrestling. It was my fault, because I started caressing him. He was turned on. It was exciting for young men. But nothing happened in the end and he wasn't mad at me. It was because of these fragments that I finally realized my sexuality.

As he grew older, David further explored his sexuality with his male cousin.

> I tried to seduce my younger cousin . . . I lived in a big house. We held a banquet one evening and all the adults went to the restaurant beforehand to play *mahjong*. I stayed at home with him, but we had nothing to do, so we went into a room. We didn't really make love though we both took our pants off. He didn't refuse. It was probably exciting for young men who were curious. We did it several times. That's how it began. We never talked about it after that. Now his daughter has even got married.

People (mainly middle class) often held house parties in the 1960s and 1970s. One of his secondary schoolmates who was also gay invited him to an all-male party in Sham Shui Po.

> I told him I had never gone to one of those parties before. He said, 'It doesn't matter, just do whatever I do.' So, I watched him the whole time. I then learnt that all of them hugged and kissed each other. If you liked someone, you just dragged him to a corner and did whatever you wanted . . . maybe kiss a little. If you wanted to do something more intimate, you had to go to the bedroom or the toilet.

The host of that party lived alone. His parties usually had twenty to thirty guests and the apartment was filled with soda, peanuts, chips, and so on. There was no alcohol in those days. They would start off with slow dancing most of the time, so people could hug and kiss.

> It was awesome! Everyone was [gay]. As they say, 'People become braver when they have company.' When a group of people who spoke the same language got together behind closed doors, they really let go.

Young, Cocky, and Surrounded by Admirers

David said he felt like a kid in a candy shop and it was an eye-opener for him, but he felt safe at the same time. He started exploring the gay community after that.

'Young', 'wild', and 'free' are probably the best words to describe David in his youth. Cheating on one's boyfriend was a cardinal sin back then. However, David dated six or even seven men at the same time. Looking back on his wild youth, David is 'somewhat proud' of himself. He thinks 'it's fine as long as you have great time management skills . . . And don't mess things up.'

But in fact, he once went to a movie with two boyfriends, making both of them miserable.

> I went to a movie with two boyfriends, one sitting on each side. We were all friends. In the middle of the movie, one of them put his hand on mine, so I held his hand. Then the other one did the same, so I held his, too. I was holding both of their hands. One of them suddenly noticed and became absolutely furious.

David dated for a while before settling down with one of the men. They moved in together and started a sort of a family. Like many other couples, passion slowly turned into attachment and the separation of love and lust. His partner started going to public toilets in 1989.

> He hid it from me in the beginning, but you know, you can't keep it a secret. So, I went ballistic. I wrote on a piece of paper what he should do—what rules he had to obey, what else he shouldn't do—and he had to tell me before doing certain things. Of course, he agreed to it at first, but he couldn't keep his promise in the end. So, I was really upset. I knew it was human nature. We were together for a long time, so it was only natural that he lost interest in sex with me . . . It was fine for me that he did those things. I wrote on another piece of paper that I didn't mind what he did outside, as long as he didn't bring anything home; as long as he didn't bring his affairs home. I also told him that I did things outside too. To be fair, you couldn't treat me like nothing, so I went out, too. I thought then, he was screwing around, so we might as well break up, but he kept begging me. I was okay with it in the end. To be honest, it's human nature . . . I was actually very sensible. I didn't even care when he brought someone home later on . . . Then he kept a 'steady friend'. I couldn't care less, as long as he didn't bring this man home.

They were together for a few years. By that time, I had met another man, so a couple eventually turned into a foursome.

Home, the Fortress of the Couple

Most people might have difficulty understanding this kind of relationship. However, the people involved were perfectly fine with it.

> When we went out or had dim sum, there were always four of us. So, we became quite close, but I kept my promise and I never let my boyfriend stay overnight.

As far as David was concerned, home was a fortress for the couple. They were having a foursome, but he wanted his home for the two of them. Even though his partner sometimes took his boyfriend home to stay the night, David kept his promise all along. He never brought anyone home to sleep over.

> It didn't matter to me that he didn't keep his promise, but I had to, because I saw him as the best person for me.

To everyone they knew, they were a couple. When David described their relationship, he said, 'We were like brothers.'

> We went everywhere together as a couple.

His partner's parents were open-minded and accepting of their relationship without problems. David treated them like his own parents as well.

> I treated them like my own father and mother. I went on a cruise with them to Xiamen. Everyone on the liner said we were great sons. Nobody knew that I wasn't their real son. He took care of his father and I took care of his mother. I literally carried her to the liner and to the car.

Unfortunately, this harmonious relationship did not last forever. In the last few years of the 1990s, David's partner ended his relationship with his boyfriend and met another man.

> The new man wasn't such a nice person. He was particularly manipulative. He didn't receive a lot of education, but he was good at scheming and messing things up. He was definitely a bad person. He was trying to get rid of me.

David knew that someone new is always better. The new boyfriend was forgiven constantly in the name of love.

> My partner knew that he was bad. He stole his money and tried to frame me for a lot of things. My partner was a university graduate like me, so he never lost his judgment. However, they had only known each other for two or three years then, so they were head over heels in love.

There was not only conflict between David and his partner, but also between his partner and the new boyfriend. 'They did break up. He threw his keys back at him. They did everything. They fought. But he was a real piece of work and he always came back.'

Illness Makes Life Unpredictable

David's partner took the new boyfriend on vacations all the time, and always paid for everything. They had a fight once and David's partner went off with other friends. The new boyfriend was furious. David thought that they would not last long. Unfortunately, his partner fell ill then, and he could not move about easily. They had insisted on living together exclusively and allowing no one else to stay, but, because of David's partner's illness, the rule was broken for the first time by the new boyfriend. He made accessories, so he could work wherever he wanted as long as he had his toolkit with him.

> We had four bedrooms, so the new boyfriend suggested working there so he could take care of my partner . . . Who knew that actually he was moving in? It was his office at first, but he lived there in the end, because he said he had to look after my partner. But he went home every night at 8 or 9 to massage my partner's mother's feet.
>
> I suggested to my partner, 'Why don't I resign so I can take care of you?' But he didn't want me to. He didn't know he would be ill for such a long time, and he said my job paid really well anyway, so I didn't insist. We were like brothers. I didn't know he was going to die.

David's partner's parents were open-minded and they always knew their son was gay. They not only accepted David, but loved him a lot like their own son. 'His father was particularly good to me. He treated me better than his own son. His mother trusted me more than him.'

However, the trust and closeness was gone after the involvement of the new boyfriend and his partner's death.

> The day my partner died, I went to the hospital in the morning. The new boyfriend wasn't there. After taking care of the business at the hospital, I went to my partner's mother's place. I rang the doorbell, but no one answered, though I could hear their television was on. So, I kept on ringing. I thought his parents must have collapsed in shock. No one answered the door for a long time, so I called them but still no one answered. After more than ten minutes, someone finally opened the door and it was their relative. I asked why no one had answered, but then his mother came out and yelled at me. She said I was responsible for the death of her son.

Her behaviour made David speechless.

> I had intended to take care of his mother until she passed away. However, that man made things up and said I was responsible for her son's death, that I was the one who made her son sick. There was nothing I could do. She was old, and it really broke my heart.

When his partner was alive, he used to tell David, 'Don't you dare die before me. I will be the first one to die.'

That is why David always thought it was his responsibility to take care of his mother. However, as things turned out, he knew there was no way for him to do that. He knew how greedy and manipulative the new boyfriend was, so he was worried he might be slandered.

> He swindled a lot of money. It was really a lot. I shared a safe deposit box with my partner. Do you know what happened when I opened the box? The staff at the bank asked me, 'Did your friend have a friend called so-and-so? You have to beware of him.' Even someone at the bank told me that! Can you imagine what he did? I asked them, but they said they couldn't say but I had to beware of him anyway.

Fortunately, David and his partner had always been financially independent. His death did not cause any financial problem for David, but it seemed to be a problem for his partner's family.

> They asked me if I knew anything about his bank accounts. I think millions were gone. I told them it wasn't my problem. We were financially independent. But in fact, I know it was definitely him.

No Need to Come Out

David was born into a big family with many siblings. He had a great relationship with them, but he never revealed his sexuality to his family.

> I never thought I needed to come out . . . Young people might be more liberal nowadays. As for older people, they might have a problem accepting it. Besides, people around me might not accept it anyway . . . Let me give you an example. My nephew is also gay. He came out when he was 21 or 22. His mother said she found a blusher in his drawer . . . I asked her not to take it too seriously, because young people were just trying to be fashionable. But then he came home drunk one night and called out someone's name all the time. It was a guy's name. So, his mother got suspicious and asked him. He admitted it. He was in his twenties. He was more liberal, so he didn't deny it. He admitted it, but so what? Every family member around us treated him nicely to his face. We talked and laughed together. However, everyone gossiped about him behind his back. They called him queer and they didn't really respect him. They weren't too respectful of gay people in general . . . Many people think that we should come out so that we can face society honestly, and it's brave or whatever. But I think coming out is not really important to me. I might be able to support the gay cause more openly if I came out, but it was better for me to stay in the closet.
>
> I think it's difficult for Chinese to accept it. I have a huge family and you can't expect ten family members to support you in a family of fifty people. I don't want people to talk behind my back.

An Almost-perfect Lie about Marriage

To cover up his identity as a gay man, David had to be extremely careful to avoid exposing himself whether at home or at work. He said 99 per cent of his co-workers did not know about his sexuality. His family did not suspect anything, either. When he was in his thirties, he had already made up a perfect lie.

> I'm very well-organized. I told my family and co-workers that I was married. I said my wife was in Thailand and my daughter was in Britain.

David had even faked his marriage when his mother was alive.

> My mother asked me to bring a wife home all the time. But I told her I couldn't do that because I was such a playboy. I told my mother that I always fooled around. She saw one woman but then another, so I had to explain to her that it was over with the first one. And then when she saw a third woman, she might ask me why I dumped the previous one. So, I asked her why I had to take all that nonsense. I could tell her everything, but I wouldn't take any woman home, not even my wife. But, actually, there wasn't any woman.

This lie was not too convincing. However, it became almost perfect because of an unexpected misunderstanding.

> I was living in Kowloon. The wife of my brother's friend told my mother one day that she saw me in Kowloon with a woman and a child. I owed her one!

Because of a friend's careless mistake, David's lie became more credible. So, he seized the chance to make the lie even stronger.

> My office was in a seven-storey mixed-use building. There was a family living at the back and they had a little daughter, who liked hanging out with my co-workers. We played and sometimes we took photos. So, I made good use of a picture with her on my lap. I put it at my bedside at my housewarming party. I was bad. I was really bad. People looked around the house during the party and they checked every room. I told all kinds of lies when they stepped into my bedroom, saying I was married with a daughter, but that they weren't in Hong Kong . . . When the guests went inside my room, I waited for them to start talking about it. Then I grabbed the photo and said, 'No, no, don't look at it.' And I threw it in my drawer. That's why they totally bought it.

David posed as a playboy. He made people think he had accidentally got his girlfriend pregnant and they had a daughter, but he just did not want to get married.

> Now I receive three red packets[1] from people during Chinese New Year, it's the most convincing trick.

He told people his wife was in Britain at first, because he went there to visit his friends and family that year. However, to keep his lie convincing, he moved

---

1. It is a Chinese tradition for married couples to hand out red packets during Chinese New Year. David received three—one for him, one for his 'wife', and one for his 'child'.

his 'wife' to Thailand, because he spent his vacations in Thailand all the time, so people thought that he was there to see his wife.

> I went to Thailand two or three times a year. I told my family that my wife had gone to Thailand to help her brother's business. Her brother needed a hand because he didn't trust the Thais, so he asked his sister to help. And my 'daughter' was studying in Britain. I'll tell them that my daughter has had an accident one day. It's fine because I never had a daughter. It's just a white lie. I never hurt anyone, so what's wrong with a little lie? My family was relieved and so was I.
>
> I prefer people to think that I'm a playboy rather than a gay man. We are in a Chinese society. Being promiscuous is better than being gay. It might not be true, but people still think that you are a playboy because you like playing around, but if you're gay, then you're a pervert. Of course, we know that we aren't perverts, but that's what people think.
>
> Whoever reads the newspaper knows that there are people out there who beat homosexuals up. I don't want to take this risk. I'm not ready to handle it.

There were homophobic co-workers at work with him. So, whenever there was the risk of being exposed, he tried his best to cover it up, but sometimes he got really close.

David was chatting with a co-worker whom he knew very well one day. They talked about hitting on women and watching pornography. There were VHS tapes back then. David was asked if he had any porn videos to lend.

> I said yes, but then I put it behind me and totally forgot about it. One day he asked me again to lend him some porn, so I said, 'Fine, I'll bring a few tapes for you tomorrow.' But after I got home, I was so careless that I didn't check. So, I ended up bringing him some gay porn. I didn't realise . . . It was a Friday. After the weekend, when I came back to the office on Monday, he said he was really mad. He asked, 'What did you give me? It was gay porn!'

There were other co-workers in the office at the time. It was a dangerous moment, and he didn't have a lot of time to think of a solution. He had to react immediately.

> I picked up the phone instantly, and made a random phone call. I didn't even know who I was calling. I said, 'What's wrong with you? What kind of tapes did you give me? Those ones last Friday!' Then I pretended to laugh and said, 'Your prank wasn't on me, but on someone else.'

Fortunately, his co-worker believed it without a doubt. David got out of the bind safely.

Hiding His Sexuality Discreetly and Meticulously

David flawlessly kept his sexuality secret. Besides being smart and quick-witted, he was extremely vigilant. When he was in front of his family, relatives, and co-workers, he had to be as meticulous as possible. He even posed as a straight man by checking out women when he had lunch with his co-workers. After his partner died, David and his boyfriend from the foursome naturally got together and became monogamous. They were not living together, but they saw each other all the time. It was impossible for them to avoid running into people they knew when they went out. To prevent people from getting suspicious, he even scripted their dialogue just in case.

> I told him all the time, 'Don't stutter when you run into someone because that's a giveaway.' It was very simple. I like playing *mahjong* and I was so much older than he was. So, he had to remember that I was his brother-in-law, that's all. When he ran into his friends, he just had to tell them, 'He's my brother-in-law. We are going to play *mahjong*.' That's it.

If they ran into a relative, David could not pose as his brother-in-law, so they had another script.

> I'd tell him, 'Go and find Nancy. They are expecting you.'

That comment implied they were not going out with each other, but with other friends as well, male and female included.

David probably went to such great lengths to hide his sexuality because of a friend, who was arrested in a sting operation when looking for a sex partner in a public toilet in the 1980s.

> It happened to some of my friends. Two of them were arrested. One called me out of the blue one night. He asked, 'David, are you free now?' I asked him what happened. I could hear it. I could feel that something was wrong. I asked him what happened. Then he said he was at Yau Ma Tei Police Station. You could sense something. So I asked him what was going on. He asked me if I could go over. I said, 'Okay, I'll be right there.' Do you know how crazy I was? I was in my shorts. I put on my shoes without my socks. And I put on a top. It was autumn. I didn't put anything else on and I rushed there right away.

> You knew something bad had happened, but you didn't know exactly what. When I got there, the police were very polite. They took me somewhere, to a cell. He broke into tears once he saw me. He was shirtless. It was quite cold during late autumn, but he was shirtless, with only a pair of jeans. I asked the cop if I could talk to him in private. It turned out he'd gone to a public toilet and hooked up with a man. They got caught *in flagrante* [Latin]. The other guy was in another cell. We talked for a while and I told him, 'You don't have to worry about anything. I'll follow up your case no matter what. But you don't have to call me.' I said that because I heard he got yelled at when he called me. I knew his situation. So I said, 'I'll follow up your case. Don't worry.' And I said to the police, I didn't know what their protocols were, but I'd like to give him my top, because he . . . [burst into tears] It was really distressing. It really was . . . In the end, my friend was bailed out. He went abroad to study afterwards.

David was still very distraught when he recounted the event.

He did not approve of 'fishing' in 'fishponds' either, in other words, looking for pick-ups in public toilets.

> There were sting operations in the 1980s and you couldn't put the blame on others. It wasn't right, and those gay men crossed the line. Honestly, those were public toilets, and it wasn't only gay men in there. When those gay men got inside, they acted like they were at home. Sometimes two men went inside one stall. They just stood there, and people could see them clearly. People knew what was going on. There was no excuse, because those gay men didn't respect themselves in the first place. It was fine if they squatted down and hid themselves, but some of them even opened their doors. Some of them flashed their dicks for others to see with the doors to the stalls open. They were trying to seduce others. They touched their junk as if they were saying, 'Do you want to play with it?' So, they clearly crossed the line. When they saw someone they liked in the opposite stall, they didn't close the door. They opened it and took off their pants. So, I thought, some people just wanted to use the toilet. Even when the cops weren't there, people called the police if they didn't like it. Therefore, the police had to do something. That's why they couldn't put the blame on others. They were the ones who didn't respect themselves.

Lust, Like a Flood, Has to Be Channelled but Not Repressed

As for David's relationship with his boyfriend, now his partner, they have been together for over a decade. His partner is a teacher, and about twenty years younger than David. They get along well. Having been with different men for a great part of his life, David has his own beliefs about handling his relationship.

> I learnt from my past experiences that you have to learn how to appreciate your partner. Sometimes you take your relationship for granted, so you take your temper out on him or you disrespect him. You don't appreciate him anymore because the two of you have been together for so long. You've seen everything. You've seen him trimming his toenails, taking a leak or a dump. So why do you have to be appreciative? But I think you do. People have to respect each other.

Having been together for more than a decade, it was not surprising they went through the 'seven-year itch'. David understands clearly that lust, which is like a flood, has to be channelled but not repressed. So, he made a pact with his new partner. When they leave Hong Kong together on vacations, they can each have affairs with others.

> I think it's human nature. That means I'd rather both of us play around together than get cheated on. We go on vacations several times every year. During that time, we make our journey 'more delightful' and more pleasurable. We're good after we've played around. We have our fun and we have our needs satisfied. I understand human nature. I can't be in denial. I have that kind of drive myself. Of course, sex with him is good. However, sometimes

we have to have fun together. You're good enough if you can control yourself. We go on vacations a few times every year anyway, so we should take the chance to let our hair down.

They often go to gay saunas during their vacations.

We handle it sensibly even though we go to saunas. If we know that place very well, we go to different saunas . . . I totally understand it. We might have reached a 'compromise', but when you see your partner hugging and kissing someone else, you get upset. So, we have our arrangement. If we aren't too familiar with a place, such as Laos or Cambodia, we go to the same sauna. It takes time to find one, so how do you find another one? One of the agreements in our arrangement is that we don't screw around in Hong Kong, but people don't believe us.

David and his current partner have complete trust in each other, and he believes that his trust is not blind at all.

I know he doesn't screw around. I trust my judgment, because he has given me everything he has. From the day we met till this day, no matter who leaves Hong Kong, we talk over the phone once every day. We must call each other no matter how busy we are. It's a must. Of course, we have dinner and go to the theatre together. What do we do if we can't make a phone call? You find time if you want to, you do . . . If he hasn't called me by late at night, I feel very uneasy. Because, first of all, I worry whether he has a problem or something, or if he has an emotional issue, not with me, but with his family, that I don't know about. His mother is very feisty . . . I know his schedule, so I don't have to check on him. Call me what you will, but I can tell you, not many people can fool me.

David believes he will not have another foursome.

Up to now, it has never crossed my mind. It was my former partner who brought someone in out of the blue last time. I didn't understand it totally before doing it. But with my new friend, so far, up to now, it has never occurred to us. To tell you the truth, I have left all my properties to him in my will and he knows it. My friends say that I'm an idiot. They don't understand why I've done it, but I tell them, 'It's fine. If he doesn't treat me well or if we can't get along anymore, I'll change my will.' However, at the moment he's the one I can rely on the most. To be honest, I don't want to leave my property to my family. I don't get along with them too well. As a gay man, he's my 'other half'. He's my wife, so why can't I leave my property to my wife?

His Will, the Last Step of a Perfect Lie

Without marriage, many gay men and lesbians are not protected by the law like heterosexuals are. So, David believes he has to take care of his will while he is still alive. Some gay couples might resent not having the protection of a marriage. However, at the same time, David thinks that a genuine relationship is not defined by a marriage certificate.

> I say all the time that it's fine as long as we have a great relationship. Let me give you an example. When we first knew each other, we were probably very sweet. We said, 'good morning' and we kissed when we woke up after spending the night together. After ten years, you might say, 'You have bad breath, go and rinse your mouth.' It's realistic and it's human. So why do we need a marriage certificate? If we get along fine, like we do now, I'll leave everything to him in my will. Otherwise, I'll just change it. We don't need a piece of paper to prove that we are a couple. That's what I believe.

David has already worked out a reasonable explanation of his estate distribution.

> I'm going to tell another lie. I'll tell my family that I have a son [i.e., his partner]. This son is older than my daughter. He was raised by his mother . . . but his mother is dead, so I have been taking care of him . . . That's my arrangement.

Becoming Totally Immune as He Matures with Age

To summarize his life as a gay man, David thinks it has been half bitter, half sweet. He admits that his life has been joyful and fun, but, deep down, he still has his regrets.

> Straight people hold hands and kiss wherever they want. Gay people can do that, but only if you are brave enough to risk everything. It's not something you can do lightly. A lot of places that you go to, like a dinner or a party, you remind yourself that you are gay, so don't be a sissy. Don't show any clues that might reveal your true identity.

> If you are a playboy or a celibate, it's better than being thought of as a gay man. It may be different decades later, but people are not open enough to accept you. It depends on tolerance and open-mindedness. They have to understand human nature. I was born gay, so you have to understand that. I said earlier that most young people accept homosexuals now, but it's just a kind of peer sympathy. They think you are just a friend and so hang out with you and accept you. That's how they see it, but maybe I'm wrong.

Tongzhi have a difficult path to walk. However, if he had another chance to live again with a choice of his own, he would still rather be gay.

> Because I like men, even though a lot of the guys are jerks. I'm not sure if it's because of my sexuality, I'm not emotionally attached to women at all. I've always been attached to guys.

After spending a large part of his life hiding his true orientation and dealing with the intangible pressure of society, sometimes David does not even know how much he has endured.

> You've lived your life for decades. You had to roll with the punches and take things as they came when you were young. I once sneaked into the toilet to cry. I don't remember why. I've forgotten about it already. Failure teaches

success, as time goes on. I can't say that I'm totally immune to everything that happens, but at least it doesn't bother me anymore.

David looks very handsome. He is still in good shape in his sixties. He was born into a middle-class family. As a university graduate, he got a good job. Now he is retired and lives at leisure. When he has time, he plays mahjong, goes to the theatre or goes on vacations. He is living in comfort. It is the kind of life many people look forward to. However, there has always been a thorn in David's side, because he has made up lie after lie to dispel people's suspicions about his sexual orientation. Although he is very happy to see the setup of Gay & Grey and participates frequently in our monthly activities, he still does not want to come out. You can imagine how great the social pressure must be for people sometimes.

In fact, it is never easy to meet the demands of society. People say that you have no future if you are not well-educated; you are worthless if you don't make a lot of money; you will never get a girl if you look ordinary; you are not masculine enough if you do not have a six-pack; you are a loser if you do not have your own apartment to house your family. The list goes on. Society is ruthless, so you cannot take any risks when it comes to your sexual orientation. I am not sure that if you were promiscuous, you would be less stigmatized than a gay man. If you do not fit into the norms of society one way or the other, you get punished somehow. I cannot help but wonder though, is there any fun in being 'normal'? No wonder queer theory always advocates the subversion of social norms as queers just cannot stand normality.

5
Robert

A Banished Expatriate Officer in the Royal Hong Kong Police (1947–)

Robert was born into a middle-class family in London in 1947. His father was the managing director for a big company and his mother was a housewife. He has two elder sisters and a younger brother. As was the custom in well-off families in those days, he was sent off to a boarding school at around the age of seven. His parents visited him once or twice a term. He went to a boy's public school when he was 12. He learnt how to take care of himself, because he lived away from home. As a good athlete and leader in school, he was a school prefect and he headed up his house.

He wanted to be a doctor, but he did not do very well academically. So, his father sent him to Scotland for a year, where he worked for an engineering company. He came back down to London and did two years of business studies, living at home and going to college every day.

Seeking Pleasure from Mutual Masturbation in Boarding School

Robert started experiencing same-gender sex play when he was at boarding school.

> I would call it, I started engaging in locker room fun, how long is yours, how long is mine . . . And I was taught to masturbate by somebody who was standing in the shower quite innocently jerking off. He said, 'If you do this, it feels good.' So, I tried and it felt good! And I got to know four or five other boys roughly the same age basically engaging in mutual masturbation . . . hanky panky . . . that's really what it was.

Losing Virginity with His First Girlfriend

When he was a young man, he was still trying to prove his heterosexuality. He shared a house in Edinburgh with four other guys who were all straight.

> I perhaps have lived a very straight life in a funny sort of way. When I studied at a university in London, I met my first girlfriend . . . We had sex and I lost my virginity, actually, at about 21. I was very late with the ladies.

He was sad when they parted, and then he met another young lady, who used to come up to his flat during weekends. But she made an interesting comment to him, 'you're very strange because you're very loving. You're very close to me most of the time, but there's something where you suddenly have to disappear, it's like you want to drop me for a couple of hours.'

Her observation was right. He liked her company, but there always came a moment when he had to find male companionship.

Experimenting with Same-sex Desire in London's Saunas

It was the early 1970s, and homosexuality had only been decriminalized in England in 1967. The whole atmosphere was still very repressive. But he secretly tested his sexuality.

> I had discovered the delights of a London sauna, which my father warned me not to go into ever. So, of course, the first thing you do is go for it . . . The only sexual exploits really were a sort of sauna bath, and it was really more sort

Robert (fourth from left, second row) in boarding school in 1959. Source: Interviewee.

of exhibitionist than anything. You didn't actually meet somebody to take them home . . . I was a really, really good looking, fit, and young public school boy. If I went to a particular sauna bath, I . . . er . . . I was in demand for the older generation. And again, it was usually fooling around there. So, I was practically trying to be gay. I thought, this isn't right. I wasn't disgusted with what I was doing or what I was, but I was trying—I was hoping it would pass, because I somehow sensed this would be a rather different life and a difficult life to lead, and something my parents were not expecting. Haha. So, I suppose having girlfriends, I was trying to just prove something . . . obviously it wasn't meant to be.

Joining the Royal Hong Kong Police to Become a 'Real' Man

In 1974, his whole life changed.

> The economy in England was dreadful. Everything was falling apart, the miners were on strike for four days a week, inflation was up at 16 per cent . . . I was sitting in a pub one Sunday on my own and I opened up the *Sunday Telegraph* colour supplement, and there was this huge advertisement—Join the Royal Hong Kong Police! I remember this [advertisement] . . . I think I've got a copy of it on my shelf . . . I read down and it said 'under 27' and I was. It said 'two A-levels minimum' and I had that. 'From a disciplined background'—yeah, and I had boarding school. Erm . . . I applied and I went and I was just under 27—that was the maximum age. I went to Hong Kong House in London . . . and a couple of months later, I found myself on an airplane with thirty other guys and girls going to Hong Kong.

He then spent eight years in the police, from 1974 to 1981. He loved the police force, so why did he leave? It was due to his sexuality. Because of the notorious John MacLennan case (see introduction), he was identified. His promotion was blocked and he then left. It was one of the most horrible times in his life.

> It was horrible, horrible, horrible . . . I also lived in single inspector quarters in Ho Man Tin . . . I didn't know John very well—we had a few beers at the bar—because we worked at different police stations and we were often on different shift duties . . . But he was a lovely guy, super guy, very polite, very gentlemanly . . . The government created the team (Special Investigation Unit, SIU) before he died. They worked in very, very underhanded ways, which would never be tolerated nowadays. And, frankly, they bullied and blackmailed people for information to such an extent that some people weakened and gave information.

Exposed as a Homosexual by a Friend and Facing Investigation

> I think I had only come out to one particular friend in the police and I can only assume that he was the one that gave my name away, and I was interviewed and basically promised that nothing would happen to my career, da-di-da-di-da. And they knew I'd never been to a [gay] bar in my life. They actually had quite a lot of information on me, so somebody had been talking.

ROYAL HONG KONG POLICE

A Career in Leadership

Join us as an Inspector and you'll soon see what we mean. In this exciting city, dynamic, prosperous, yet unbelievably crowded, all kinds of situations can build up thick and fast.

You must be able to make swift decisions, and know with confidence that those under your command will readily follow you. You must show the kind of tact and good judgement that can quickly defuse a difficult situation; possess the determination and stamina that keeps you going when others are exhausted; and demonstrate an uncompromising integrity at all times. In short, you need leadership qualities in abundance.

To apply, you must be a single man between 18½ and 27 years of age with at least 2 'A' levels and 3 'O' levels, including English Language. If you have a degree, so much the better, you would then qualify for a higher salary. You must also be over 5' 7" tall, physically fit and have good eyesight.

After a thorough training you will become a Police Inspector, with up to 40 disciplined men ready to carry out your orders.

What we can offer you:

- Approximately £12,000* total salary for first three year tour — this is currently under review.
- 25% gratuity on salary.
- Good promotion prospects.
- Subsidised accommodation.
- Free medical treatment.
- Free passage.
- Low tax area.
- 4½ months leave on full pay on completion of tour.

If you are interested and qualified, please write for further details and an application form to The Police Appointments Officer, at the Hong Kong Government Office, 6 Grafton Street, London W1X 3LB — quoting ref ST/20/1.

*Based on current exchange rate of HK$10.80 = £1.00. (These rates are subject to fluctuation.)

 **Royal Hong Kong Police**

Advertisement for the Royal Hong Kong Police in 1974. Source: Interviewee.

HONG KONG GOVERNMENT OFFICE
6 GRAFTON STREET LONDON W1X 3LB

Our Ref. 3rd September, 1974

Kensington,
London W.14

Dear Sir,

    I am pleased to inform you that you have been selected for appointment as an Inspector in the Royal Hong Kong Police Force at a commencing salary of HK$ 2,410 per month.

    I should be grateful if you would use the attached letter to indicate whether you wish to be appointed on agreement for three years or on probation. Would you please also indicate whether a departure date of 1st November, 1974* would be acceptable.

    On receipt of your reply an air passage will be booked and a letter of appointment and form of agreement will be prepared and forwarded to you.

    A current paper of particulars of the post is enclosed. You are advised to study this carefully as it may not correspond in all respects to that previously issued.

    A stamped addressed envelope is enclosed for your reply.

Yours faithfully,

(G. Sherry)
for Commissioner

* on or about 1st November 1974

TELEPHONE: 01-499 9821   CABLES: HONGAID LONDON W1

Employment letter from the Hong Kong Government Office. Source: Interviewee.

They said, 'Don't worry. We know you are on the periphery, but we need to have a chat with you.' And they blew me down. I found out two years later, my promotion was being blocked . . . I had done very well and was being fast-tracked to a higher position. I was actually going after chief inspector, two years earlier than most people, and I was passing the interviews. I had done the exams, obviously. Then I got the interviews and I was passing it and was coming roughly second or third out of roughly sixty people . . . but not getting promoted. The first time this happened, my friends looked at me and said, 'This is strange. What's going on?' And I knew then what was going on. I didn't know why it was happening, but I suspected of course. I couldn't tell them. I was still, you know, in the closet, and when it happened the second time, because it only happened once a year, then I knew.

My boss called me and said, 'You must realise what they are doing. They sent the list of candidates who had passed to CID [Criminal Investigation Division] to check criminal record, to ICAC [Independent Commission Against Corruption] to check if they have anything on you, to Special Branch to see if there is any secret political thing about you, and to SIU, and SIU keeps posting a black mark against you . . . But, sadly, SIU kept on.' This is what he told me. I can only assume that that was what was happening. So, um, that was a nasty time . . . and right after I left the police, we were still under . . . there were a couple of scary times, I heard some guys got raided in the middle of the night . . . They were still searching and then eventually in . . . 1983, it all calmed down a bit.

Finding Love after Leaving the Police Force

He had a police friend who called him up and invited him to join his newly established financial advisory company. He then changed his field completely from policing to business. He stayed in his friend's company for seven years and went to many different places in Asia, including Burma, Thailand, Singapore, and Indonesia. He was later headhunted into a big insurance multinational.

But life is always full of surprises. While he lost his job, he found love. As he said, 'a very black cloud with a silver lining'.

He did not get into the gay scene until he left the police force. 'It wasn't until I left the police that I was really introduced to the gay scene in Hong Kong, and even in other countries. I knew two gay policemen in training with me, but we seldom talked about it. I think we were too frightened. We were scared because it was illegal, and you could go to prison for a very long time. Yes, it was a really repressed time. It was the same for everybody, not just for the police. That was Hong Kong.'

Meeting a Young Local Boyfriend on a Junk Boat Trip

Nevertheless, Robert then tried out the gay scene in Hong Kong. He hung out at train stations, and sometimes went to a famous sauna with a substantial gay clientele at the President Hotel. As he had a car, he sometimes drove to Repulse Bay to cruise. He always hung out at Dateline, which was 'a major, major meeting place and it was fun and a bar, I don't think they were gay actually . . . it just had the right atmosphere and I used to meet up all of my European friends there.'

Then one day, he told his gay police friend, 'I need to meet some likeminded people.' His friend said, 'Okay, we have a junk trip on the last Sunday of every month.' He joined an expatriate group of gay men who went out with Chinese gay boys. These expatriates were all professionals, such as senior civil servants, bankers, and engineers. And they were all in their mid-thirties, but their Chinese boyfriends were all in their mid-twenties.

He went on a junk boat trip and met his first love.

> So, I went on board and I saw this really handsome guy in the background, phwoar, um . . . and, yes, I chatted to him but I was very careful. 'How nice . . .' and so on, and it wasn't until 6 that evening that he got off the boat and I saw him get off alone. So, I went up to him and said, 'Are you alone?' And he said, 'Yes. Yes, I am.' I said, 'Well, would you like a coffee?' There was no Starbucks in those days (*haha*), so one thing led to another.

This Chinese young chap, Peter, became his first boyfriend, and they have been together since. That was June 1981, a month after he left the police force.

Coming out to His Family and Clearing the Air

In 1988, one of his sisters came to visit him in Hong Kong. He told his partner,

> Peter, 'Look, my sister's coming over. She doesn't know about us. Would it be awful if you leave me for a bit and stay with your mother?' And graciously he agreed to do so and one night my sister was looking through photos and stuff in my apartment, and she said, 'You know if you don't get married soon, we're going to think you're gay.' Haha . . . I thought this was the perfect opportunity.

So, he came out to his sister, basically 'ruining' her holiday. She ran off, rang her husband, and cried. But she is now totally supportive of his sexuality.

But he begged his sister not to tell his parents, 'They are both in their seventies, they don't need to know. If they know, they know already, but let's not worry them in their old age. They are now living 6,000 miles away.'

> And, of course, she went home and told them indirectly, but it obviously came out. Erm, and they never spoke about it with me, and they didn't love me any less. I was welcome to stay with them during my summer holidays, but they knew that I knew they knew.

As for his brother, 'My brother apparently had a complete sort of fit. He didn't believe my older sister and called her a liar and everything, because he worshipped me. But he's come around now, and he loves Peter and both of us are absolutely accepted into the family.'

Besides respecting Robert's personal choice, they accepted him because the UK was getting more and more open about homosexuality as well.

Getting His Partner a British Passport and Getting Civil Partnership

In 2000, they went back to London as he wanted to get Peter a British passport. He got a job in London, but the company needed Robert to go back to Hong Kong four times a year to do some training. That was the first time he and Peter had been apart for a considerable length of time, as he had to stay for one more year to qualify for his passport.

They registered for civil partnership in 2004.

> A number of reasons, economic. We knew the emotion was there. Well, actually, we thought of it twice, the first time being seriously, because we were sort of slightly alarmed about 1997. 'Oh gosh, we better get you a passport in case we need to run away.' But we never got around to it, frankly. The opportunity wasn't there. We both had good jobs, we didn't want to give up our jobs. And it wasn't really until about 2000 when I was getting older and thinking actually about tax and it would be valuable if we were partners . . . And one of our friends had already done it and we thought, 'It's not that difficult.' But we were a bit put off by the bureaucracy of it. And when we went to London on a trip, we actually thought, 'Come on, let's register our names and see how difficult it is.' And we went to the registry office and registered our names, and they said, 'Fine, you got three months to actually do this.' Um . . . no, we had up to a year, actually. You got to register your desire to get married, and then you have a year to actually do it. It's a two-stage process and so it happens that about six months later, we had to go to London again. I can't remember the reason and we said, 'Let's go for it.' But, basically, it's more for economic reasons.

> And I must say, the embassy was fantastic. We obviously had to declare we were gay. No problem at all, and then I had to put together a dossier proving that we had lived together for a certain time, so we made a copy of the passport, got letters from family. They said, 'Right,' stamped the passport, 'Permitted to enter the UK without a visa' or something . . . My brother and sisters were very happy and even went to the civil ceremony.

Accepted by His Partner's Family and Having a Harmonious Relationship

His boyfriend, Peter, who is ten years younger than him, comes from a working class Chinese family. He has many siblings, two mothers, and one father: a very traditional Chinese family. He had to leave school at 16 and worked in a factory. From Robert's perspective, 'He always worked responsible jobs. In fact, his family rely on him heavily now because of his language, his intelligence, and maturity.' It seems that Peter is still very involved with his family: 'He's forever getting phone calls from his sisters, who are older than him.' And Robert seems to be accepted by his family: 'I'm Uncle Robert . . . We know that they know . . . I mean, a European and a Chinese living together, so they must be stupid if they don't.'

> I am always invited to Chinese New Year. I am invited round to most activities by one particular niece. She's got two kids and she's got fluent English. She works in Central, and Chinese New Year, most of the family seems to go to her apartment. I am always involved in that. I take the daughter with Peter to the ballet sometimes, because she loves dancing. I take the boy to a country club for swimming. It's good fun.

Long-term Monogamous Relationship and Occasional Hook-ups

In fact, Peter was the first person he ever lived with, and they have taken care of each other as a couple.

> We have basically lived our whole life here. We had a coffee this morning. We are a very strange couple, actually. We don't hang around each other. We live together. If I want to go and have a swim, he doesn't have to come with me. If I want to go eat sometimes at the country club, I say, 'Do you mind? Do you want to come?' He always says 'No', because he doesn't actually like the country club much. I say, "Do you mind if I go?' He says, 'Fine, go.' It's the way we've always been. Some of our friends find it quite strange. Like yesterday I went hill walking. He doesn't like hill walking. Crazy to try to bully him into hill walking, that would break the relationship. So, I say, 'Are you really okay spending Sunday on your own?' He said, 'Fine, I could sleep in. I could go to my family.' Ah, because we know the relationship is absolutely rock solid. If I go to . . . um . . . to Bangkok, he knows I'm not going to sit in my hotel room knitting socks. I am going to be out in the gay scene. It doesn't worry him. He thinks I am mature enough and old enough not to get into too much trouble, and he just doesn't want to know. If he did something, I wouldn't want to know. What goes on when you're away . . . don't be silly, don't get into trouble.

So, they practise the 'don't talk, don't tell' policy.

> I would never lie and say I didn't go out, because he wouldn't believe me. Here, occasionally I would go for a massage. I won't cruise anymore. I don't know how to cruise anymore. But if I want some release, I may well go to a massage establishment. There are plenty here. I often tell him—not always, to be honest. I don't think he needs to know every time. I tell him I'm off for a massage and go. There is no question when I'm back. Sometimes we joke about it . . . Everyone knows about the happy ending . . . It's stock knowledge nowadays. Perhaps I'm a bit of a coward. I don't tell him every time I go, but I don't go that often, so it doesn't matter . . . Even in Bangkok, these little guys sometimes they would give you their numbers. I would tear them up at the

airport. He's too . . . it sounds romantic, but it's too precious to ruin a relationship for a ten-minute quickie. That's how I view it.

An Interracial Gay Couple with Their Own Rules

So, what are the differences between an interracial couple and a non-interracial couple living together? Robert knows some expats who are going out with Chinese men.

> In all we had twenty expats, all were there. We know a lot more who didn't have partners, but they had all been brought up in the old way. We were all similar ages. Relationships were valuable in those days. Of course, you couldn't hop around too much, because it was illegal. So, I suppose if you found someone, you tended to hang on to them as you felt comfortable. And the other thing is, we were both working. If I went to work and Peter just stayed at home all day watching TV, going out to the store in the afternoon, Middle Bay Beach [a popular gay beach], I would become envious and jealous and suspicious, and he would have nothing really to talk about in the evening. If you're both working, then you're both obviously contributing financially for the family. I mean, basically in any relationship between *gwailo*[1] and Chinese, the *gwailo* tends to foot the serious bills, because our salaries are so much more, um, but they . . . There is an unwritten rule of a *gwailo* meets a Chinese, the *gwailo* pays the big bills. But, equally, like most of my friends, Peter has his own pride. I say to him, 'You have to contribute, I'll do the holidays, I'll do the mortgage or whatever . . . but your everyday expenses . . . you know I could afford it' . . . but he's fine. He would want to contribute, he would actually want to contribute. He'd be very offended . . . In fact, he said to me, 'I'm not a money boy, you know.'

But in 2005, Robert got cancer, and it took four and half years to recover. That's when he gave up work. 'I thought this is crazy. I can't do chemotherapy and radiotherapy and keep on working.' His health is just fine but unfortunately he has undergone a major surgery this year. Whilst experiencing ageing and thinking about the health and financial implications in the future, Robert is considering whether he would stay in Hong Kong, go back to the UK or find another cheaper place to live with his partner.

Looking Back on His Life: The Depressing Early Days

Now Robert keeps himself busy: he teaches at an international school, works as an extra for television soap operas and advertisements, and does a lot of sports

---

1. The term *gwailo* (or *gweilo*) literally means 'ghost man/men', but is often translated as 'foreign devil(s)'. It has been used widely in Hong Kong to refer to Caucasian men, and with a long history of derogatory racial condemnation. Nowadays, it has a much less negative connotation and may even be a neutral term as used by some Caucasians.

like working out, swimming, and hiking. When he looks back, the career change was the major event of his life.

> Nowadays, if a young policeman gets into a little trouble, he would have his union representative with him and all that. We were very much left out those days. Nobody wanted to touch us. I think, looking back, had I been more mature and talked to different people I'd still be in the police. When I left, it hurt, it hurt badly. But I shook myself down and got on with my life, and, actually, I've probably had more of a fun life since then than had I stayed in the police. I could meet somebody, meet somebody I loved, I could travel to other countries, so actually although it was painful, you've got to move on.

Through Robert's story, we catch a glimpse of the life of gay London in the 1960s and 1970s. He came to Hong Kong with great ambition when he was young and joined the Royal Hong Kong Police to become a 'real' man. However, he left because his promotion was blocked due to the John MacLennan case. It is depressing to hear that. As long as there is no legislation against discrimination on the grounds of sexual orientation, such prejudice will continue to prevail.

Something else that makes this interview interesting is that Robert thinks the society was generally repressive towards homosexuality in the 1970s and 1980s in Hong Kong, but the Chinese interviewees, especially those from the working class, clearly did not think so. I believe this difference is a matter of social class and social status. The colonial government in the early days was more concerned about the image of senior civil servants, and so it was all about 'saving face' for the government.

Nevertheless, after losing the job he liked, Robert met the love of his life, and their relationship was accepted by their families, so the situation can be considered a blessing in disguise. Interracial gay relationships between a Caucasian and an Asian man are a very common topic of interest in Western societies (e.g., Leong 1996; Jackson 2000; Eng 2001; Manalansan 2003; Lim 2014; Nguyen 2014). It was a prominent phenomenon in Hong Kong in the 1980s and 1990s which has received attention in academic discussions, with the focal point being how power and desire are implicated in such interracial relationships (Ho and Tsang 2000; Kong 2002, 2004).

6
Jonathan

A Gay Gambler Who Turned over a New Leaf (1948–)

Born in 1948, Jonathan came from Shenzhen. His grandfather was a village head and a landlord, so his family used to be well-off. Unfortunately, his father was also a gambler who spent the family fortune. As a result, his father was forced to become a seaman and sail the high seas for a living. Jonathan did not spend a lot of time with his father. The only thing he remembers about his father is the constant fights with his mother over money. Jonathan cannot help but wonder why, even though he and his two brothers were not educated by their father, they have ended up becoming gamblers too.

A Smart Child Who Went to a Good Secondary School

Jonathan came to live in Hong Kong around 1958. He claimed to be three years younger when he arrived in Hong Kong, so his birth year (on record) became 1951. He is the eldest son, and did well in school, coming first every year, so he was also the favourite child. His mother was especially fond of him.

> Everyone in my family spoilt me a lot, including my grannies, my two aunties, and two so-called 'aunts', who were actually my aunties' maids . . . Before my youngest brother was born, my parents had only two sons, and my mum spoilt me so much that even I felt bad . . . I was such a picky eater when I was little. I ate chicken, and I remember I had minced pork, steamed eggs, pork ribs, but nothing else. I didn't eat vegetables or fish. Most families had chicken during New Year or other holiday seasons. I liked having chicken legs and I was always given both the chicken's legs. I gave one to my little brother once, but I was told not to.

Jonathan was always top of his class. After graduating from primary school, he went to a famous secondary school in town.

> After taking the Secondary School Entrance Examination, I was the first student in my primary school to get into that famous secondary school, so of course everyone was impressed. My primary school even made a cardboard stand-up figure with my photo as a promotion . . . I received a full

scholarship because I came in about 400th in the examination out of over 20,000 candidates.

Jonathan received good grades, but it also became a pressure for him.

> I don't know why, my mum always spoke highly of me in front of people, and it became a problem for me, because I didn't know how to handle it. I was too well-protected growing up. First of all, people took care of me all the time. Moreover, I never experienced any failure before that. So, I was destined to fail in secondary school. Why's that? It's very simple. I came from a primary school in the New Territories before entering a famous English-speaking secondary school. You were encouraged to speak English even during recess. But I wasn't good enough. I was out of my league. However, my mum used to tell everyone how good I was, so I couldn't contradict her . . . I felt a lot of pressure, but I couldn't tell anyone. So, I wasn't too well-adjusted then.

With huge academic pressure and a money-minded nature, Jonathan quit school in Form 6.

> I was qualified for Form 6, but I quit by myself. I told my mum I wasn't accepted by any school and so I would look for a job. I got myself a job in a bank in the end. I graduated in 1968. My mum asked me to go back to school. I took some classes but I wasn't too serious about it. Then I went to a school in Yuen Long and became a substitute teacher. I taught in a primary school. I was lucky enough to be recommended by someone, because I wasn't even qualified to teach students in Primary 1 or 2. Qualifications weren't checked out thoroughly then.

Jonathan picked up gambling even when he was in school. Moreover, the luxurious lifestyle of his rich schoolmates in primary school was another incentive for Jonathan to quit school early and get a job.

> I was gambling all the time. I played *mahjong* and poker with my schoolmates. I didn't bet big and I wasn't in a lot of debt, but money was always short for me. Besides, the schoolmates around me were thoroughly pampered. They went to high-end places such as The Peninsula or Hugo's at Hyatt to have high tea. Spending HK$5 for a cup of coffee was a lot of money, really expensive. So, I became a big spender. I got used to it and I couldn't change. I sunk really low. I lost all my motivation. I didn't want to go to school. I just wanted to make money, so I looked for a job and got one in a bank.

First Sexual Experience at the Old Kowloon Train Station

Jonathan realized his sexuality for the first time shortly after he entered secondary school. He lived in Tai Po, so he had to take the train to the old Kowloon train station to go to school every day. However, the service was not frequent then.

> While you were waiting for a train, you might have to go to the toilet at the train station sometimes. I remember between Form 1 and Form 2 . . . I was studying in Form 1 in 1963. When I went into the toilet, I didn't know why someone was looking at me when he stood beside me. I didn't pay attention

to him, but then he seemed to be . . . He seemed to be stroking himself. We called it 'stacking the deck' then. He touched himself and got really excited. I got a hard-on myself when I saw that. I didn't know what was happening. I was scared, so I ran away. It was kind of my light bulb moment.

When Jonathan was in Form 1, he had a classmate who befriended an expatriate man. Jonathan and other classmates were often invited to the expat's home.

> I had a classmate, I think he took part in a territory-wide dance competition later on and came in the top three or something. Then he became a flight attendant. He even worked for Cathay Pacific. Now he lives in Canada. He was dating an expat, who lived in Tsim Sha Tsui. My classmate was in Form 1 and he invited us to the expat's home all the time. It was the second term. We didn't know what was going on. We hung out at their place, but we didn't know if they were a couple or what. We saw the two of them kissing, but we thought it was nothing. We saw it in movies, so we believed it was a Western etiquette.

> Of course, we only drank orange juice or milk, nothing else. There was a guy, I know he came from Shanghai. His family had a jewellery shop. He felt me up all the time. Sometimes he would hold me and kiss me all of a sudden. I found him very annoying, so I pushed him away. But he was the only annoying one, because he stuck his tongue out when he kissed me. It was very disgusting. I didn't like it. It felt dirty.

However, Jonathan was not upset about anything else. He was exposed to some foreign gay magazines at the expatriate's home, and he liked them very much.

> Playgirl wasn't even published then. But the expat boyfriend got his hands on some foreign magazines with nude photos. The models had great bodies. I was turned on whenever I saw them.

He did not realize his sexuality at first. But in Form 4 or Form 5, he met a rich schoolmate with a generous father. He was taken to Empress Pavilion every weekend.

> I was there almost every Saturday night, ball night at Empress Pavilion. It was a restaurant and a nightclub . . . Chang Loo [famous songstress] was resident there, with a Filipino band. My schoolmate's father had a table there every night, and I was one of his guests. He was unbelievably generous. I didn't know it then. For a regular job such as a postman, you made about HK$100 or 150 a month. But he gave me a red packet at Chinese New Year with HK$500 in it. So, I probably picked up my extravagant habits from him.

His schoolmate's father often took them to Shanghainese bathhouses in Jordan or Tsim Sha Tsui. Those bathhouses were not specifically for the straight or gay crowd, but Jonathan realized his sexuality through the intimacy of back scrubbing.

> There were many Shanghainese bathhouses, especially in Jordan . . . I went there all the time. There was one in Tsim Sha Tsui, and another one in Jordan

> called Cheung Lok or something. We mostly went to the one in Tsim Sha Tsui, where his jewellery shop was located. It was a place for straight guys, but it wasn't exclusive. There was no way to tell. We were asked to get our backs scrubbed. Of course, I was turned on when my back was scrubbed. I was embarrassed, but it felt wonderful. I didn't understand it.
>
> Then one day he took me home. He led me into his room and showed me some magazines. After that, we jerked each other off until we came. He was the first person I had sex with. I don't know why we were so bold. We groped each other all the time in class after that. I don't know if our classmates figured out what was going on with us. There was no way that they didn't know.

After having his first sexual experience, Jonathan could not stop thinking about it. He wanted to do it so badly. However, he said they 'didn't know any better' because all they did was masturbate each other.

The first time he had anal sex was with a man he always saw on the train.

> I remember it very well. I saw him many times. It was very late that night. I was taking the last train, at a quarter to 10, and it went from Tsim Sha Tsui to Lo Wu. I went to the toilet while I was waiting for the train. I saw him and he tried to seduce me again. I was turned on when I saw that. He pulled me into his stall all of a sudden. He was turned on and he screwed me. It was my first anal sex. He fucked me. I was so scared after doing it. I was scared for a whole month or at least a few weeks. But I couldn't stop thinking about it either.

That man later asked Jonathan out to watch a movie at the London Theatre in Jordan.

> Half past nine at night was pretty late for me, because it would be after 11 p.m. when I left the theatre. I had to go back to Tai Po after that. There were no trains or buses, only minibuses. I had to go to Jordan Road Ferry Pier, which is the West Kowloon Cultural District now, to take a minibus.

Memba-only in the Mezzanine Seats

However, that man did not show up that night, so Jonathan watched the movie alone.

> When I entered the movie theatre . . . I don't remember what movie was screening, but I remember in the mezzanine seats, oh my, they were all *memba*. They went into the toilet constantly, but I didn't know what they were doing. Then I noticed a guy. It was summer. He wore a white shirt and it was almost see-through. People didn't go to the gym then and they weren't too masculine. However, that guy had a great body. I was so attracted to him, but I didn't have the guts to do anything until the movie ended.

The two of them bumped into each other after the movie.

> We walked on the same street, so we ran into each other. We looked at each other. It was quite funny because then, when we cruised, we were all very nervous. Cruising was very embarrassing. We were quite conservative.

Jonathan followed him and walked along Nathan Road.

> I wanted to leave so badly, but when I saw him walking ahead, I just followed him. When I saw him stop, I stopped. My heart was pounding. I didn't know if I should go on following him . . . So, we kept going in circles. I followed him to Bowring Street. I followed him for a long time, almost half an hour I think. It was like that then. You can imagine the situation.

They kept flirting for half an hour.

> He finally stopped and smiled at me, so I smiled back.

They went to a motel room in the end.

> Oh, God! The place was terrible. It was a motel in an apartment building. The hygiene was nothing compared to what we see today. When I got inside, I felt—How should I put it?—I was used to the best things in life, so I wasn't too comfortable. Why was the bed so dirty? I couldn't use those towels and I didn't want to touch anything. But I was so turned on when I saw that guy. I had sex with him. I let him fuck me. He called me the next day at my office. Then he picked me up at work that evening and saw me home to Tai Po. He did it for weeks.

> I don't know how to explain it, but I was obsessed. It was like I couldn't live without him. Nobody had ever treated me like that before. He lived in Lower Ngau Tau Kok Estate, and he was in the tailoring industry. His workshop was in Tsim Sha Tsui and it was very dirty. I went to his place to sleep at night all the time. He came to my place sometimes. I thought we were dating . . . He lived with his family. We slept on the same bed with his father, but we had sex on his bed anyway. I don't know why we did that, but we did it for years.

Fighting over Jealousy in All-male Parties

There was no internet or emails back then, so gay men spread news on their parties by word of mouth. They, sometimes, did not even know the hosts.

> When you went to those parties, you didn't have to pay if you were invited. If you did have to chip in, it would just be HK$10 or 20. We would hang out for a whole night drinking soda. We didn't usually drink alcohol. We just danced. But my boyfriend, he was a real dick. He fooled around with other guys whenever he went to these parties. He hugged and kissed them when he danced, and I got jealous easily. I knew he sometimes took them to the toilet to screw them. I would get mad and leave. I wanted to dump him all the time, but we were kind of on again, off again. We were together for about thirteen years in all.

Besides going to parties, gay men liked to have high tea during that time, and they were not straight-acting at all.

> We were like a bunch of girls chatting and gossiping. We talked a lot and we were loud. We liked putting on all the trendiest clothes, so when we went out, people probably knew. But I wasn't so flamboyant. People were skinnier then. I don't know why. I looked alright, but I was kind of camp and twinky (i.e., boyish) in appearance.

Jonathan described his life this way:

> There was a girl who was really funny. She liked hanging out with us. She wasn't gay, but she hung out with us for two to three years. There was also a screenwriter for a TV station. We got together all the time. It was very common then, but it was silly. People hung out in groups. It was really silly. We would just sit there at Ocean Terminal. There was a cafe between Ocean Terminal and Ocean Centre. You just had to order a cup of coffee and you could sit there for the entire afternoon. Sometimes the screenwriter had a deadline the next day, but he just sat there and he couldn't write. Still, the TV series went on as usual. I don't know how he did it.
>
> That was how I passed the time every day. If I felt like going up-market, we went to The Peninsula to have high tea. We hung out with lots of celebrities. We went to a bar called Dateline at night. It was very famous. It was a formal restaurant during the day. However, after 9 at night, it turned into a gay bar in an instant. We went to Dateline first. The place was clearly divided. There was a corner for 'potato queens' [Asian men who like Caucasian men]. People who didn't like Caucasian men sat down at the tables. 'Sticky rice' [Asian men who like Asian men] and Caucasian men were all separated. Later, we later went to D.D. (Disco Disco, a night club). D.D. was more fun. Everyone went crazy. We would go there early, but I don't remember when. We went there almost every night. We were always there after it opened, every Friday and Saturday.

Having Sex Wherever He Went

Jonathan and his boyfriend passed their time by having dim sum, watching movies, and swimming at Repulse Bay or sometimes in Stanley. They went to Macao a lot for a while.

> During my time, of course we went for dim sum or watched movies. Then we went swimming at Repulse Bay. We didn't go to Middle Bay or South Bay. It was common to go to Middle Bay or South Bay later on . . . Sometimes we went to Stanley. My boyfriend and I, we were crazy. I can't explain why we were so crazy. We were insane. I mean we were crazy in terms of sex. We had sex wherever we went, even in broad daylight, on the beach, in the water, or on a small hill in Stanley. People below seemed tiny when we were high up the hill. But then when we went down and looked up from the beach, oh God, people could have seen us easily. And we went between the rocks on Stanley Beach. We got to know more *memba* later on, and we went to Macao. It was a very popular destination. We gathered a group of friends to go on trips . . . I only had one boyfriend then. I never met anyone else, and I didn't go cruising for other guys. I don't know why I was so devoted. In the last few

years of our relationship, I was on again, off again with him. I wanted to end things with him so many times. I wanted to break up, but I couldn't do it.

You Do Not Marry the One You Love

After going through ups and downs, Jonathan chose marriage in the end. However, he did not fall in love with a woman, and it was not revenge against his boyfriend's infidelity.

> I got married for two reasons. First of all, I gambled. Actually, I speculated in gold in the 1970s during the oil crisis, so the price went up and down. Gold trading became very popular in Hong Kong. Next door to me was a gold trading room. I heard all their noise when they were trading. I lost HK$300,000 in the end. I made about HK$3,000 a month, so there was no way for me to clear my debt. But my wife came from a rich family. She had wanted to be with me for seven years, but I just kept her hanging. I didn't want to turn down the benefits she could give me. In order to please me, she asked my boyfriend to make her clothes, to make Mandarin gowns. She went to his tailor shop to approach me indirectly. She probably knew about us.

Jonathan treated this rich girl very badly. However, the worse he treated her, the more obsessed she became with him.

> I often asked her out and then ignored her. I avoided her on purpose and I left. So, then she would come to my house. My mother, who came from a country town, was very traditional. She even asked me to get married when I was in primary school. It was funny . . . Don't laugh. Almost all of my female classmates got married in Primary 5 or 6 when they were 11 or 12. They usually got married and moved to London, Amsterdam, Belgium, or some other places. They all tried to make money from foreign exchange dealings. It was very popular in those country towns. They weren't well-educated and they didn't have a lot of skills. So, my wife went to my mother, and my mother was thrilled when I had a female visitor. She was very welcome. So, my mother invited her in. She was asked to go into my bedroom, not just into our living room. Then she went through my stuff. When I came home, I saw her going through my photo albums as well as my letters. There was one which was particularly cheesy. It said something like "Jonathan, how are you? How's your sex life with your husband?" There was no way that she didn't know after reading that letter. I was so furious, but I was quite quick-witted so I made a huge scene. I yelled at her. I confronted her and asked her why she read my letters. After that, I put it behind us.

Of course, Jonathan did not have any feelings for her. The only thing he wanted was her money.

> I had to pay off my debts, so I lied to her. I asked her once to clear a debt of HK$300,000. She was very disappointed and left me for a while. Then I coaxed her into getting back with me. But I dumped her again after she paid off my debt.

Jonathan's mother got sick and her illness changed things.

> She was delusional. She was lying in bed and she opened the door saying that someone was trying to kill her. She called her friends and relatives in the middle of the night and accused them of harming her or poisoning her . . . I didn't have a choice. I asked her to see a doctor. I was superstitious and I thought I should get married for my mum, so that she would get better. Besides, although my wife had cleared a debt of HK$300,000 for me, it doesn't mean that I quit gambling once and for all. I kept on gambling, so my finances weren't too good. But my career was quite a success . . . I started a bonding company with some partners in early 1980. There were four of us. I made HK$40,000 a month, excluding bonuses . . . I married my wife later on. First of all, I did it for my mother's health. I thought she might get better. Furthermore, I thought I had a certain social status, and so there was a lot of pressure.

A Strange Bedfellow and Reluctant Sex

It is obvious to say this marriage did not bring Jonathan happiness. In some ways, it was even torture.

> Actually, I couldn't have sex with her. However, it wasn't until . . . I don't know, sometime in August. It was summer and I got turned on easily during summer sometimes, especially in the morning. It's hot in the summer. When she started feeling me up, I got turned on. It worked eventually and I was hard. After entering her for the first time, everything changed. After that, it became easier, and I could do it a second, and then a third time.

However, Jonathan did not enjoy it. 'Not at all. I had to fantasize about other things. I had to find a substitute. In fact, I found it disgusting, because it felt dirty. I don't know why I felt this way about her . . . even to this day. I could smell something. Whenever there was fluid, it felt . . . revolting.'

Jonathan wanted to get his wife pregnant, to fulfil his duty to get married and have children, so as to appease his family.

> The only thing everyone cared about was that I had to make a baby as quickly as possible. My duty would be fulfilled and everybody would be satisfied . . . However, we had a miscarriage the first time. Someone came to improve the *feng shui* of our house. So, we relocated our stove and our doors. We had to put some stuff in our house. Then my wife really gave birth to a son, so things got easier for me. We had another son soon after.

Jonathan appeared to have a happy family, but in fact, it was not that way at all, especially his relationship with his wife.

> I actually counted: after we got married, we probably had sex no more than ten times. We rarely did it. I don't know why it didn't bother her, though. However, she wanted it very badly every time it happened. She said she wanted it, but I always pushed her away. She masturbated sometimes.

Or she'd ask me to hold her. She said she'd be satisfied if I held her, but I detested it.

He suspects his wife of knowing about his sexuality all along.

> She is supposedly very open-minded. She's supposedly worldly, so she must know what being gay is. And she must know her husband very well. She must have felt it. Women are more sensitive. Men don't usually find out nowadays, but women sense us. Take my colleagues at work as examples, the first ones who found out were mostly women, but men didn't know. They were such fools.

Jonathan married in early 1980, but he did not have a stable boyfriend for six or seven years. When he had needs, he went cruising or visited saunas. His former boyfriend met another man, and they have remained a couple for a couple of years.

Gambling Heavily as He Got Wealthier

Gambling has been a problem for Jonathan since he was young. After getting married, he became wealthier, but was emotionally destitute at the same time, so he gambled more heavily. He spent millions betting on foreign exchange such as British pounds, Deutschmarks, Japanese yen, and Swiss francs. To acquire the latest news, he turned night into day.

> Sometimes at night—It wasn't so advanced and we didn't have computers or the internet —we'd use our pagers to receive market information. They would beep and flash as prices changed . . . I stayed up late every night. Sometimes I went to bathhouses . . . or a proper place to get massages by women. Sometimes I went to that sauna in The President Hotel to get massages by men . . . Anyway, I went to those places and got massages at night. I didn't go home until it was really late. I was probably trying to avoid my wife.

Besides speculating in foreign exchange, he gambled in other ways as well.

> I sometimes went to snooker clubs, but I would play only one or two rounds, then I'd go play Chinese dominoes or baccarat. I went to illegal casinos sometimes, making bets of hundreds of thousands of dollars. I was out of control. When I was doing well, I was even coaxed into joining the board of directors of a charity group.

Jonathan's wife moved to New York with their sons around 1990 because of work, and they lived there for four years. He gambled excessively and ran up huge debts.

> I lied to my wife and asked her to clear a debt of a few million dollars. As for my monthly salary, I made over HK$200,000 in as early as 1987. It was a lot of money. I could buy an apartment whenever I wanted.

In 1989, Jonathan said he was 'gambling like crazy'. He met his second boyfriend, Ken, who was 19 then. Jonathan started a relationship with him within a week. He rented an apartment for his boyfriend, so that they could get together more easily. He even hired Ken to help him in his company.

Waking up from His Fantasy and Getting a Divorce

After his wife returned to Hong Kong in 1993, Jonathan still slept over at his boyfriend's apartment from time to time. His peaceful life was finally turned upside down in 1997.

> I cleared all my previous debts. Everything was fine and life was peaceful. However, one day out of the blue, I don't know what happened . . . My smallest son was in Primary 1. After signing his homework,[1] I left home in my T-shirt, jeans, and trainers, and I never went back.

He went to Ken's apartment. He did not tell anyone and he did not contact anyone. The only people who knew his whereabouts were Ken and Jonathan's brother, who was living in Shenzhen.

> I don't know why, but I slept through the entire time. I slept for over three months.

After vanishing for almost four months, it was Jonathan's eldest son's birthday. He had a sudden whim to take a birthday cake and go see his son.

> He usually took the school bus. It was a Saturday. I didn't know my wife would pick him up in her car, so I ran into her before I saw him. She said I shouldn't see my sons. Their father had suddenly disappeared and they had only just calmed down. She had had a hard time explaining to them why their father had disappeared. They didn't know what had happened. Then she asked about me. I said I was staying at a friend's place. I didn't tell her about my lover or whatever. The truth hasn't come out even now. She said, 'Don't bother your friend anymore. Go and rent your own place. I'll pay for it.' Then she suggested a divorce.

To avoid Jonathan's debt affecting her and the children, his wife did not want any alimony.

> I didn't have to pay for anything, not even alimony. I paid HK$1 as a token and she took care of everything. She only needed my signature. So, we were officially divorced.

Jonathan could not work the entire time. He just wanted to sleep.

> It took three months before we finally got a divorce. We went to court. I fell asleep whenever my head hit the pillow, but I couldn't sleep properly. I would break out in cold sweat. When I thought about what I had done, I

---

1. It is a common practice in primary and secondary schools in Hong Kong that parents are asked to check their children's homework and sign a homework checklist handbook.

> loathed myself. What was it for? I had everything, why did I end up doing that? I couldn't explain it myself. I just felt that it was great being a beggar. I had nightmares whenever I fell asleep . . . I'd be covered in sweat whenever I woke up. After falling asleep, I'd sit up suddenly; I'd even jump up sometimes. I couldn't go to work. Luckily, cable television had started in Hong Kong. Cable channels broadcast twenty-four hours a day, so I watched TV all day. I'd watch until I was really tired. I'd go to bed at 9 a.m. or 10.30 a.m. in the morning. I'd get up at 6 p.m. in the evening and grab something to eat. Then I'd go back to bed to watch TV. I didn't want to watch TV in the living room. That was how I lived my life.

He kept on living like that for several months, until his younger brother brought his wife back from mainland China. Jonathan did not want to bother his brother who supported him financially, so he started looking for a job.

A Helping Hand When Hitting Rock Bottom

Jonathan worked many different jobs, including as a telebet operator, insurance agent, and survey taker. He returned to his former industry in the end, becoming a securities trader in a bank. After all, he had worked in the industry for a long time and was widely known. He made HK$40,000 to 50,000 a month in the beginning. His salary was eventually raised to HK$100,000. Even with a great job and a high income, it did not solve his financial problems.

> It doesn't mean that I quit gambling. I made smaller bets. At least I didn't make offshore bets and I didn't go short when I gambled. I played *mahjong*, but I didn't go to illegal casinos. And no, I didn't go to Macao to gamble, either.

However, the biggest issue was tax.

> I owed the Inland Revenue Department over HK$500,000. It accumulated into over HK$700,000 including interests . . . So, I knew I was doomed even though I kept working. That's why I filed for bankruptcy in the end. I must say it was quite a record. I had been gambling since the 1970s. I roughly calculated it and figured out that I had lost over HK$20 million . . . It was a good thing being flat broke, though. You couldn't get a loan easily anymore. It was kind of a constraint on my own behaviour. I had to refrain.

When Jonathan hit rock bottom, someone lent him a helping hand. It was his eldest sister-in-law, who was a devoted Christian.

> My eldest sister-in-law never gave up on me. She wanted me to get back together with my wife all along. She tried very hard, taking me to different churches . . . I followed her to her church every week after I married her sister, because she was very devoted. She never skipped a day. Her two children were baptized and they both served at the church.

However, Jonathan did not get initiated into the church.

> Christians were overfriendly. They were so friendly that they scared me. I was afraid of being exposed. You couldn't tell them you're gay; you couldn't tell them you gamble; and you couldn't tell them you went bankrupt. I was afraid that people would find out about me.

His feelings changed when he went to another church.

> The congregation was different in this church . . . The people were all very nice. They gave people a lot of space and they didn't ask about your personal life.

He started going to a Christian gambling rehabilitation group in 2002. He was dragged there by his eldest sister-in-law.

> She said she paid HK$900 for the course, and it was a twelve-step program. I attended the class, then I had to go to the next room for sharing. We were in groups. I wasn't comfortable when I started sharing. What were they talking about? I lost more money than all of them put together . . . I started believing it eventually, but I still gambled.

Coming to His Senses One Day with a Hundred Years of Remorse

Jonathan finally became a Christian in September 2005. He quit gambling and found himself with the help of his faith.

> I started volunteering at the group and I started realizing my own identity. Besides, after working for some time, I began to find my true self. It was my identity to help out at the gambling rehabilitation group. It would have been embarrassing if I had been seen in a gambling venue. Moreover, I felt joy when I helped people. After all, money is not the most important thing. It was different from the thrills I got after winning a game. It's important to be recognized by others. It gives you value.

When Jonathan looked back, he finally realized he had not only lost money, but also his health and his time.

> I turned night into day. I didn't know my body was failing, but all sorts of complications started to show up when I finally understood. I had lost a lot of time as well. I always say, if I had spent my time studying, I could have got a PhD.

He tried hard to fix his relationship with his family, but not everything could be repaired.

> I've lost a lot in my relationships. Even though I'm slowly fixing them, it still doesn't feel good enough. When my wife went to New York to look after our two kids, I went there once or twice every year, and she came back at least three or four times a year. My sons still treat me as their father. She treats me as her husband and I call her my wife.

After starting to face his true self, Jonathan gradually understand why he left home in the first place.

> I was told later that I suffered from depression during those two years. I was slightly depressed. Could that help to explain why I did that? The pressure she put on me seemed to be less (after our divorce). After our separation, I was probably more relaxed. I could do whatever I wanted.

He still feels pressure after getting back with his wife, and sex is the source of his pressure as always.

> Oh, my, it sucks. I have to sleep with her again. Fortunately, she has lost her sex drive since last year, probably because of her age. So, she doesn't ask for it that much. I guess it's a kind of relief for me. It's great now. I've got used to this kind of life.

'Homosexuality Is Not a Disease, and It's Not a Sin.'

His young lover Ken is now in his forties. And Jonathan feels very guilty about him.

> I think I've dragged him down. It feels that way. He told me some time ago he wasn't too happy, because he felt like it was his fault that he couldn't change me . . . There were debt collectors coming after us for a while. I couldn't pay for my offshore bets. He was terrified when people came in the middle of the night. Things were okay in the end, but I feel bad about it. Besides, he never complained, not even once.

Ken met another guy in the end and became very distressed. He eventually confessed everything to Jonathan.

> He drank all the time. He got dead drunk and cried. I asked him what was going on, but he wouldn't say. In the end, he told me about the other guy and said he couldn't choose between us. So, I told him we should split up. Breaking up is not a big deal. To say the least, I've seen everything, and done everything, but not him. He still had his chances. He should try to have fun if that was what he wanted . . . He was such an innocent boy. He didn't ask for material satisfaction, but I tried my best to make him happy and satisfy him. We went on vacations, and had fun together. But he refused whenever I tried giving him something. He didn't want me to buy him anything. He wasn't into brands. That's why I feel guilty about him.

The two of them have turned from lovers into best friends.

> And then I met a guy in a sauna and we got into a relationship. But it was quite funny because it was similar to my relationship with my first boyfriend. It was very unusual. We phoned each other once or twice every day. I went to his place for dinner once a week, to enjoy some home cooking. He always left me some soup made by his mother.

Besides going to his usual church, Jonathan goes to the Blessed Minority Christian Fellowship (a *tongzhi* religious group) as well. Looking back on the larger part of his life, Jonathan thinks he has lost many things which are irretrievable.

> I know that I acted selfishly. To be honest, I'm helping myself when I try helping others to quit gambling, because I have a high risk of going back to gambling. I'm not someone who doesn't know how to gamble, and it's not like I can simply hit 'Delete' on the computer and unlearn it. Through helping others, it's my way of helping myself, because I can stay vigilant all the time. Moreover, I hope I can strengthen myself through spirituality. I hope I can be calmer, and find peace and joy. I hope I can stop over-thinking. I used to have so many thoughts in my head. However, as for my gay life, I'm still a little bit confused. I wonder if everything will really be fine if I just confess and repent after committing something bad? Do I just confess again if I do it repeatedly? We genuinely repent, but we keep doing it. Does it really work this way?

Jonathan seemed to have found his answer the moment he said that.

> I admire former Archbishop Peter Kwong for the things he has said. He said, 'Homosexuality is not a disease, and it's not a sin. They just don't know what they are doing. They can't control their behaviour.'

Now, coming out to his sons is Jonathan's greatest wish.

> I'd really like to tell my two sons. I'd like to come out to them. I've thought about it many times. My sons are quite easy-going. I don't want to die without them knowing.

Jonathan is very gentle and polite. He does not talk a lot at our gatherings. He is rather reserved. However, his story is so dramatic that it could be adapted for the big screen.

Everyone has many different identities. To Jonathan, he is gay, but also a gambler and a Christian. These three identities changed his whole life. Had he not been a gambler, he would not have found God. Had he not been a Christian, he would not have seen his sexuality as a sin, something that had to be 'cured' like his gambling habit. Among these three roles, his sexual identity is the most difficult one to come to terms with.

Tam (2013) argues that the incarnation of Jesus Christ is like the Lord coming out. It shows His love and breaks the boundary between God and humanity. At the same time, when sexual minorities come out, it shows their courage in staying true to themselves. However, many people, including Jonathan, might not agree with this kind of queer theology. I hope Jonathan will understand one day that the coming out of homosexuals is not always in conflict with his Christian faith.

Jonathan has had a dramatic and eventful life. Shortly before I first interviewed him in 2010, he was diagnosed HIV+. In recent years, he has also developed the early stage of Parkinson's disease. He is now living in an apartment with his previous boyfriend Ken who is taking care of him as a friend. He is currently going out with a 20-ish young man. He still keeps a good relationship with his wife. I am always curious about the stories of his wife, who never left him, and Ken, who goes through thick and thin with him. What are their sides of the story? In China, there are two main strategies that gay men use to deal with their sexuality under family pressure to get married. The first is to get married to a heterosexual woman and either suppress their same-sex desires or have a secret homosexual life outside the marriage (e.g., Kong 2011, 145–73). These women are called 'homowives'. The second strategy is cooperative marriage, in which a gay man marries a lesbian (e.g., Fu 2012, 139–66; Wei and Cai 2012).

Letters Provided by Interviewees

　　中年男男，您好！我叫＿＿＿＿，您可稱呼我「安仔」，看見您的廣告，我想我應適合您的要求！

　　首先，要說的是我很少寫中文，如果有任何錯漏請原諒，另外也請原諒我的字体不靚！

　　今天是公眾假期，又不想「去蒲」，又沒有人在身邊，寂莫實在難奈！看見朋友給我的「大紙」，您的廣告很是吸引！於是便⋯寫給您！

　　或者我該形容一下自己：28歲，身高6呎，重140磅，比較瘦弱，但現在已積極練身，希望身形會好看一點！四眼，方面，比較內向，不怎愛說話但愛細心聽人家的話！喜愛獨個兒聽音樂，這也是每日必做的事，沒有音樂不行！運動方面，羽毛球是我的強項！

　　其實找一個適合自己的人是很困難的，若不然我怎會到現在也是孤身一個；也就是從來沒有戀愛經驗，不知究是何滋味！或者您已有無數經驗，始終沒有找到個合適的，在此祝您成功！

　　關於我的工作，請看看信頂的「Logo」，相信您已知道我是做甚麼工作的！

　　最後，給您我的電話"＿＿＿＿"，歡迎隨時來電，因為我與家人「分居」了，也就是一個人住！也請給我一個機會每您認識！

　　祝健康快樂！

P.S. 為何自稱「中年男男」？

Hi, *Chung Nin Nam Nam* (lit. 'middle aged Southern Man'), my name is XXX. You can call me *Onjai* (lit. 'little brother *On*'). I saw your advertisement, and I think I would fit what you're looking for.

First, I'd like to let you know I rarely write in Chinese, so please forgive me if I make any mistakes. Also, please forgive my terrible handwriting!

It's a public holiday today but I don't want to go clubbing. And I have no one to spend the day with. Such loneliness is quite unbearable! While I was looking through a copy of the newspaper my friend gave me, I saw your advertisement and it was really compelling. So . . . I decided to write to you.

Maybe I should introduce myself. I'm 28 years old, 6 feet tall, and I weigh 140 pounds. I have a rather frail frame but I'm trying my best to work out. Hopefully I'll have a better-looking body soon. I wear glasses and I've a rather square-shaped face. I'm quite introverted; I don't talk a lot but I'm a very good listener! I like listening to music on my own—it's something that I must do every day. I can't live without music! In terms of sports, badminton is the one I'm best at!

Actually, finding the perfect one is very hard indeed. Otherwise, I wouldn't still be single. I've never fallen in love before, so I have no idea what that feels like. Perhaps you have a lot more experience than I have, but it just so happens you haven't found the right person yet. I wish you all the best on this!

Regarding my occupation, please take a look at the letterhead and you'll know what I do for a living [NB: Coat of arms of British crown colony Hong Kong].

Lastly, here's my telephone number—XXX. You're welcome to call anytime! I live alone because I have 'separated' from my family. Please do give me a chance to know you!

Wishing you health and happiness.

P.S. Why do you call yourself *Chung Nin Nam Nam*?

XXX

Hi! 你好嗎? 很開心從這个机会認識你。由於我的中文字体較差及如有錯字, 望能兒諒! ok!

首先自我介紹一下, 叙名叫 ____, 28, 5'10", 斯文, 思想成熟, 樣子一般, 有時和朋友話的似看某份 (即鬼鬼嘅), 但我係100% Local Chinese, 性格: 較靜, 有空此会打 Tenis 健談, 喜歡聽 Classic Music & Love Songs (中英也). 睇小說, 睇戲 (Love Story), 旅行等. 現任職 Designer. 但由於經濟較差, 故此我也可能轉為 Freelance Designer.

為何我会回信給你, 理由很简单, 希望藉著多次机会能找到一个可以互相関心, 恒久而稳重的感情.

曾經我雅有过一段刻骨銘心的爱情故事, 但他已去了一个很遠很遠的地方, 永遠不能再相見, 如有机会才再慢慢告訴你, 好嗎?

真實我已 28 3. 轉眼間便收到 30. 我不想再沒有目的地飄漂泊泊向前走, 很想停下來. 我知道外边圈子裡生活多姿多彩, 五光十色, 但外圍重是離離合合. Easy Come Easy Go. 我想我並不是尋找這樣生活方式的人. 而我只希望二人走在一起渡過餘下的光陰. 你有同感嗎?

現時我和父母住在香港岛, 你呢?

我是个喜和了解別人的人, 也是个不懂表達自己的人, 可能这亦是能需不说醫吧!

好了. 下次再談! 如果能繼續寫下去. 我相信你会悶死的. 你可否介紹多一点你自己嗎? 如你有問題也可以問我的. 現寫下我的電郵地址, 期待你的回信!

Bye! Bye! .....

Yours Pen Friend

Address:

Hi! How are you? I'm really happy to get to know you through this experience. My Chinese handwriting is pretty bad, and if I use the wrong Chinese characters, please forgive me. Okay!

Let me introduce myself. My name is XXX. I'm 28 years old and 5'10". I am polite, mature, and average looking. My friends sometimes say I seem like a 'banana' [NB: an Asian person living in a Western country], but I'm 100% local Chinese. Regarding my personality, I'm a pretty quiet person. In my free time, I play tennis. I'm quite chatty and I love listening to classical music and love songs (Chinese, English, and Mandarin [Taiwan]). I like reading novels and watching movies (love stories), and going out as well. I'm currently a designer, but given how bad the economy has been, I'm considering becoming a freelance designer.

The reason I'm writing back to you is simple. Through this experience, I hope I can find a mutually caring, eternal, and committed relationship.

I once had an unforgettable relationship, but he has since moved to a faraway place. I don't think I'll ever see him again. I'll tell you more about it if we get the chance to meet, okay?

In fact, I'm 28, and will be turning 30 years old pretty soon. I don't want to just be drifting anymore. I want to settle down. I know life in the (gay) community is fun, colourful, and glamorous, but those relationships tend to be on and off—easy come easy go. It's not the type of lifestyle that I'm seeking for. I just want to spend the rest of my life with someone and walk this path together. Do you feel the same?

I'm currently living on Hong Kong Island with my parents. What about you?

I'd like to describe myself as kind and caring, but at the same time I'm not good at expressing myself. Perhaps it's like what others say, 'a doctor can't cure himself'!

Anyway, let's talk again soon! I'm afraid that I'll bore you to death if I keep rambling on. Could you tell me a little more about yourself? If you have any questions for me, I'll gladly answer! I leave my correspondence address here. Looking forward to your reply! Bye, bye!

Yours, Pen Friend XXX.

Address: G.P.O Box XXX Hong Kong.

Photo Exhibition of *An Oral History of Older Gay Men in Hong Kong* (2014)

Bobby K. H. SHAM (Bobpin)

Photo Title: Ordinary People (Senior Comrades)

Artist's statement

Through the process of taking photos, I am interested in communicating with people and knowing their stories. Sometimes their dreams can be reflected from the combination of their choice of clothes (or of being naked), makeup (or no makeup), their gesture, position, and choice of venue and any particular photographic objects around them.

Bobby K. H. SHAM (Bobpin) is a Hong Kong photo artist, photo art administrator, curator, and educator. He is now a part-time lecturer in the School of Journalism and Communication, Chinese University of Hong Kong and the Initiator of the Hong Kong International Photo Festival (HKIPF). He has had solo photo exhibitions and joined many international and local group shows during the past twenty years, e.g., *Small Shops (2013, 2014, 2015), INKcarnation: Literary Tattoos* (2015). He curated photo exhibition *1000 Families* for HKIPF in 2016.

Photo Exhibition of *An Oral History of Older Gay Men in Hong Kong*

WONG Kan-Tai

Photo Title: Photo Project 2014 for Dr. Travis Kong's 'Gay and Grey'

Artist's statement

Thanks to the people who allowed me to take their pictures even though they prefer hiding their face in the shade.

WONG Kan-Tai is a photographer born on Lantau Island, Hong Kong, in 1957. He joined Hong Kong Press in the late 1970s, after which he became a photojournalist. From 1982 to 1986, he pursued a photography course in Japan. His published photographic collections include *'89 Tiananmen*, *Land Reclaim* and *Hong Kong Walled City 2002–2007*. Wong works as a freelance photographer.

Acknowledgements

Dustin Shum (Saltyard) and Wong Kin Yin (Excellent Colour Ltd)

Photo Exhibition of *An Oral History of Older Gay Men in Hong Kong*

Gyorgy Ali PALOS

Photo Title: Meeting Points

Artist's statement

The most challenging part of making portraits is to create a dialogue between the person and the photographer. The still photo should reflect that short moment.

Gyorgy Ali Palos

Born in 1959, in Cairo, Egypt, Gyorgy Ali Palos is a Hungarian producer, film director, director of photography, scriptwriter, and photographer. He is also a board member of the Independent Hungarian Filmmakers Society and a member of the Hungarian Film Directors Society. He was a visiting faculty member in the School of Creative Media, City University of Hong Kong.

CHAN Ka-Kei

Photo Title: Meeting Points

Artist's statement

I am lucky to participate in this interesting project. Thanks to those who let me record their lives.

Chan Ka-Kei, 'K'

Born in Shanghai, raised in Hong Kong and studied in the UK, K is a freelance graphic designer who has been working in 2D images and design for over a decade.

7
Uncle Lee
A Sunset Tongzhi *(1940–2016)*

Uncle Lee was born in Guangdong in 1940. Since his family had some farmland, they were considered landlords, so life became miserable for them when the Communists took over in 1949. He, his mother, and his elder brother were persecuted and condemned to hard labour. His father died early so he did not experience the torment. Although Uncle Lee was the son of a landlord, his family was actually rather poor, and therefore he did not have the chance to receive formal education. He went to school for two years and dropped out when he was nine years old. That explains why he cannot read.

Risking His Life to Enter Hong Kong Illegally by Boat

In 1966, Uncle Lee was 26 years old when the Cultural Revolution started. He risked his life to come to Hong Kong.

> I came alone, because my mother had already died. I took a boat with other stowaways. When any stowaways got caught, they were put in prison or even shot.

For Uncle Lee, risking his life this way was clearly worthwhile.

> It was tragic being a landlord's son. I didn't have enough food. I was persecuted. I had to do whatever I was asked. So, I came for freedom. I didn't come here to get rich, but only for freedom. I wasn't free then. I was totally denied of my freedom.

Uncle Lee has a few siblings, but he was the only one who came to Hong Kong.

> I have six or seven brothers and sisters . . . My father lived in Cambodia, but he died when I was very young. My eldest sister, she came to Hong Kong before going to Cambodia, but we lost contact with her after that.

There were over twenty people on the boat. Most of them were from the same place. There was no trafficker, only a group of stowaways banding together.

Okay, there was a boat. So, we went.

The voyage took three days and nights. On top of the risk of getting caught, they had to go against wind and tide.

> The seas were rough. They were very rough the whole way. We thought we were going to die. There were boats where everyone on board died. We were so frightened of getting killed.

Lee was very lucky to have arrived in Hong Kong safe and sound.

> I got to Hong Kong. A relative picked me up. I think it cost over HK$100. I was notified when he arrived. HK$100 was a lot of money then. My relative picked me up. I left everything in mainland China. I only had a pair of underpants. He picked me up and took me downtown. So long as I got there, everything would be OK. If a stowaway got caught in the countryside, he would be deported . . . I came onshore in Tai Au Mun in Sai Kung. Then I took a car. I wasn't afraid, because I was already in the city.

The economy of Hong Kong started to take off in the 1960s. Everything was booming even when riots were breaking out.

> We arrived downtown. We got there one day, and I started working the next. There were lots of vacancies in different factories. Workers were provided with bed and board.

Uncle Lee got his first job in a plastics factory.

> It was November when I got here, and I worked there until Chinese New Year around February. Then I went to a grocery store and delivered goods for a year. I even carried a bag of rice of over a hundred catties on my shoulder to a flat on the seventh floor. I was from a country town. I farmed, so I was hardy. I travelled around and took car rides sometimes . . . I delivered rice for a year before becoming a street hawker, an itinerant one without a stall. I put up a stand so I didn't have to pay any rent or apply for anything.

Uncle Lee ran his small business for over thirty years until the market area was demolished. He supported his wife and six children by running his little stand.

> I kept working and working. I went to my stand early in the morning and came home late at night. I would be so tired after having dinner that I just went straight to bed. My kids would all be in bed already. When I left home in the morning, all my kids would still be in bed.

Uncle Lee took the opportunity to retire when his business was closed. However, he was still in good shape and he could not stand leading an idle life, so he went back to work after taking a short break.

He worked in Shenzhen and then worked as a cleaner in a gay sauna.

> I sold cooked food. I did it for over a year. It didn't work, so I handed it over to my nephew and looked for another job instead. A friend of mine said he

needed my help, so I started working here [a gay sauna]. I have been in this business for over three years.

He enjoys his work a lot.

> I clean. I wash towels, tidy things up, look after the plants. There are lots of flowers, so I have to take care of them. I water the plants . . . I enjoy it. When I come here to help out and talk to people, it makes me happy. I want to work here, because it comforts my soul. When I have someone to talk to or do something with, I feel happy.

Looking back on his life, Uncle Lee has worked for almost fifty years and he cannot help but sigh:

> I told people it was like being in jail. It feels like I've been in jail for my entire life . . . When my wife brought me food, it felt like I was being visited in prison. I was working all day from dawn till dusk on the street.

Realizing His Same-sex Attraction When He Was Young

Uncle Lee married when he was 32. His wife was Chinese Cambodian. He did not marry for romantic love, but to comply with societal expectations of marriage and family. Uncle Lee did not even get to meet his fiancée before he married.

> My elder sister introduced me to her, but she only gave me a photo album. She said I should go to Cambodia to get married, but the place wasn't safe, so I said we shouldn't go . . . So, they sent someone over from Cambodia. They held a wedding banquet there. I didn't want to hold one, but they insisted because their family was quite rich. It was cheap holding a banquet over there anyway. I remember it cost only a little over HK$300, so we hosted a dozen tables of guests.

Uncle Lee's relationship with his wife was based on a sense of responsibility. There was not a lot of communication between the two.

> Times were different back then. Now, old people are all married. But many younger people, like those in their forties, are not married.

Uncle Lee rented a flat in Kwun Tong later and moved there. His wife did not work. She was a stay-at-home mother who took care of the family. When it came to sex, both of them were uninterested, seeing it as solely for procreation.

> My wife didn't ask for it. She never asked for it. I declined when she offered it, then she put it behind her . . . She never worked. She came here and started having children. We had six children in six years—one every year, literally. I didn't go and play around then. I didn't even go to prostitutes.

Uncle Lee realized he was attracted to men when he was young.

> I had this kind of tendency when I was young while I was in the Mainland, but it was nothing. It was a tendency. I liked to watch but I wouldn't dare do it. I never even played around with others from my village. We might sleep in

the same bed with other guys, and maybe touch a little, but we would have no idea what we were doing.

Uncle Lee always behaved like a regular guy before 1997. He had no same-sex experience before that.

> I never did it. I'm married . . . I might have felt this way, but I didn't know what to do . . . I didn't know what it was. The only thing I cared about was my job. I was waiting for my children to grow up and I felt that was my responsibility. I finally entered the gay circle after my children had all grown up. It's been over ten years.

Meeting His First Love in His Sixties

In 1997, Uncle Lee's children had finally grown up. He passed by a public toilet in Kwun Tong while he was still a hawker.

> Oh, my . . . I was so scared at first. I wasn't curious; I just went to the toilet because I needed to, and then I saw some people there. They looked at me while they were messing around. I was frightened. They just got together and did it. I stayed and watched, out of curiosity. 'Why would people peek at others in public toilets?' So, I watched them. I was in a stall later when somebody peeped at me. He asked if I was this kind of person. He asked me that . . . But he said he was in a hurry, so he left me his number. He asked me to go out and have dinner some time.

This man became Lee's first boyfriend.

> He was the first one who brought me into the gay circle.

Lee was in his sixties then, but his boyfriend was only in his thirties.

> He showed me around. It was like another world to me. He liked taking me to different places to eat. He always took me around . . . I didn't know those places in the beginning. He told me to go to a gay sauna called Tai Fan [defunct], but I didn't know that place, so he took me there. He showed me the place because he knew I was curious. 'I just want to show you the place, but don't come back on your own.' I went there anyway. He asked if I knew what kind of place it was. I said I did. He said someone would give me a towel when I got there, and so on and so forth. Oh, my! When I got there, people threw themselves at me. Oh, my! I was terrified.

Uncle Lee fell in love for the first time. And this man opened the door for him to another world. They saw each other frequently after that. They went out together and had dinner. Uncle Lee did not have another boyfriend in the six years that they were together.

> I went to his place once a week . . . Yes, I liked him a lot. He was my first and I liked him very much. I told him my heart was pounding when we were together for the first time. It was funny . . . We went around town. He took me everywhere to eat and have drinks. I didn't go out a lot before, not to those

places . . . He was the one who brought me into the community. I was really happy . . . I went to his place on Chinese New Year's Eve to spend the night and hang out with him on New Year's Day. We did it every year . . . I told my family that I played *mahjong* all night. I went home on New Year's Day. I kept secrets from my wife all the time. I told all kinds of lies, haha.

There was no 'top' or 'bottom' in Lee's same-sex relationship, contrary to most people's expectations.

When it came to sex, I could only do it with my wife, but not with others . . . I tried it, but I couldn't. So, I have no idea what kind of person I am. I couldn't enter anyone else, and I couldn't let someone enter me either. We only hugged and kissed. It was fine as long as we were happy.

They were happy together, but they had to split up in the end, because Uncle Lee values his family a lot.

He asked me to leave my family, but I said I couldn't . . . It was one thing that we were madly in love and were having an affair; asking me to leave my family was something else. He said we couldn't be like that anymore, so we broke up. I felt miserable at first. I didn't have any friends, not in the gay circle. So, I went to gay saunas.

However, the two of them did not discuss splitting up.

We just didn't see each other. He didn't call me. I thought he'd call, but he didn't. Finally, we lost contact.

And just like that, the two of them separated naturally.

Family Always Comes First

Family has always been Uncle Lee's top priority throughout his life. He didn't marry his wife because of love, and he is not close to his children. However, he supported his family. It is an accomplishment he is proud of.

It's an achievement for me to have brought up my six children. It doesn't matter what people say. I have no money, but my seven family members are all I have in Hong Kong. They are my joy, my six children that I've brought up, as well as wife. I never felt angry . . . I'm happy with my family. It gives me much contentment. When you have six or seven children, they fight and argue sometimes. It's quite funny. Having brought up six children, sometimes I joke that I could have bought six apartments.

Family has always been Uncle Lee's rock. Same-sex relationships are rather illusory.

I have great affection for my family . . . As for the gay circle, I work for the community and it feels . . . quite insecure. You see someone with this guy today, but he's with another guy tomorrow. People come and go easily. I've worked in a sauna and observed the circle for a few years.

After breaking up with his first boyfriend, Uncle Lee met another guy. They started working in a gay sauna together.

> We got along well. To be honest, we're both monogamous, so we got involved. We're committed and we don't screw around.

His current boyfriend is in his forties and unmarried.

> He said he couldn't. His mother urges him to get married all the time. But times are different now . . . When I'm with him, we don't go out a lot. We have dim sum, have dinner and go to my sauna. Now we work together, so we're used to seeing each other every day.

In the beginning, Uncle Lee was still in contact with his first boyfriend, but they became estranged because of his current boyfriend.

> He [his first boyfriend] hasn't come to my sauna for some time. He came here to watch me work after we broke up. We talked sometimes . . . But he didn't get along with my current boyfriend, so it didn't work out. He didn't want me to be caught in the middle, so that was it. We don't see each other very often.

Uncle Lee's impression is that it is very common for a young gay man to get involved with an older person on the gay scene.

> I don't understand what they think. I found it very funny when I first saw those people. A guy, who is pretty and young, falls for an old man. Like I said before, I'm so old but still so many people like me. I went to mainland China and a 16 or 17-year-old boy came on to me. I said, 'No way, you're under-aged!' Sometimes I ask them why they like me. They're so pretty, but they fall for an ugly old man.

Catching up on All the Fun He Missed

To cover up his homosexuality, Lee tried going to prostitutes with his friends when he was young, but he would pay the prostitute and leave. Now he sometimes volunteers to help people. His children have all grown up. He does not have to worry about money. And with a trusting wife, Uncle Lee feels that he has a lot more freedom, so he tries to catch up on all the fun he missed.

> I told my children I'm in my later years. It's fine as long as I'm happy. That's the attitude I have . . . I've met a lot of people in the gay circle over the past few years. We chat, joke, and laugh with each other. I'm glad. We chat with each other, gossip with each other.
>
> I'm even more fortunate now with a family, as well as a boyfriend . . . My boyfriend told me, I have a wife at home. When I arrive home after work, I have a home-cooked meal with soup. I should be glad. I have no regrets. I feel blissful. My first boyfriend is a single child. I said he should get married. He yelled at me and said I was crazy. He said, 'No way! How could I get

married?' I told him he should do what I did. Just get married and he could screw around after having a son.

Uncle Lee does not feel guilty about his 'deviant behaviour', but there is no way for him to reveal his sexuality to his family.

> We're having a secret affair. Nobody knows about it. I don't know what others might think about me, so why bother? Neither my wife nor my children know about it. I tell them I have to work, or play *mahjong*. Better keep it a secret. I'm very devoted to my family. So, I save myself some trouble by keeping it from them. My attitude is that I'm just fooling around . . . Even if you find out or if you see us, I won't talk about it. As for my boyfriend, when my children got married, I invited him to their wedding banquets. He's the only one I invited in the gay circle. I told people he's my friend. We're colleagues after all.

However, what if his children or grandchildren are gay?

> Well, it doesn't matter nowadays, as long as they find someone they like . . . My children are all very liberal. I told them honestly, they can't choose their parents, but they have their own choices in their relationships. They can choose to be with whoever they want. So, they are very open-minded.

He is quite satisfied with his life right now.

> I have no problem financially. I have enough money to spend. My children are all great and they give me pocket money. I tell them I don't need it. I have money; I don't need it . . . When I volunteer, I don't have to spend a dime and I'm happy. I'm happy when my current boyfriend and I work together . . . I don't smoke, drink, or whatever. I always have breakfast at home. My health is fine. I haven't been really sick since I came to Hong Kong. I was a farmer. I've never been to a hospital since I came here. I always joke with my friends that I'll probably drop dead if I ever fall ill. I get a body check every year. My blood pressure is fine. I'm perfectly fine and I don't need to take any pills. I go swimming all the time.

Looking back on his life, he has his own definitions of success and failure.

> I really have no idea. I don't know how to define success or failure. People think someone is successful if he has money or a great reputation. My life is quiet and ordinary, but it's fine. When I go home, I have home-cooked meals and soup. When I go out, I have fun. Then I go back home and it's peaceful. I don't complicate things. I don't care what people say about me . . . It's fine as long as I'm happy.

When I asked him if he had any regrets, he said he felt very content about his life.

> No, I don't. I have both male and female partners. I had this path laid before me and I took it, and I'm glad. And this path . . . It led me to another world and I'm very pleased.

Uncle Lee's story of coming to Hong Kong from mainland China reminds me of Ann Hui's movie **Boat People**. *It is about the pursuit of freedom and never giving up. Uncle Lee's hard scrabble life in Hong Kong also reminds me of Lui's (2007) observations about the 'first generation' of Hong Kong people who helped found modern Hong Kong after coming from the Mainland during the Second Sino-Japanese War. They are hardworking, earnest, and down-to-earth, but they are also stubborn, rigid, and patriarchal. Some of them have repressed desires, but they still have to be like other men and struggle to support their families, and fulfil their responsibilities as husbands and fathers.*

Uncle Lee started realizing his real needs when he was in his late fifties. What struck me most was that he met his first love when he was almost 60. When he told his first boyfriend 'I like you', his heart was pounding. What do you call that if not love? It might be late because he waited for it for half a century, but I think it was totally worth it. No wonder he laughed a lot like a 16-year-old during my interview. His 'gay age' was only 16!

Uncle Lee passed away in early 2016.

8
May Wu

A Divine Woman's Poisons of Ignorance, Attachment, and Aversion (1940–)

Nicknamed the Divine Woman, May Wu came from Zhongshan, Guangdong. He was born in Shaoguan in 1940 during the Second Sino-Japanese War. May's ancestors were tailors, but his father, who passed away when May was young, sold kerosene for a living. May had an elder brother, but he died of hepatitis B in his forties or fifties. He has a nephew, who is a doctor, but they do not keep in touch. May is a Buddhist. He has been a worshipper since he was young.

'I Worked Every Job Possible'

With the help of his mother, who moved early on to Hong Kong to work, May migrated to Macao.

> After going to Macao, I went to the Immigration Department to apply to migrate to Hong Kong. However, I didn't know how to fill in the form and there was no one to do it for me. I came from a village and I was a hick. I hired someone to fill it in for me. He asked, 'How old are you, kiddo?' I said I didn't know. 'Then, when were you born?' I didn't know that either. So, he made it up for me and wrote 1946.

Actually, May was born in 1940, but that person made him six years younger.

> I didn't want to change it back. I became younger. I wasn't too old, so it would be easier for me to get a job, and I could probably work for a few more years. I didn't know how things would work out. Now you retire sooner if you're older, and you can get your benefits earlier.

May's mother worked as a maid in an expatriate family after coming to Hong Kong.

> I worked many factory jobs. I did everything, because I didn't know anything. I started working in a printing house and operating carbon lamps. Whenever someone worked in the darkroom, I would go inside to watch. Those masters wouldn't teach me anything, so I had to learn by watching them. I went to work early. I had to boil water, make tea, and sweep the floor. I went through

a rough time. I really did. I worked every job possible. I was in the printing business. I made radios, cameras . . . They were all factories . . . It didn't matter how good I was at my job, because I didn't have the qualifications or literacy.

May did not receive a formal education, not even graduating from primary school. That is why he resorted to any type of work he could get but found it difficult to get a promotion.

Losing 'Her' Virginity in a Treehouse

As a child, May lived in a farming village in the Mainland.

I pretended to be a girl all the time, trying to hang out with other girls. But they didn't want to play with me.

His schoolmates built a treehouse in their schoolyard. It was here he lost 'her' virginity.

I 'played' with others in the treehouse. By 'playing' I mean fooling around with them and grabbing each other here and there. I was with the boys . . . They were herding cattle . . . I pretended to be sleeping in the cowshed . . . I was only pretending. Then they took off all my clothes. They tickled me and grabbed me. It felt great. I didn't know anything, but it felt wonderful.

May did not know anything about homosexuality. The only thing he knew was that he was attracted to boys.

I knew it when I was in the Mainland, but I didn't know what homosexuality was. I just knew that I preferred boys to girls.

Injected with Androgens to Convert His Sexual Orientation

After coming to Hong Kong, May's relatives felt that he was 'weird'. So, he was referred to a doctor at Queen Mary Hospital.

They said I was shy and I didn't talk to people, but I liked anything bling-bling. And they said I was in my twenties, but I didn't know any girls, so I was taken to a doctor at Queen Mary Hospital. The hospital proved that I had excessive oestrogen.

The doctor injected him with androgens for a time after that, but of course it did not work. May still did not know anything about homosexuality.

However, I knew that whenever I saw a guy, especially a handsome guy, I felt so happy. God, I was so thrilled!

On the contrary, May was not interested in women at all. He could not even tolerate the slightest physical contact with women.

Even when my mum, who brought me up, touched me I'd jump . . . I worked in a sugar refinery. Those female workers played tricks on me all the time. They poked me in the back and my whole body jumped. Then I had goose bumps all over.

May entered the gay circle after 1963 or 1964, when he started posting personal advertisements in a newspaper.

What was the newspaper called? People put up personal ads in it to meet friends. There was only one, but I forget its name . . . That's how it began. I posted personal ads to meet people.

May mostly wrote that he was 'an introvert' and wanted to 'know friends who liked meeting guys' in his personals. It goes without saying that May simply wanted to meet male 'friends', but he was also hoping to come in contact with other gay men through these ads.

May was an assistant in a Christian voluntary group at the time. According to May, he was one of the trendiest teenagers.

I looked the same in all the photos I took when I was young, with a really short top . . . If I wore brown, I was brown from top to bottom . . . The pants were usually bell-bottoms. Moreover, I had those bangs with curls in front. When I was young, I went to those places for what we called 'tea dances'. I went there to let my hair down with a group of friends. I was a frequent attendee. It was hip, very hip.

May in his twenties. Source: interviewee.

Getting Caught and Then Fired for Having Office Sex

May met some gay men through the personals. He met up with one of them every weekend at a department store in Central. He would have sex with them in the office, if they had eyes for each other.

> The doorman asked me all the time, 'Why do you take your friends here every Saturday?' I said we were great friends and we hadn't seen each other for a long time, but I only brought them there once in a while.

So, his office became the place for May to fool around and seek pleasure.

> I went back to my office. I did it on my manager's desk . . . There was a studio, a dance studio. The four walls around . . . they were fitted with mirrors, except for the wall with the door, which was covered with boards. So I moved all the boards and opened every door, and the mirrors were totally unblocked. We played in the room. We put some yoga mats on the floor and had sex.

May was a bottom and those guys were tops. They used saliva or shower gel as lubricant. And so a life of sexual escapades began.

Besides putting up personals, May tried his best to look for possibilities around his office as well. One of May's most memorable hook-ups was with a waiter in a restaurant near his office.

> I didn't know if he was gay, but he was willing to do it with me. He was ladling soup and I went next to him to watch at first. I grabbed him here and there sometimes . . . He didn't respond even when I grabbed his dick, so I went down on him. That's how it happened. I risked everything.

Unfortunately, the good times did not last. May's colleagues found out about his gay pen pals as well as his hook-ups with the restaurant staff, so the Christian voluntary group forced him to resign on the pretext of religious difference, because he was a Buddhist. May became furious and threw a large pile of letters away.

After leaving the voluntary group, May had no choice but to take his hook-ups home to Shau Kei Wan. He lived with his mother, so he had to make excuses to send his mother away, or take his hook-ups home after his mother went to work. As someone who liked adding zest to his life, May sometimes cooked and fed his hook-ups well before they had sex.

> When I took someone home, I would cook a few dishes. I know how to cook. If he liked Western cuisine, I'd make soup and whatever, with a steak. We'd have sex after finishing the steak and all the food.

May met up with his old colleagues from the factories and the voluntary group regularly. They might have suspected that he was gay, but May never admitted it.

> I made up an excuse . . . I told them a fortune teller said I might get my parents, my wife, and my children killed. And then I told everyone I got my wife killed and even my children killed, so it was okay.

Unrequited Love with a Straight Man

May started to work at a sugar refinery in 1979 making golden syrup. He worked there for 14 years until he was laid off because the refinery moved to the Mainland.

> After entering the sugar refinery, I became very open and flamboyant. Nobody could be as open as I was.

When asked how open he was, he said,

> When I liked someone, I would give him anything he wanted. I'd kiss him, touch him here and grab him there. Everybody knew about it, even my boss. Everyone knew.

May was particularly emotionally attached to the manager of the refinery.

> I didn't want him to leave. I gave him a fountain pen when he left. It was a Parker pen and it was very expensive. I didn't go to work that day on purpose, and I asked someone else to give it to him . . . I told him, 'Take me with you if you want the best for me.' I liked the manager a lot.

Besides the manager, May had a 'hubby' in the refinery that everyone knew about. He joked around with his hubby in front of his colleagues without any hesitation.

> I patted his face or whatever, and I hugged him.

It was common for May to give him bear hugs or sit on his lap. It was something May and his colleagues enjoyed having fun with.

> One of my colleagues dared me to kiss my hubby. I said it was a piece of cake, but I needed an incentive. So, I asked for a can of soda for myself and a can of beer for him . . . It was morning and all the staff were waiting for the coach. Our manager sat on one side. My hubby sat on the other side and I sat somewhere in between. So, I said to him, 'Hey, hubby, turn around. Turn around now.' And I kissed him when he turned around. Everyone watched me kissing him and they couldn't get out of their promise. So, he got a can of beer and I got a can of soda. When we took photos on company outings, we had to hold hands and interlock fingers. But he actually had a wife, so it was just a nickname. Anyway, he called me by my name and I called him 'hubby'. Everybody knew about it. They called him my hubby when they talked to me.

May never hid his homosexuality from his colleagues.

> If that guy, I mean the guy I liked, didn't feel too well, I would go over immediately and touch him, and ask him how he was feeling. I would feel his forehead. I'd show my kindness and get him medicine.

His colleagues knew he was attracted to men, and they weren't homophobic or discriminatory. They mostly played it down by making jokes about it.

> Everyone in my company said that, 'Your hubby is sick and he isn't coming into the office today.' I'd call him immediately whenever he called in sick.

May is still in contact with the 'hubby' he met at work when he was young, which is admirable.

> He calls me once in a while, probably once or twice a year. He's a doorman and he has a wife. But I call him my 'hubby' even in front of his wife. It has become a habit and it has stuck.

Having Sex behind Closed Doors with His Apprentices

Of course, joking around did not fulfil May's sexual desires. May prefers young men, so his apprentices at the sugar refinery naturally became the objects of his desire. The workshop in which May worked became the place for him to develop workplace hook-ups behind closed doors. He fooled around with them while teaching them how to make golden syrup.

> One of my apprentices was about 20 years old . . . There was a room in one of the departments for making golden syrup. There was a large vat inside the room . . . He followed me inside, then I closed the doors and turned on the red light, because nobody else could enter when I was making syrup or teaching . . . So, I fondled him inside. I stroked him. I grabbed him here and there. He grabbed me as well, so I grabbed him back. After much grabbing, I took his hand and put it on me, then he started grabbing me.

May only had sex with three of his apprentices in the sugar refinery, but he did it so many times when he was an assistant at the Christian voluntary group that he cannot recount the number anymore.

> There was no way of telling in the voluntary group. How can I remember? Sometimes I brought two people up a day, one in the morning and another in the afternoon.

May did not go cruising in 'fishponds'—public bathrooms and toilets—until years later.

> I started going to fishponds when I was living in Shau Kei Wan. I had no shower at home, so I had to wash my clothes in a fishpond. You know what position I prefer . . . I can't be a top, so I stuck my ass out and let people touch my butt. I did everything with them after closing the door . . . We would go our separate ways after having fun. Then I'd wring my clothes dry and leave. There was plenty of space in a toilet stall.

May did not have shower facilities at home, and there was hot and cold water in public bathrooms. So, he went there to take a shower and wash his clothes every night, giving him plenty of opportunities to hook up with people. Public toilets were his main venue to meet gay men. The spots that he frequented the most included Tsim Sha Tsui Ferry Pier, Tsim Sha Tsui Train Station, a gas station in Mong Kok, and toilets in Yau Ma Tei.

May never had the courage to go to gay bars, because he was afraid of getting arrested.

> I never went [to gay bars] because I was scared. I'm very insecure and I'm always afraid of something. I don't ever want to go near a police station or a courthouse. I don't ever want to get arrested.

One of his friends was arrested in the bar area in Lan Kwai Fong in the 1970s.

> That guy was working in the Correctional Services Department. He got caught . . . So, he told people his identity. He said he was also a law enforcement officer who worked in the Correctional Services Department. But it made things worse. They wanted to nail him even more. It was just a few years before his retirement, and his whole pension was gone because of that.

Forced to Be 'the Principal Wife' by a Two-timing Boyfriend

May met a gay man through his personals early on when he was working in the Christian voluntary group. They moved in together and lived together for over twenty years. However, the relationship between the two was not always smooth sailing, because this boyfriend was seeing another guy when he was with May. He got intimate and slept with his new lover all the time, leaving May miserable and alone.

> I slept in one room and the two of them slept in another room. When it was really hot during summer, my boyfriend asked that guy to let me sleep over, because there was no air-conditioning in my room. It was miserable for me. They held each other and played around on their bed. It was really annoying when I was sleeping beside them on the floor. I slept there twice, but never again, even if the heat would kill me. The two of them held each other and fooled around on their bed. My boyfriend even told me he wasn't in love with that guy. It was that guy who fell for him and he couldn't stop someone from falling in love with him.

With a two-timing boyfriend, May felt like he had become the other man. He even became 'the principal wife' for a period of time.

> One day I came home from work, and he had met another guy. This guy was in the movie industry and he was an extra. When I got home, that guy poured me a cup of tea as soon as I set foot inside. He called me his godfather and

> poured me a cup of tea!¹ And my boyfriend said, 'He's just pouring you a cup of tea, do you really have to sit down to take it?' So, I asked them, 'What's the matter? I just got home from work. It's normal to sit down and have a cup of tea, so what's the problem?'

May's boyfriend's new lover was called Dee. However, May does not speak English, so he mispronounced it as *yi* (meaning 'two' or 'the second' in Cantonese), so May naturally became 'the principal wife'.

May had a relationship with his boyfriend for many years, but was swindled of his savings.

> I was laid off by the sugar refinery. So, he said I received so much severance pay from the refinery—over HK$200,000—I would lose all my social benefits . . . He said I should transfer all my money to his bank account and I could get it back any time I wanted . . . We didn't sign anything, but I gave him over HK$200,000 just like that.

May demanded his money back afterwards; his boyfriend refused initially. However, he was given some money back eventually. About HK$60,000 to 70,000 have been returned in recent years.

Seeking Pleasure across the Border and Hiring Male Prostitutes in Shenzhen

Besides putting up personals and hooking up with other gay men in public toilets, May started hiring male sex workers from the 1990s. He was working as a security guard and he went to Shenzhen to buy sex with a colleague. His colleague hired women and May hired men.

> He asked me why I hired a man . . . Of course, I made an excuse, because I couldn't tell him bluntly that I'm gay. He knew that I prefer masseurs, so I explained to him that male masseurs have stronger fingers. Women aren't strong enough.

May started hiring masseurs to relax his tendons because he had foot cramps. However, he was pleasantly surprised.

> He massaged my back . . . Then he grabbed me there. But why did he grab me there for no reason? That was how I found out that he could do something more. He massaged my back, then he grabbed me here and there. And he touched me occasionally when he massaged my thighs. He got close to my sensitive parts. I never got a hard-on when a woman touched me, but when I was touched by somebody I liked, my dick would get hard.

May kept hiring the same masseur after that and they even had anal sex. He kept in touch with the masseur until recently, when the masseur decided to retire

---

1. It is a Chinese custom to pour one's godfather a cup of tea as part of a sponsorship ceremony.

from the business. He gave May a coat as well as some money as a farewell gift. He even took May to a restaurant to thank May for taking care of him for years.

After being laid off by the sugar refinery, May worked as a security guard and is now retired. He lives a normal retired life like anyone else.

> I wake up at 4 in the morning. Then I just wait for things to happen. It's what I do day and night. If I can't sleep, I go out and eat with other old people. It's really boring. I sit all day and come home at night at 9. I have nothing to do even if I can't sleep. Sometimes I watch video discs, but I get bored if I watch too many of them. So, I go to have dim sum at 8. After having dim sum, I go to the old people's centre in the neighbourhood. I sit there all day, but I go and have afternoon tea at 4. I don't have lunch after having dim sum in the morning. I just have a few biscuits if I get hungry. Then I have afternoon tea at 4. I don't eat at night. I just boil some vegetables when I'm hungry.

Coming out to His Mother

May's elder brother worked in a sports club and lived in a dormitory, so May and his mother lived on their own. May's brother was nice to him. As May did not receive a lot of education, his brother gave him some money for a computer course. However, May spent the money on himself since he did not like studying. As for his mother, May thinks she was an amazing woman.

> She worked for an expat family. My mother spoke good English, but I didn't know anything. She even went to Britain with her boss. She spoke fluent English. I asked my mother where she had learnt English. She said she didn't speak it in the beginning. Her boss taught her word by word and did it by showing her everything around them. My mum knew how to make Western dishes. She did everything herself. She did the laundry and ironing. She waxed the floor.

As a gay man, May had to deal with his family asking questions about his love life.

> My mother asked me all the time, 'Why haven't you gone out with a girl all these years?' My boyfriend came and slept with me all the time. My mother slept on the bottom bunk and I slept on the top bunk. We spoke softly and laughed loudly. My mum didn't like it.

So, May simply came out to his mother in his fifties.

> I came out to her. I came clean with her and said, 'Mum, I like men but not women. I'm sure that I'm in love with him.' I said he was the only one for me.

May's mother seemed to have accepted her gay son, as well as his boyfriend, in the end.

> When my mum was dying—she died in her eighties—all her friends and relatives came to her deathbed, but she still hung on. So, I called my boyfriend

and told him he was the only one who hadn't come. He had to be there so my mum could leave peacefully. He waited until it was really late. He came at 1 a.m. He never left work that late, but he did it intentionally. He came at 1 a.m. After seeing him, my mum died at around 4.

Flirting with His Neighbour

May is now living mainly on social benefits.

> I've been retired for a few years . . . When I retired, I didn't have a son, a daughter, or a wife. I had nothing. So, I was advised to apply for social benefits . . . The Social Welfare Department said I was all alone, so they gave me benefits after some investigation.

May retired when he reached 65, as per his legal age on his identity card, and then he applied for social benefits. He gets HK$2,800 a month. With the addition of his disability and tenancy allowance, his total is about HK$4,000 a month. He has been living in subsidized apartments for over twenty years, paying HK$900 a month. He used to live in a medium-sized apartment with his mother. After his mother passed away, he felt uncomfortable living there, so he applied for a transfer to a smaller apartment and has been living there ever since.

Most of May's neighbours know about his sexuality because of his flamboyant behaviour.

Recent photos of May. Source: Wong Kan-tai.

> I walked around in a pair of rainbow pants and they talked about it. Those men asked me why I was so 'trendy'. I said, 'I woke up like this. It's my pyjamas.'

The interaction is actually quite interesting between him and his neighbours.

> There's a straight guy. He kissed me twice . . . He kissed me on my cheeks out of the blue . . . I cooked for him the other day, and he kissed me all of a sudden. It gave me the creeps. Actually, I like him a lot. But it gave me the creeps because he has a girlfriend (i.e., his wife). That's what I hate the most.

May gets along well with his neighbours. He spent his last birthday with them.

> I had dinner at a Chinese restaurant nearby on my last birthday. It was my treat. I told them it was my treat. My neighbours are my close friends. It cost about HK$900, but they gave me red packets over HK$1,000, so it evened out. I didn't ask them to pay, but they gave me HK$100 each. There were seven of us, including me, at the restaurant. Five of them gave me HK$100 each and another gave me HK$500. So, I got HK$1,000, but it only cost me HK900 plus. It was a great deal.

May is a devoted Buddhist. He has been worshipping different Chinese gods and Buddha since he was young in the Mainland. 'Of course, I believe in Him. Otherwise I wouldn't have put Him in a shrine at home.' Having lived to this age, May thinks that he does not have any regrets.

> I have no regrets. Look at my life. Having lived to this age, it's a blessing for me . . . I have no regrets. I'm really glad.

May's friend Shmily gave him the nickname, 'the Divine Woman', because he thought May was garrulous, like a neurotic. They are funny and witty and they are like a pair of sisters, but they call each other 'mother and daughter'. May seeks advice from his 'Mum' Shmily whenever something happens to him. They always go to pride parade in drag together. However, the 'women' get competitive sometimes, even though they are great friends. When people said Shmily looked like the movie star Carol 'Do Do' Cheng during the Hong Kong Pride Parade in 2013, May became a little sulky and moody, since his make-up did not look too good that year. Moreover, he had not been feeling too well, so he looked haggard and a bit wan. But May got over it quickly and took photos with Shmily like normal.

Apart from Shmily, May is another out older gay man in Hong Kong. A mainstream television programme featured May's story and captured him on film saying 'I am gay'. After the programme was broadcast, his friends from a local elderly day centre who had watched it said bluntly to him, 'Oh, you are gay!' They then distanced themselves from him and stopped inviting him to social activities. He was saddened by their behaviour, but coming out always has a price. May just said, 'I am who I am!' May still lives his life the way he wants in his seventies. He laughed when he talked about his romances during his youth. Many people might find him weird, but I admire him for his strong character and quirkiness. He is still deeply in love with his ex-boyfriend, who cheated on him on so many occasions. He died last year and May put his photo next to his mother in the same altar at home.

People usually ask, 'What makes a person homosexual?' This is not the appropriate question, as the person is called to account for the 'reasons', leaving the institutional framework (e.g., sexual and gender norms) unquestioned. Moreover, the implication of this question is usually to 'convert' or 'cure' homosexuals. The more appropriate question is, 'What's wrong with being gay?' It brings the discussion to a sociological level, examining dominant ideologies that govern gender and sexuality (e.g., homophobia, heterosexism, heteronormativity) and thus opening up the possibility to understand the labelling of gay men and male stereotypes. It also enables us to challenge the hetero-homosexual binary as a master framework for constructing the self, sexual knowledge, and social institutions.

May was injected with androgens by a doctor to 'cure' his homosexuality when he was young. This kind of treatment has proved ineffective. Besides labelling homosexuality as a 'disorder', it also harms homosexuals physically and psychologically. However, this kind of reparative therapy has reappeared in recent years, which is something we should be alert to.

May is a devoted Buddhist. He worships Guanyin at home and has a lot of prayer beads and ritual implements. He goes to Buddhist events regularly, so he is literally 'the Divine Woman'. He wears a 'silent teacher' tag around his neck, showing that he is willing to donate his body to medical science and education after his death. In recent years, his health has gone downhill. He has difficulty walking and needs a walking stick or wheelchair to join our gatherings and other public events. He is optimistic and happy with his life in general. However, with a houseful of Hello Kitty dolls and products, May cannot help moaning about his loneliness. 'So, I talk to the flowers when I'm bored.' That is why he totally supports any social services catering to older **tongzhi** in Hong Kong such as residential home care, day centres, and nursing homes.

9
Brother Shing

Only Men Understand Me (1944–)

Brother Shing was born into a lower middle-class family in Hong Kong in 1944. His father was a businessman while his mother was a housewife. He is the eldest son, has five siblings, and is a middle school graduate. Although born during the war, he does not remember the hardships of that time because it ended not long after his birth. Brother Shing grew up at a time when most people did not know anything about homosexuality. He did not understand it either, but he was vaguely aware of his same-sex attraction.

> Yes, I was a little curious back then, but our times . . . were rather conservative. Also, we didn't have the chance to meet other people, even though we knew we liked men. We couldn't look for others. There was no internet. We didn't have many ways to communicate. Nothing really . . . I was just more interested in boys. You'd meet other gay people after you started working.

It was during the 1960s when Brother Shing joined the workforce and became an apprentice mechanic. As an adolescent with sexual needs, Brother Shing started having ambiguous same-sex experiences.

> I went on vacation with my male colleagues. I slept on the same bed with another guy, which was perfectly common. When I touched him, he didn't resist. But I only touched his body with my hands and that was it. I didn't know what to do anyway. [His understanding of sex was completely different from today.] Teenagers know everything now.

He did not have the chance for sexual experimentation. They never talked about it after their trip.

> We acted like nothing had happened. [Brother Shing slept over at his colleague's home later on, but it did not lead to anything more.] I went to his place a lot after that . . . We played *mahjong* overnight on weekends. I touched him a little and it went on for a few years . . . He wasn't gay. Boys do that all the time during puberty. It was just me who carried on with it, but it was only a phase for him. We touched each other, and acted like normal after getting off.

Looking for Boyfriends in Tabloids

However, Brother Shing's same-sex attraction did not go away. He started meeting other gay men when he was about 24 years old. There were not many ways for gay men to meet then. However, there were readers' sections in some tabloids and even in a weekly youth newspaper. Many gay men used these sections to meet friends and get to know people with similar interests, and so did Brother Shing.

> It was a single-sheet tabloid. There wasn't anything special, but there was a readers' section. It wasn't only for people like us, so it wasn't just for gay men. It was for all kinds of people, like an advice column. There was a doctor called Doctor Henry who answered questions. People asked him questions. Of course, I was curious, so I read how he answered. The doctor also screened those letters . . . You sent a letter to the newspaper office, and it'd get forwarded to Doctor Henry. When he got your letter, he'd send it to another reader at your request. I didn't know if it was true or not, so I never made a request. Anyway, sometimes he'd print some addresses in his column. So, if you had a post office box, it would be more direct. I didn't have one though . . . but some had and got some letters back. And I met some men through this method. Let's say someone named Wai, who wrote that he wanted to meet a male friend and develop friendship. Then you could write him back, saying that you'd like to make friends with him. You would usually write your age, height, weight, and hobbies. We'd meet if we were both interested. If we got along, we'd stay friends. I left my address but I used a fake name.

> When someone wrote that he was 'looking for male friends' as a pen friend, and wasn't looking for a girlfriend, you'd know.

> I made friends with someone and he was great. He was very genuine and well-educated. So, we became friends, and he introduced me to other friends. That was how we made friends in a tiny circle. We all did that back then.

Yuk Tak Chee, the Pleasure-seeking Bathhouse

There was no gay sauna then, so Yuk Tak Chee was a famous cruising spot for the gay community. Brother Shing found it funny because when he first went there, he did not know the cues of cruising so he did not enjoy the pleasure of cruising there until a friend taught him the tricks.

> People talked about Yuk Tak Chee all the time. It was funny when people talked about it. People would ask if you had been there or not. We were very conservative. So, we tried looking for cues. When we had our backs rubbed then, we took all our clothes off. It was a guy, so I was really turned on when he rubbed my back. I had massages after taking showers. After having massages, people sat there and watched TV. There were no individual rooms . . . So, what was the fun? There was nothing we could do! People just walked around and they were all gone after a while. I thought there was nothing going on after visiting just once or twice. After making more friends later on,

one of them told me, 'You're wrong. You have to stay. It starts after 3 a.m.' So, it happened in the middle of the night. The door was closed after 3 a.m. Some people left, others went wild. There were some rooms. So, if you were lucky, you could occupy the whole room yourself. If you got a bed, it would be more comfortable for you, because others might come in to check on you. If you didn't have a bed, you just walked around. You couldn't lock your door. People could open it and come in. They kept coming for you no matter how tired you were, and they kept doing it until you were totally exhausted. The sauna would reopen again at 7 . . . Then everyone gradually left, but some of them stayed till 9 or 10 in the morning.

There was another bathhouse in the basement of a hotel in Wanchai. It was not exactly a gay sauna, but there was not another similar venue that targeted the gay community then. So, many gay men visited, with masseurs providing extra services.

People sometimes met for business there while they had massages. Massages were provided in the bathhouse. Those masseurs were very smart . . . If you got turned on, they gave you hand jobs. And they got bigger tips after getting you off.

Gay patrons hooked up with each other as well.

They [gay men] could tell. They wouldn't do anything to you if you weren't gay. When you were soaking in the tub, they touched your legs with their feet. When you were leaning against the bathtub, they jerked you off until you came. There wasn't much privacy though . . . It was in the 1980s, but it was over by the end of the decade. Gay saunas started to do business at the end of the 1980s.

The Public Toilet above Lan Kwai Fong

Besides advice columns in tabloids, bathhouses, and saunas, public restrooms were popular spots for gay men to meet. However, Brother Shing did not like this kind of venues.

I thought it was silly. I heard people went to those toilets all the time. They liked them a lot. But I thought they weren't so convenient. People got arrested. Besides, it felt weird when you were inside. The toilet in Lan Kwai Fong was very famous. Of course, I mean then, not now. Before it was renovated, it was very popular. In the toilet above Lan Kwai Fong, people stood inside the stalls, which were all occupied. They all stuck their heads out to peek at each other. I thought it was silly. I went there once because I heard so much about it. Those people never left, but nothing went on inside. They just looked at each other. There was another one on Ice House Street, but I didn't want to go. The one at Beaconsfield House was very popular, that's the toilet next to the Hilton Hotel below the post office. It was very famous. I went there once but there wasn't anyone inside. I probably wasn't used to those places, so I wasn't comfortable. If I'd stayed there, someone certainly would have come. If I'd stayed for an hour, pretended to wash my hands, comb my hair, and take a leak . . . But I wasn't used to it. I took a look and left, so nothing happened to me. I wouldn't dare even if something had happened . . . There were cops doing sting operations, even during the later years. I would've been caught in one. The cops were so macho, so handsome, so young, so pretty, and so great. I'm sure I would've been caught in a sting operation. Many people were arrested.

Gay bars were popular venues for gay men to meet as well. However, Brother Shing had hesitations about these places.

> I didn't go to gay bars because I neither smoked nor drank, and I thought it was a waste of time sitting there. You had to wait, chat someone up, or wait for someone to chat with you. What was the point? After hooking up with someone, you had to look for a place. You couldn't bring him home. It would be better if you lived by yourself. You could take him home. But you'd be damned if you hooked up with the wrong guy. He might come back and blackmail you.

Heading North When a Sea Change Took Place

Mainland China changed drastically after the economic reform in 1978. One of the changes was gay men started to become more active. So Brother Shing began going to the Mainland to meet men.

> It was during the 1980s. I met some friends and they said they did it in the Mainland. There were many of them in Guangzhou. And they said you had to be really careful when you met someone in the north, because all they cared about was money. I didn't know a lot about them. But I heard they came from other provinces to make money, so they extorted money from their targets. I didn't know many guys like them . . . I went to the Mainland with a friend. My friend had eyes for a guy, but he didn't have the guts to approach him. So, I became the go-between, and talked to the other guy. 'A friend of mine wants to know you. He likes you a lot.' But he said he liked me, not my friend. That's how I met him and I took him back to my hotel. It was funny.

Meeting Taiwanese Soldiers and Cruising at the Red House

Besides mainland China, Taiwan and Thailand were popular destinations for gay men. Brother Shing liked Taiwan, mostly because of the people there.

> There were soldiers in Taiwan. Some of them looked for hook-ups on their days off. Those soldiers had great bodies and they knew how to have fun. Even though sometimes they weren't soldiers, Taiwanese guys were so good-looking.

Brother Shing met a holiday romance at 228 Peace Memorial Park, a famous gay cruising spot in Taipei. He was in his thirties, believing he was very popular in the gay circle.

> I sat on a bench, looking at the entrance of the toilet. I saw two boys, in their twenties . . . I think one of them was about 24 years old and the other one was 28. I thought both of them looked good. The two of them went in and one of them came back out; that meant they didn't have eyes for each other. It was strange that they didn't like each other. After one of them came out, I went in. I stood there and the other one stayed. He didn't leave. I stood there and watched. I was more experienced by then. I wasn't bold enough at first, so I just watched. He didn't leave and he didn't seem uncomfortable. He responded a little, so I went over. In the end, we got into a stall at the back. It was quiet. There was nobody else. I wasn't afraid of getting robbed then.
>
> Taiwan was very popular, probably because of its atmosphere. There was conscription, so people had to join the army. There were plenty of opportunities. There still are, especially between the officers and soldiers, because . . . How should I put it? Some of them don't mind even though they have families. Their families accept it. It was very common during those times. The Red House is now renovated. It's not a cinema anymore. It used to be one. But people didn't go for movies. If they liked someone sitting beside them, they just . . . The Red House was very famous.

Brother Shing had a boyfriend in Hong Kong, who was about 24 then. They met through personals in tabloids. They were about the same age and they were together for over a decade. Then Brother Shing's boyfriend married a woman without telling him. However, Brother Shing was not angry about it.

> I didn't ask him to live with me. It was okay as long as both of us were comfortable with our living arrangement. I didn't ask my partner for anything like people do nowadays.

It was difficult for gay couples to establish permanent relationships then, and it was unacceptable for two men to live together. So, Brother Shing got married at 28 when he could not deal with the social pressure anymore.

> I wouldn't have got married if I had the choice. It's fine to stay single nowadays even if you're the only son, but our families pushed us back then. I was almost 30 years old, so I dated women. We went out and broke up after a few dates. It was over if I didn't keep on asking them out. So, it was just on and off. I was then urged to get married after some time. It'd be great if I hadn't got married. I could have lived the way I wanted, but I did it anyway. [His wife was a friend of his family.] After I stopped dating, my family found a wife for me.

Satisfying His Lover, but Upsetting His Wife

He got married to fulfil his duty and going out with her was a routine for him at first. The marriage was practically doomed from the outset. Brother Shing believes his wife never suspected his sexual orientation, but he obviously was not a good husband.

> I was so bad. Why? I cared only about myself, but not her. When I went to factory outings, usually you could bring a family member, but I never asked her. I didn't like it. What's wrong if I liked going on my own? She went back to her family whenever she was upset. She had no choice but to come home every time, and everything went back to normal.

They got a divorce three to four years later. He had a son from his short marriage, but his wife did not fight for their son's custody. Brother Shing understands his ex-wife.

> It was probably more convenient, in case she wanted to have another family. You know women, unless they never marry again . . . It's simpler if they remarry without children.

Brother Shing has lived with his son, who is now in his thirties, ever since. His son is married and has a son of his own. They all live together and they get along well.

Brother Shing hangs out with his male friends all the time, but his son has never asked any questions.

> My son doesn't pay me a lot of attention. He's never asked. It's possible that he knows about it but he never says anything . . . I guess he knows. I have been single all along, but I've never met another woman. Young people nowadays . . . How should I put it? They have all that information, and knowledge. They are well-educated. Besides, he had many gay schoolmates. He went to a boys' school. I could tell that his best friends were gay just by looking at them. That means he didn't think much about it. He accepted them. So even though he knows, he doesn't mind.

Brother Shing is not very keen to find a male partner to settle down with, probably because he is living with his son.

> I've got used to being single anyway. If I move in with someone else, you know how difficult it might be. You have to accommodate and adapt to each other. Two people must have different habits, so you have to understand each other, tolerate each other, and adjust to each other. When you fall in love with someone, you can tolerate anything. But after being together for a long time, you start getting bored, and you become intolerant of many things. 'Why don't you tidy up your things?' 'Look at the toothpaste! You have to push it down, instead of pushing it up.' 'You haven't flushed the toilet again!' You see a lot of flaws. It affects your friendship when you fight, so it's not that simple.

A Cheating Arrangement and an Open Relationship

At the same time, Brother Shing knows that he is not going to 'give up a forest for one tree'. He has been making like-minded friends since he was young.

> I'm a playboy, that's who I am. I date a lot of guys at the same time. People introduce friends to each other, so we meet a lot of guys. You must know that people in this circle are not particularly devoted. They cheat even though they're in a relationship. They might be able to hide it, but some of them don't like that. Even if you screw around, you have to avoid running into your partner. When people are together for over a decade, their relationship must fade. [Many gay couples have 'cheating arrangements'.] It's okay when they go abroad, but not in Hong Kong. When a couple goes on vacation in Thailand, they can do it together. They go and screw other people separately. That's what some people do nowadays.

Brother Shing is very open when it comes to same-sex relationships. He once introduced his boyfriend to another friend, who stole his boyfriend from him in the end.

> My boyfriend said he didn't have other friends after being with me, and I had so many friends, so I should be fine if I lost one. That's why I thought it was me who had dug my own grave. I introduced them and thought they were just friends. But I lost two friends after setting them up. Anyway, I'm quite open-minded. If I were more stubborn, I would have done so many stupid things.

Would Brother Shing want to be gay if he had the choice?

> I think it's great. Whatever I needed, my partners were able to give me. They knew what I wanted. We satisfied each other's needs. Sometimes, we didn't even have to ask. However, women might not be able to satisfy me. They might not understand me. Their needs are different from mine, or I couldn't satisfy their needs. So, I think being gay is a great thing. [However, Brother Shing knows that physical contact is not the most important thing. Sex without love does not satisfy him.] Unless he's your lover . . . otherwise . . . those people want quickies. They are in such a hurry that you can't even enjoy it. It's just meaningless.

Brother Shing was particularly careful when it came to work.

> I was afraid that people would not approve of me, or they would talk behind my back. There were so many things they could talk about, so I didn't want that, not even after working there for many years. I was very careful at work.

An Elderly Gay Romance

When people grow old, their bodies weaken and that is hard to bear. Brother Shing is no exception.

> My body is changing with age. I can't do three or four people a night anymore. That's for sure. I'm degenerating everywhere, mentally and physically. I can't compare myself to people your age . . . How could I face it? I already have one foot in the grave. It won't be long before I'm sleeping in it.

> I rarely go to saunas. I did it till I was 60 years old, and then I thought I should retire . . . I thought I couldn't pull anymore. Nobody would want an

old man like me in those places, no matter how long I lingered. So what was the point? That was bad for my ego. I used to be popular. A lot of people approached me in saunas.

However, time heals anything. He willingly accepts his current state, now that he has got used to it.

> Once I calmed down, it didn't bother me anymore. It's totally fine. Now I'm more optimistic and cheerful. Sometimes I volunteer. I have some friends. I have a lot of friends, so life is good.

Many gay men remain single, and experience feelings of loneliness and helplessness. Gay people with different backgrounds live very differently.

> It depends on your expectations. If you ask me, some of them are rather miserable. Some people who are single, who don't have much money, they can be quite lonely. It's fine if they have enough friends, not just lovers. They can chat with their friends. It's not that bad in Hong Kong. Government supports some poor people. Some of them live quite opulently, and they live rather comfortably.

Homosexuality has been better accepted and understood in Hong Kong in recent years. Brother Shing finds that the society has changed a lot since he was young.

> It's certainly different. Many gay men were in the closet then. Now people come out step by step. They are more courageous. They are not afraid to try. There are many of them around today. Many men and women aren't afraid of telling the world.

People had to speculate if someone was gay or not in the past, but it is slightly different now. Brother Shing thinks that 'people still speculate, but they are mostly right when they suspect someone. They are mostly right, because gay people are more open about it now. When people suspected someone in the past, no one ever admitted it.'

'I Enjoy Every Day That God Gives Me.'

Brother Shing had a Christian boyfriend, so he tried to learn more about his boyfriend's religion. Now he considers himself half a Christian.

> He is right. He is a Christian and he said he will go to Heaven when he dies. He hopes that I'll go with him, instead of going God-knows-where. That's what most Christians believe. He believes in it, so he asked me to listen to their sermons. That's okay for me. His church is not around here; he introduced me to a nearby church. He asked me to go, so I go to their sermons.

Many Christians disapprove of homosexuality, so a group of gay Christians initiated the Blessed Minority Christian Fellowship. Shing has been there once or twice.

> They are all Christians in the fellowship. Their sexuality wasn't acknowledged elsewhere, so they got together and started a fellowship, which is quite successful.

Brother Shing is very calm when it comes to life and death, growing old, and getting sick.

> You don't have to worry about that. Once you're born, death is a reality everyone has to face. No one knows when it is going to happen. Look at Princess Diana. She was loved by almost everyone in the world, but her life was taken away all of a sudden. There's no way of knowing. Those balconies looked so sturdy. When Wing On House was being built, a balcony collapsed while someone was walking underneath. A car might hit you out of the blue when it passes by. You can't tell when you're going to die. Nobody has a say in it. So, have I ever thought about when I'm going to die? How would I know? It'd be great if I could tell.
>
> I enjoy every day that God gives me. It's a gift from Him that I'm still living today, so I enjoy my life today. I live happily, and I try to make myself as happy as possible. It's my philosophy of life.

Brother Shing is one of my divorced interviewees. He married when he was only 32 years old. It was during the 1970s when divorce was still culturally frowned upon. He did not want to talk about it, so I did not ask much because I did not want to embarrass him. However, there was an upside of being divorced: he fulfilled his filial responsibility to continue the family line but without holding his wife back. He lives with his son's family now, and he quite enjoys being a father and grandfather. Sometimes I wonder if there are any children and grandchildren who understand and accept their gay father or grandfather? It is difficult for children to come out to their parents, but it is even more difficult for parents or grandparents to come out to their children. It is probably a burden too heavy to bear, so Brother Shing still stays in the closet.

Brother Shing was diagnosed HIV+ when he was in his forties. His HIV status was slowly revealed when we got closer and deep trust was built between us. He once had a boyfriend who was also HIV+ whom he met in an AIDS clinic. They spent some wonderful time together before the man passed away. The man's family knew about Brother Shing and treated him as a family member. Brother Shing still remembers vividly how he cleaned his body and said goodbye to him right before he died. His own health has gone downhill. He does not come to our Gay & Grey gathering that often, as he has difficulty in walking.

10
Uncle Leung

A Lifelong Libertine Who 'Queered' around Hong Kong, Macao, and Canton (1945–)

Born in 1945 in Guangzhou (also known as Canton), Uncle Leung is the eleventh child in his family. His father has three wives and fourteen children in total, and he is the son of the third wife. His family, being affluent, gradually moved to Hong Kong when landlords and the bourgeoisie were persecuted in mainland China in the Cultural Revolution (1966–1976).

His grandfather established a paper mill in Guangzhou and his family made 'foreign' paper after that.

> It was foreign paper. Paper was all imported then. People weren't educated in China and Chinese paper was terrible. People used it to wipe their asses, because it was so coarse. Foreign paper was better . . . Our business was quite good. Otherwise my grandfather wouldn't have got so many wives and had over a dozen children. For God's sake, he had to hire a whole bunch of helpers.

Leaving for Montreal after the Decline of His Family

Uncle Leung's family business started to decline after coming to Hong Kong. They first lived in an apartment of 3000 square feet in Happy Valley. Then their homes became smaller and smaller. In 1967, the family business failed. His father lost a large amount of money on the stock exchange and in real estate, so he filed for bankruptcy. Uncle Leung had some brothers in Montreal, so he emigrated with his whole family.

Uncle Leung worked in his brother's trading company in Canada. However, he never got used to it, since he did not speak French.

> I was too old to learn. I couldn't have picked it up in my twenties, for God's sake. When I went to school in Hong Kong, I went to the United College. It was only a diploma mill. The University of Hong Kong was the only university in Hong Kong back then. The United College merged into the Chinese University of Hong Kong after I graduated. I majored in economics. My

> father wanted all his children to get rich. I could do business after studying economics, so I could make money.

Uncle Leung stayed overseas for over a decade, only returning to Hong Kong in 1980.

> Living abroad was a nightmare. To be honest, I didn't have the qualifications to compete with others... The government didn't recognize mine.

The government later introduced new measures. After finishing the senior year and submitting graduation papers, United College graduates received a Chinese University of Hong Kong degree certificate, which was recognized by the government. However, Leung did not finish his senior year.

> No, I didn't. Why bother? I was already in my forties when I came back... Having a degree wouldn't have made any difference.

Uncle Leung eventually worked in a former schoolmate's company, doing stock market trading. It was a popular business in the 1980s.

> It was fine, but working for him was annoying nonetheless, because he never worked. He never did anything. He relied on his younger cousin to do everything. Sometimes he dragged me off to fool around with him. We went out here and there all the time. We got off work at 5 p.m. His father left at 4:30 p.m. and once his father had left, he would drag me with him and leave the office. We went to Kowloon City to watch striptease, play *mahjong*, or eat dog meat. His cousin was such a bore, so of course he never brought his cousin along. That was why his cousin hated my guts, not because his cousin thought I was a bad influence, but because I never finished the work I was supposed to do before he dragged me away. That's why his cousin never liked me.

Eventually, his schoolmate's father died and the cousin took over the company. Uncle Leung became an eyesore for the cousin and it was difficult for him to go on working there.

> I went to the Labour Department for advice one day, and I said I wanted to quit my job. He asked me how long I had worked in the company. I said I had been working there for ten years. Then he said I wouldn't be given a cent if I quit, unless I was fired. But that cousin sneered at me all the time. He always sneered at me. He knew that I had quite a temper, so he thought I'd quit if he always sneered at me, and then he wouldn't have to pay me a cent. However, he was the one who couldn't take it anymore in the end. He fired me in the end. I got almost HK$500,000... It was a lot of money, but I made almost HK$40,000 a month then.

Working Wherever He Wanted during His Prime

Uncle Leung was in his forties—still prime age for men.

> After getting that much money, I became so complacent. I didn't want to work. Damn it! It wasn't too difficult to get a job anyway, right? So, it didn't matter even if I lost my job. I could get another one easily. A job is just a job. You do it when you like it, and you quit when you don't. Don't you agree?

Uncle Leung planned a trip to Europe before running into a friend who was in the printing industry. Uncle Leung was hired as a sales executive. He ran into another friend not long after. His friend worked in a multinational corporation and referred him to some printing jobs.

> I struck a deal just like that. He asked me to bring him some samples . . . and I sent him all the quotations. Then he sent me all the printing costs for his company, and that was it . . . It was my first deal, and I got more and more after that.

Uncle Leung met more people in the industry after taking up this job. Some of them encouraged him to start his own business, so Uncle Leung founded his own company in about 1993.

> I hired a printer and a delivery man. I met some clients occasionally. I slept till noon and then I had dim sum. I took calls sometimes after 1 p.m. . . . Oh my! That was a great time. I made HK$30,000 to 40,000 a month quite casually and I didn't have to work. I played *mahjong* whenever I liked. It was much better than working for someone else. I had quite a laid-back life.

Having a Stroke, and Being down and out after the Handover in 1997

In an unfortunate turn of events, there was a wave of mass migrations from Hong Kong before 1997. Uncle Leung's business went down because some of his frequent patrons and old schoolmates emigrated.

> My business kept dropping then. My major clients were all gone, and I was left with minimal orders. I was doomed. They were so minimal that the shop made HK$20,000 to 30,000 a month. But I had a lot of expenses to pay, man! I fired the delivery guy instantly, but I had to keep the printer. I didn't know how to do it myself.

The printer taught Leung all the basics before he left later. Leung eventually ran his business on his own, taking orders one at a time to make ends meet.

However, misfortunes never come singly, and Uncle Leung had a stroke two years later.

> It happened right after I took a vacation to Taiwan. I probably took too many dips in the hot springs. I spent hours dipping and playing in the springs, and I didn't know my blood pressure had already rocketed. I was sleeping and bang, it happened in the middle of the night. I couldn't move my limbs and I was hospitalized for months. I called my clients, because they kept calling me. They asked me how I was doing and I told them I quit. I couldn't move then,

so how could I work? I had to sell all my machines at low prices. Fortunately, there were still some people reselling those machines in mainland China.

After being forced to close his printing business, Uncle Leung was desperate and he thought about applying for social benefits. When his younger sister found out, she gave him HK$8,000 a month to cover his living expenses.

> She said, 'What are you thinking? It's a disgrace to the whole family if you apply for social benefits . . . I'll give you money.' My sister had gone to Canada for some time. She came back after getting her passport. Her husband opened a factory in Shenzhen. They invested in real estate or something too, so they were rich.

However, not everyone in the family was willing to help him.

> Like my elder sister, she doesn't even know I was so broke that I almost had to apply for social benefits. We don't share the same mother. Siblings usually aren't too close in a big family, not at all. So, don't think that it's so great being born into a big rich family.

Looking back on the ups and downs of his early life, Uncle Leung admitted that he once lived luxuriously.

> I lived very well for a decade. I lived in a big house and I made lots and lots of money. It wasn't a big deal to spend over HK$30,000 for dinner, having rice with shark fin. It cost HK$2,500 for an abalone at Fook Lam Moon [a luxurious Chinese restaurant] then. I went there with a friend. Each of us had two abalones, then we each had two bowls of shark fin soup . . . as well as bird's nest soup. It cost tens of thousands of dollars, and I tipped the waiter a few hundred at least.

Being Touched all over When He Was Young and Curious

When asked about his homosexuality, Uncle Leung recalled that he was interested in other boys at primary school.

> I was in Primary 5. After I left school . . . I went to a public toilet on Wellington Street in Central. The stalls had no doors then, so I went there with my schoolbag on my back, to watch an old man taking a dump. I thought it was funny . . . I was about 11 or 12 years old then, I hadn't even begun puberty, and his dickhead looked funny. 'Why does it look different than mine? It's wrapped. And I don't have hair like him. Oh my, when I grow up, is it going to be itchy with that hair?' I squatted down opposite him. He was quite old . . . He couldn't have known that I was peeping . . . I was so turned on when I peeked at him. However, all I did was watch. I didn't have the nerve to touch anyone . . . Nobody talked about it then, not in the papers, magazines, or on TV. Nothing, so I didn't know anything.

It was not until he was in Form 3 in secondary school that he started going to Tai Tat Tei in Sheung Wan. The area has now been gentrified.

> There were lots of people selling things and singing in Tai Tat Tei. It was so crowded. But I was too young to understand what was going on. I just went into the crowd to see what was happening. Then an old man suddenly touched me. I thought, 'That's strange.' I got scared and I fled. I was too young. I was only 16 or 17 years old. When that old man touched me, he was afraid of me, too. I was too young, so he didn't try to chase me down. Knowing that people might touch me, I went there as soon as I finished dinner and homework, to get felt up by someone. I would stand in the crowd for people to touch me. People touched me all the time . . . I was touched by old men. There were old men and young men. The place was wild. There was an expatriate inspector. Oh my, he stood behind me with his pants unzipped. I didn't realize at first. Then the person beside me began to shiver! As it turned out, that inspector had put his dick inside him, so he kept moving . . . The place was packed, but only people like us noticed these things. They wouldn't notice anything if they weren't gay, would they? If they weren't interested, they would pay attention to the singer, but not to the others.
>
> Those old men brought me to the trucks sometimes. We would walk all the way to Sai Wan or Sai Ying Pun, where many trucks were parked. There were no semi-trailer trucks in Hong Kong, only mini-trucks covered with canvas in case of rain. The trucks were unloaded at night, and the empty trucks were parked at the seaside. Nobody went to the seaside at night. So, we got on the trucks and fooled around under the canvas.

Uncle Leung recounted his experiences of getting felt up in detail. He enjoyed being touched at different cinemas before he migrated to Canada with his whole family.

> I went to the cinemas in Lai Chi Kok Amusement Park or Kai Tak. Yeah, it was really common. It happened as soon as you stood there . . . I went to a cinema, and there were two screens, one for imported films and the other for local films. It was really dark inside, and it would happen as soon as I stood there. I would get felt up as soon as I stood there. They'd touch me gently to see if I would respond. We'd get on with it once I reacted.

Learning from the Old Men

Uncle Leung actively participated in the gay community in the 1960s just before he emigrated to Canada.

> I was young. I had just graduated and started working. So, I went out all the time . . . I would go to Beaconsfield House in Central as soon as I got off work. [Once] I ran into a famous singer, but he was so camp. For God's sake, I worked in Central . . . And I ran into a colleague . . . I was damned. One of my best friends wanted to screw the singer, because the singer was handsome. However, he was a bottom, and my friend was a bottom too. 'So, what if you were both bottoms?' I told him it was fine. Lesbos could be fun, too.

Leung teased them for making out like lesbians.

He got acquainted with some older gay men then, and picked up a lot of gay community idioms from them.

> *Pit* meant 'top', or 'front and back', where 'front' meant giving and 'back' meant receiving . . . Some of them were called *lanchik* ('wrecked mat'), which meant they both gave and received. There were lots of idioms. I knew a lot of old people then. I met one at the Lai Chi Kok Amusement Park . . . He was a *fadan* [the female lead] in a Chinese opera troupe. He was very popular, one of most famous *fadan* in Guangzhou. There were both male and female *fadan* then. They had to be screwed. If they weren't, they wouldn't be queer enough, which meant that their hands were not soft enough with their dance gestures.

Uncle Leung was once courted by an old man. He even wanted to marry his own daughter to Uncle Leung, because he did not want his daughter to be ill-treated by other men. Uncle Leung was shocked. He knew he was not interested in women, so he turned down 'the good intentions' of the old man right away.

> That old man said that if I married his daughter, he would give me his entire business, because he only had one daughter. But I said to him, 'If I ever marry your daughter, what am I going to do when you want to sleep with me?' I'd be sleeping with my father-in-law, which is wrong, isn't it?

He heard a lot of stories about the community from the old man.

> Most of the old men liked young boys . . . He was in his fifties or sixties, but I was no more than 20 years old . . . We often got together to chat over dim sum. He told me his stories. He said nobody could be queerer than him, so I asked him how queer he was. 'I married my "wife"!' Then I asked him how he did it. 'I lived with him for 18 years. He was put in a red sedan chair [a Chinese wedding custom] and we held a banquet of over twenty tables in a restaurant in Central.' That was something . . . 'Did your parents know?' 'They did!' 'Were you in Chinese wedding outfits?' 'We were.' 'How about bowing to each other?' [A Chinese wedding ritual] 'Of course!' I finally said, 'You are certainly the queerest. How did you do all that?' He said, 'Why not?' They lived together for eighteen years. Then he married his second 'wife' and they held another banquet . . . Yes, they were all men! He married another man.
>
> It was certainly a queer thing when a 'tranny' from Hong Kong made a scene at the Hotel Lisboa in Macao. It happened in the 1960s . . . It made headlines in Hong Kong! He held a press conference at the Carlton Hotel after he came back. The papers said a tranny from Hong Kong made a scene at the Hotel Lisboa when he went into the men's room dressed as a woman, so he had to explain.

Rendezvous in Toilets after the Chinese Economic Reform

Uncle Leung returned to Hong Kong from Canada in the 1980s. He realized that gay activities had started taking place secretly in Guangzhou.

> Oh my! It was very popular in Guangzhou, even more popular than in Hong Kong! It was in Guangzhou Culture Park. That guy suggested going to Guangzhou, but I was scared hearing the word Guangzhou . . . 'Let's go. The place is different now. It's more open.'

Guangzhou Culture Park is a public amusement park, similar to the Lai Chi Kok Amusement Park in Hong Kong.

> There was a cinema as well as vaudeville performances, wooden doll-makers, and singing. There were lots of events going on inside. The entrance fee cost only 20 cents. It was cheap. When I stood in the crowd, oh my, I was scared shitless. They surrounded me from all over. I said, 'It's crazy. There are so many of them.' I was so scared that I wanted to leave, but I couldn't move. Oh, God! Do you know what happened in the cinema? It was mad and wild. The place closed quite early, at about 10 p.m. So where could we go after it closed? A guy said, 'Just follow me. Let's have more fun!' I said, 'What? There's more? The lights are all out and it's pitch dark.' There was a 'garden' [public toilet and cruising spot] at the seaside. People peed on the ground floor and pooped upstairs. He said we should go inside, but I said, 'Oh no, there's only one bulb and it's dark inside. What the hell is going on, man?' He said there were lots of things going on inside. So, I said, 'Fine.' I came back out instantly once I got inside. He asked me why, and I said there was no room to stand inside! So many things were happening. They were giving blow jobs, hand jobs. Some of them were washing up. Everything happened under one bulb. It scared me!

He thought gay men in Guangzhou were too 'queer'.

> That means they were too wild. They were chasing after one another in the streets. People complained about them, so the police had to arrest them. Some old men from Hong Kong went there all the time to look for young boys . . . People couldn't quite accept it when China started opening up. They might tolerate it now. It happens more often now, but it only happens discreetly, unlike Hong Kong. The Mainland is not like Hong Kong anyway.

The gay community in Canada seemed different from China for Uncle Leung as well.

> The gay bars in Canada were much worse. They were too much for me. People smoked weed. There were masochists . . . They were terrifying.

Rendezvous in a Sauna Where a Young Man Fell for Old Leung

Uncle Leung met a young man in a sauna recently.

> We're kind of in a relationship. He likes to be with me all the time . . . I met him here [the gay sauna where we did the interview]. I didn't really like young guys at first. He's in his twenties. I'm living with him now. He bought a three-million apartment. He lets me stay with him, so he's fine. He's been quite good to me. I asked him why he followed me. There are so many old men and some of them are really rich. But he doesn't like them and he wants

me. I'm crippled. I'm poor. I have nothing. I asked him, 'I'm old and I'm broke, so why do you like me?' And he said he didn't know, either.

Uncle Leung had a story about this kind of Electra complex. It happened in the 1960s and it is about a gay father and a gay son.

> The father was into young boys, but his son liked old guys. Then a man met this father-and-son pair on different occasions, without knowing the relationship between them.
>
> The man said to that son, 'I'm introducing you to an old man . . . He's quite handsome. Let's go to a restaurant and have tea sometime.' So, they met. When the son got there and opened the door, he saw his friend sitting with his own father. Of course, he recognized his father, so he left straightaway.

However, the story did not end there.

> When the son left, his friend didn't know the relationship between them. 'Hey, why did you leave? Don't you like him?' 'It's not that.' 'What is it then?' 'He's my dad.'

The punchline is that Leung knew the father and the son as well.

> I knew both of them, but I never had sex with them. The father was quite handsome and I saw him cruising all the time.

Uncle Leung had a stroke in 1999. His mobility on one side of his body and his verbal ability has been reduced since then. I interviewed him in the karaoke room of a gay sauna and it took a few goes to finish the interview. Uncle Leung talked enthusiastically with abundant facial expressions. He laughed and cried while he talked. I couldn't tell sometimes what was real and what was not. He started swearing when he became worked up, and I had to stop him all the time. His young lover got so impatient waiting outside once that he interrupted and yelled at me for keeping an old man from his rest.

Uncle Leung has gone through ups and downs in his life, from living in an apartment of several thousand square feet to a few hundred square feet; from being a boss to receiving social benefits; from having rice with shark fin to having coarse fare. It seems that he never fell head over heels in love in his relationships, and it was probably because of his happy-go-lucky nature. To most of the older generation in Hong Kong, the 1960s was the golden age, and that is true for Uncle Leung as well. He was so curious about sex and his sex life was very wild. In the past, public toilets were called gardens in gay slang. But, for him, everywhere could be his cruising spot. In fact, not only public toilets were his 'gardens'; the whole of Hong Kong was his playground!

Uncle Leung is the only interviewee whom I have lost contact with. I hope he is still alive. I miss his laughs and cries.

11
Tommy

A Bisexual Butterfly (1949–)

Tommy's family had land and fields in mainland China. His older brothers and sisters were born there. However, the family fortune was lost because his father and uncle were always gambling.

His father came to Hong Kong to find a job before the establishment of the People's Republic of China in 1949. Tommy was born and raised in Hong Kong.

Young and Innocent, Enlightened Sexually by a Rice Delivery Guy

Tommy differs from the other interviewees, because he had same-sex experiences much earlier than the rest. He remembers that he was only six years old and living in a wooden hut in Hung Hom. His neighbours in the community were close and friendly, so everyone left their doors open all the time. When people bought rice back then, coolies would deliver it to their homes. The same man always delivered to Tommy's neighbourhood.

> One day after delivering rice to my house, he took me downhill. We lived on a hill . . . and there was a steep slope. My elder brother and some older neighbours went there to play football. It was probably an afternoon and there was no one around. I remember that he took my pants off and grabbed me. I think he came in the end.

Tommy was too young to know what had happened, so he was not too frightened. 'I remember what happened, but it only happened once and never again.'

Another experience around the same time struck him profoundly.

> One of my neighbours was a single middle-aged man. Young children went to bed early at about 7 or 8 p.m. then, but I played around on my own . . . I was young and I went into everybody's house, wherever there was someone at home. I wasn't too naughty when I was young. However, when I went to his place, I don't remember why, but I fell asleep. And I remember that

> he touched me. I don't know why but I touched him back when he touched me. It felt weird, because children and adults are different. When I touched his pubes, I thought it was funny, but I don't remember if anything else happened in the end. Then my mum called out to me at about 8 or 9 p.m., so I went home. After that, he gave me ten cents for snacks whenever he saw me. It was a lot of money then.

Having Secret Sex as an Apprentice in the Workshop

After finishing primary school, Tommy apprenticed with his brother-in-law as a tailor. It was during the Vietnam War, when a lot of American soldiers were sent to Asia, and so there was high demand for tailored suits. Tommy was only 13. He went to school in the morning, then to work in the afternoon till night. When business was good, they had to finish a suit in one or two days, so they often had to work overnight. Tommy had reached puberty when he became an apprentice. He lived with a group of apprentices about the same age and the apprentices often engaged in homosexual acts.

> We lived together . . . So, we often touched each other. They even taught me how to jerk off. One of them 'played' with me. He made me play with him. Some of the tailors did it, too. I sometimes fooled around with some younger apprentices.

Tommy's brother-in-law had a room in the workshop where he slept when he had to work overnight. The room became vacant when his brother-in-law bought his own apartment. It became the place where Tommy explored his same-sex desire with a tailor.

> One of the tailors was quite handsome . . . We were left alone one day, so I locked the door when I got in the room, almost like I was going to rape him. He probably wasn't gay. He was only in his twenties . . . I remember that he asked me to blow him, but I didn't know how to give blow jobs. I liked giving hand jobs, but he wanted to fuck me and of course I couldn't possibly do that. So, I jerked him off in the end. We saw each other all the time, so we had lots of chances to get together. I was the one who tried to get into his pants and seduce him mostly.

These sexual acts were carried out on the quiet, so it remained a secret between them and they never talked about it.

Those Were the Days When They Went Cruising Together

Tommy, like the other interviewees, met other gay people through tabloids when he was young. They wrote their personals in code.

> We never wrote that we were looking for dates. We might say that we were going on an outing, and we actually were. We set a date and a meeting place. We went to Sai Kung most of the time, or went hiking sometimes. It was

totally healthy. If two people had eyes for each other during our outings, they'd talk more and get to know one another. Then they might exchange numbers at the end.

Moreover, Tommy had two close friends nicknamed 'Big Bro' and 'Little Bro', who took him to parties and cruising.

> It happened every Saturday, which was like a party, but it wasn't exclusively gay. Both men and women went and had fun. However, my two brothers were more flamboyant. So, when I was there, people came to me and hugged me. We went cruising at Tsim Sha Tsui Star Ferry Pier then . . . There was a toilet on the observation deck. They knew their way around, so they went off cruising. It was probably a cruising spot . . . I just sat there and flirted with people . . . They were mostly Chinese. I was so silly. I wanted someone to come over so badly, but when someone came, I was so scared. My heart pounded so hard.

Tommy sat there coyly in the beginning when his friends were cruising like past masters. Eventually, Tommy got used to cruising and had sex with another man for the first time.

> When people flirted with me, I flirted back. There was a guy . . . I'd seen him before, but I'd never talked to him. Then one day . . . I followed him home. He was in his thirties and he was from another province in China. It was my first time taking all my clothes off with another guy. I had never done it before. He had an amazing cock. Perhaps because it was my first time, I remember I couldn't manage it even with both hands. Then he said he wanted to fuck me, but I had never done it before, so we didn't do it. I can't remember how it ended. I probably left or something.

Losing His Virginity to a Doctor

Tommy said he would not call that episode his first time. The first time he had 'real' sex, it was with a middle-aged obstetrician.

> When I got there, he wanted to do it with me. He had everything he needed, probably because he was a doctor. We used lube. He used a lot of lube. He knew what he was doing and he was very careful. I didn't object like before. However, I was completely inexperienced, so I was very nervous, even when he touched me. I had to go to the bathroom when he entered me only a little way. So, we didn't go through with it in the end.

Tommy found out later that the obstetrician already had a boyfriend, who did not like Tommy very much of course, so he did not keep in contact with the obstetrician.

Tommy was very casual back then, and never had a serious relationship with another man. All he knew was that he preferred men when it came to sex. He had a girlfriend once. They had known each other since they were young, so they were basically childhood sweethearts.

> All our parents wanted us to be together . . . She never met another guy. We had been together until we were in our twenties, so our parents wanted us to get married. Then I grew tired of her, because we were of similar height. It wasn't a problem at first, but then I thought girls should wear high heels. However, she was taller than me in heels, and it hurt my self-esteem.

Tommy had had sex with other women before, but he never did it with his girlfriend, because she was older than him. He eventually distanced himself from her.

> It was fine in the beginning. We went out, we went on dates. But then it didn't feel right. She felt like my elder sister, so I distanced myself gradually. She got married a lot later. When she finally met someone, she got married after just a few months.

When the United States withdrew from Vietnam, the tailoring industry started to decline. So, Tommy studied fashion design. He entered some competitions and won. After entering the fashion industry, it became easier for him to meet other gay people and even expatriates.

A Party Monster

Many Chinese gays then preferred dating expatriates, who generally had higher socioeconomic status. Tommy had similar experiences but he was not particularly keen.

> I started working very early. It was thirty or forty years ago, and I made HK$500 a month. Think about it, I spent HK$10 a night for a movie, sitting in a mezzanine seat and having chocolates. So, I thought, 'Why date an expat?'

However, he did hang out with expatriates who worked as traders and journalists. They went out, had dinner, and went to the movies, but Tommy never thought that they were dating, because he knew very well that those expatriates all had partners.

> I was with a French guy for a period of time. He was a trader and he came to see me every time he was in town. We went out to watch movies or have dinner sometimes. But I didn't think that we were dating. There was another guy, but I'm not sure if he was a reporter. He took me to the Foreign Correspondents' Club to have lunch or dinner all the time, but he already had a 'lover'. I never really dated an expat but I didn't resist going out with them.

Besides hanging out with expatriates occasionally, Tommy went clubbing with his Big Bro and Little Bro in Central when he was young. He knew the gay bars very well then.

> At Dateline in Central, it cost HK$5 for a drink. After taking a shower and getting dressed up at home, we'd go to Hilton for a drink. We'd go to D.D. at about 9. We'd stay there till 2 or 3. Sometimes, when it was fun, we'd hang

out until the place closed. We danced. We competed with each other to see who made more new friends or who hit on more people. We just danced, but we danced flirtatiously. People hit on me, but they were mostly expats, not Chinese. I went home with expats once or twice.

Complicated Relationships

Tommy had three boyfriends at the same time once, having long-term, mid-term, and short-term relationships with them.

> It sounds like I was playing the field, but actually I never ran too wild in terms of sex, so I can still go out and have fun even now.

As for his long-term boyfriend, they were together for twelve years and they met in a cinema.

> I went to a movie. The leading actor was quite handsome, but there wasn't a large audience. I sat in the middle of the cinema . . . He sat on the left near the aisle, but two rows behind me. He was watching it on his own, too. There weren't many people. The movie was a bit pornographic, and the leading actor was quite good looking. I had been in the gay circle for some time. I was in my twenties then and it had been a long time since I was six years old, so I could tell if someone was straight or gay. Then I thought, 'The guy two rows behind me is quite weird. He follows me to the toilet, so he must be gay.' This guy, who had a long-term relationship with me in the end, took me to a motel when we left. It was my first time going to a motel.

After meeting this long-term boyfriend, the two of them became inseparable.

> After getting more serious with him, he changed drastically. He followed me everywhere. I tried to ditch him, but it didn't work. He said he wanted to come to my place. I said, 'Fine, if that's what you want.' I left home after he arrived. He followed me, so I circled around the place. I lost him . . . But then he went back to my place to wait for me.

Tommy lived with his family at the time, and some people thought the two of them were getting too close.

> They said we were both single, but we behaved like husband and wife.

However, people did not have the concept of homosexuality then, so no one suspected them.

> We didn't know about it then ourselves, so how could they know about us? But my elder sister might know now. It's been a long time, but so what? She knew it in her heart.

Tommy was of a similar age to his long-term boyfriend, who had a great personality. He knew that Tommy had a lot of boyfriends, but he never left him, so Tommy did not care if he got angry or not.

There was no point for him to get mad. I'm a really laidback kind of guy. I kept my mouth shut when he yelled at me. And I said it'd be great if he stopped coming by, because I could find another guy. I was too arrogant to care.

'I Never Blamed Him for Getting Married.'

Tommy and his long-term boyfriend got together in their twenties. Twelve years later, when they went to Macao one day, a piece of news struck him like lightning.

> I remember it was during the night after having a whole day of fun. We were having a drink in a restaurant. He said, 'I'm getting married tomorrow.' [Tommy had never suspected anything before that.] Then I told him, 'It's fine by me.' But after they got back to Hong Kong, he really did get married. It hurt a little for a while. However, I never blamed him for getting married. It was hurtful when he did it. We had been together for a long time after all.

Tommy received a wedding invitation from his long-term boyfriend and he attended his boyfriend's wedding.

> The funny thing was that he asked me out on his wedding night . . . So, I said, 'Now that you're married, to be honest, asking me out is trying to have your cake and eat it. It isn't fair to your 'wife', and it isn't fair to me.' For God's sake, I was turned into the other man suddenly.

Tommy did not go out with his long-term boyfriend that night.

Before his long-term boyfriend got married, Tommy met a boat captain in a sauna. There was also a business associate who had been in love with him for a long time. The night his long-term boyfriend got married, he went to the captain's home on Cheung Chau (island). The captain sent love letters to Tommy every time he left Hong Kong, and he stored all his valuables at Tommy's place.

> I hadn't known him for a long time. It was just a few months. Then he left everything with me, including his bankbooks. It was fine by me. I couldn't have stolen his money anyway.

The captain had to stay in Osaka once because of work. Tommy happened to be free, so he visited him in Osaka to surprise the captain.

> He stared at me when I got there, so I asked him, 'Why are you staring at me?' He said, 'Look at your clothes, and look at your hair. You can't come to my room.' To be fair, I was fashionable, but people wouldn't be able to tell I was gay just by looking at me.

Tommy was disheartened by the cold shoulder from the captain, so he rented a hotel room himself. He went touring in Osaka on his own and came back to Hong Kong two or three days later.

> I just thought no matter how I dressed, I flew there to visit him. So, what did he think I was when he treated me like that? He sent me letter after letter, but

> I ignored him. Finally, he came looking for me after he came back, so I gave everything back to him. That's insane. What was the point of keeping them? It ended between us after that. We lost contact.

They ran into each other in gay venues afterwards and became friends again.

When Tommy was with his long-term boyfriend, there was a friend who had always been in love with him. This man ran a clothing business as well. Tommy says he was a nice guy. They tried and lived together for over a year later, but Tommy could not fake a relationship in the end, because he had always only seen this man as a friend.

> I went cruising when I was with him and he knew it, but he wasn't happy about it. I wasn't interested in him sexually.

This backup boyfriend later moved to Canada. Tommy went to Canada and chose a house with him.

> But we were already over when we went to Canada. Otherwise, he wouldn't have moved abroad. He went there because he wasn't happy, and he wanted me to be there with him.

Tommy, still in his thirties, came back to Hong Kong by himself in the end.

Loyal Friends and Self-seekers in the Gay Community

There were many loyal friends in the gay community, but there were self-seekers who took advantage of others as well. Tommy knew some of them. He met someone who claimed to be in the finance industry at a sauna, who tried to talk Tommy into investing soon after. 'I don't remember if I invested in the end. Even if I did, it would have been a small amount, maybe HK$10,000 or HK$20,000. I don't remember. I probably did.' Tommy began dating the finance guy, who spent the night at Tommy's all the time. The finance guy later lost his job, and he always went out and played the field when Tommy was not in town.

To Tommy, it was not something unforgivable when the guy used his money to play around. 'Okay, it was fine for him to fool around . . . I went to Taiwan for fun. I didn't mind that.' However, the most unacceptable thing for Tommy was that the guy did not have good personal hygiene when he had casual sex. 'He got himself some parasites. He got lice, crab lice. I told him, "You have to be hygienic when you fool around."'

That guy was already in his forties then, but he did not have a serious job and he went to gay saunas as soon as he left work. After finding out the truth about him, Tommy distanced himself from him eventually.

> He called me one day. It was probably a day off, so I was home, and I hadn't even put my *mahjong* tiles away after playing with my friends. He said he'd like to come, so I asked him what for? 'I need to talk to you.' So, I said yes. He helped me to pack the tiles once he got there. I asked him what was going

Membership cards of some defunct gay saunas. Source: Interviewee.

on and he said he owed taxes. So, I open-mindedly asked him how much he wanted. And I told him to bring me his tax bill, but he had it with him. I took a look and it was probably about HK$2,000 or HK$3,000. I said, 'Fine, but I don't have money at home.' I suggested going to his neighbourhood. Then I took him home and he said he had to go up to get something. I asked him to go while I got some money from the cash machine nearby. So, he went up and I left . . . Of course, I thought, why do I have to get you some money? After I left, he called me, but I didn't call him back. I sometimes ran into him years later in Thailand. He was with some older men.

A Lingering Relationship in Taiwan

Tommy went to Taiwan a lot. He has been a frequent visitor ever since the end of the 1970s and the reason is quite simple. First of all, Taiwan and Hong Kong share the same language. He can read even if he cannot understand what people say. Moreover, one of the friends he met through personals studied in Taiwan. Tommy was 21 or 22 years old the first time he went there.

> I won a bet in horse racing, but it wasn't a lot of money, just over HK$1,000. Then I went there . . . The bus in Taiwan cost only 20 cents then. When I got there, there weren't any gay places in Taiwan. They opened later on, and I went to gay bars then. However, there weren't any when I went there for the first time. I just went sightseeing. I was so silly that I took an eight-hour bus ride from Taipei to Kaohsiung. However, I only went to gay bars and saunas later on. I got very carried away playing around there, because there weren't places like them in Hong Kong. I went there at least four times a year.

Since he went to Taiwan a lot, Tommy started another relationship there about ten years ago. He went to Taiwan on a Friday and met a young man in a sauna, who had been eyeing Tommy all along.

> He said he liked older guys. But he didn't know quite how much older than him I was.

Tommy originally wanted to take a rest in the sauna, but he took the opportunity to have sex with the young man.

> I said I had to go, but he tagged along. So, I asked if he wanted to have some food and he said yes. We went to a restaurant after we left. When we finished . . . he suggested taking a drive . . . Then I knew he had a car. We went to Yangmingshan and we had sex again in his car.

> He wanted to take me to a hot spring the next day. The place was very famous and beautiful. I asked him how much it cost, and it was quite expensive. So, I said we shouldn't go, there was no point anyway. We ended up having sex in his car again. And we drove around after that. We drove a long way for a long time. It was night by the time we arrived in Keelung. We got a hotel room for the night. It was Sunday the next day and I had to leave Taiwan . . . In the end . . . I called him and told him that I was leaving for the airport. He asked me why I was going to the airport, so I explained I was from Hong Kong and left that day.

The Taiwanese guy did not get angry when Tommy returned to Hong Kong. He phoned Tommy and came to Hong Kong a few days later. Their relationship started then. Tommy kept flying between Hong Kong and Taiwan, and he stayed in the young man's home at first.

> He asked me to stay at his place. It was fine by me because it was more convenient. Everything was fine in the beginning when I stayed there. However, he had to work, so it felt awkward for me to stay there. It felt like what I did to the finance guy who took money from me. I left home with him when he went to work, but I was just visiting my godmother or going to have some fun.

The Taiwanese guy lived with his family. So, his father and elder brother became suspicious when Tommy showed up. Eventually, he moved out because of it.

> He looked for an apartment the next day, and he found one that same day, so he moved out right away. But I told him his family behaved like that because they cared about him. To be honest, they didn't know what kind of a person I was. If I really was a bad guy, even though I might not take all his money, I might steal something. All parents in the world worry about that, so he shouldn't be angry. I never put the blame on his father and his brother as they suspected me might do something bad to him. It was their responsibility anyway. What if something really happened in the end? Isn't that right?

Irresistible Lust and Complicated Love

The relationship between Tommy and the Taiwanese guy is quite stable now. However, like between most couples, passion will eventually turn bland with time, especially in the bedroom. Tommy believes it is probably due to his boyfriend's reserved personality.

> He doesn't go out at all. He stays home all the time. He stays home on his days off. He only goes to the riverside with his three dogs on his days off. And he isn't too active in bed. He doesn't like it . . . How should I put it? It wasn't like this in the beginning. He used to be very demanding. He had to do it all the time.

Tommy goes out and fools around behind his boyfriend's back now.

> So, I go out on my own . . . Of course, I don't tell him. Sometimes he asks me why my phone is off. I tell him that I left it at home, because I forget it all the time, and I don't answer it at home.

Tommy feels guilty about cheating, because he is grateful that his boyfriend has left his family for him. On the other hand, cheating is an irresistible temptation for him.

> It's an emotional need. It still is, but it doesn't happen as often as before. My shape is not as good as it used to be after all. Besides, when you go to those places . . . you feel a bit guilty . . . That's how I feel, so I don't go out that often anymore. I probably . . . go out once every two or three months, because I have to behave like a thief when I fool around, or I have to wait until he goes on a business trip.

There are many challenges a couple has to face when they turn mere lust into a relationship.

Tommy still has his aspirations in life.

> There are lots of possibilities in Taiwan. There are lots of stores on the streets. You can be a florist if you like flowers.

However, he has not made his plans yet.

> The only thing is that I'll be with him [his Taiwanese boyfriend].

He is very close to his family members. He is very fond of his little sister, who is near his age, but he is even closer to his elder sister. After his siblings married, Tommy lived with and cared for his parents.

> My father was a gambler, but there was nothing I could do. I couldn't talk him out of it or beat him up . . . Then he got older. He became incontinent and all that. I had no choice but to talk to my brothers and sisters. I asked them what to do. We put him into a nursing home. However, it didn't take long. He was gone in a few months. That's why I didn't want to put my mother in

a nursing home after that, but we had no choice in the end. We sent her to a home and she was gone not long after as well.

Since Tommy had girlfriends before, his family only asked him to get married when he was young, but they never suspected his sexuality. Tommy is ambivalent about his sexual orientation. Tommy is bisexual by behaviour, because he has had different girlfriends through the years, and some of them even fought for Tommy. Tommy's life would have been totally different if he had no same-sex experiences. However, he does not seem to regret it.

I wouldn't have led such a colourful life. I wouldn't want that.

If he had the choice, he said he would want to be a bisexual man who is inclined more towards men in his next life.

Tommy is one of my youngest interviewees. He is more experienced with dating expatriates, which is the most obvious difference compared to the other interviewees. Dating expats probably happened because of his work. People who date mostly Caucasians are called 'potato queens' in the community. It was a common phenomenon in the 1970s to the early 1990s. After all, expatriates were richer and more open then, so they were more attractive to local young men in a more conservative era, especially when society was generally poorer. They symbolized sophistication and modernity and the possibility for upward social mobility for local young gay men (see Ho and Tsang 2000; Kong 2002, 2004). However, Tommy kept long-term relationships with mostly Chinese, because there was still a language barrier with expatriates. He had a wonderful love life, including 'straight' relationships with women, as well as long-, medium-, and short-term relationships with men. The joy and pain of hovering around different flowers is not shared by most other interviewees. However, this butterfly seems to have stopped flitting about. I visited Tommy in Taiwan in 2017. He is living there with his Taiwanese boyfriend. They have been together for more than a decade.

12
Tony
The Bear Chaser (1950–)

Tony has been an electronics technician for decades. He was born in Kwong Wah Hospital in 1950. Not everyone had the privilege to be born in a hospital then.

> My father knew a doctor. I was so lucky that he was there when I was born . . . There were only midwives then and babies weren't born in hospitals. But I was given a birth certificate, which was special.

His father, who repaired electrical appliances for a living, was from a small family and had only one elder sister. That is why his father wanted more children and so he had six in the end.

Children from Poor Families Taking up Their Responsibilities Early On

Life was hard for most people in Hong Kong then. Tony is the eldest son in the family with five younger siblings. His mother was a housewife, so his father had to support a family of eight alone by repairing appliances.

> We lived in an apartment building shared by fourteen families. It was tough. Some tenants had to live in the kitchen. Even a tiny space below the roof was turned into a room. The tenant had to climb up the stairs to get inside. That kind of space was mostly rented by single men. If a tenant wanted a better space, he could rent a bunk. There were two bunk beds in the living room, occupied by four families. [Tony lived in an old building with a balcony on each side of the building.] We lived on the balcony. Luckily, we had a bunk bed. I slept on the floor. My parents slept on the lower bunk. My younger brothers and sisters had to be packed like sardines.

When life was tough, Tony, as the eldest son, had to learn how to take care of his younger siblings and do housework.

> My mother gave birth to a lot of children and we didn't have a lot of money. She couldn't take good care of her body, so her health wasn't too good. I was almost 10 years old when she gave birth to my youngest brother. And I had to

> do housework. My father had to work, so no one gave her postpartum care. My mother had to stay home; I had to take my little brother with me when I went to the market or cooked. I had to peel ginger and prepare soup for my mother. When I did it for the first time, I found that my hands felt hot when I peeled them. People my age had to do housework starting when we were really young.

Education was not free in those days, so, with lots of siblings in a deprived family, it was difficult for Tony to go to school. He failed and had to repeat Form 4 in evening school. Unfortunately, his father lost his job in 1960. Because his family had lost their major source of income, Tony decided to go to work and take up family responsibilities.

> So, I started working. My two younger sisters and I had to work . . . I was apprenticed to my father and we worked on electric lights. My little sister sewed clothes. I worked with my dad and learnt from him after that.

Tony's family was finally given a public housing flat in 1963 or 1964. The entire family was over the moon. They lived there for over forty years.

Pursuing Further Education for Knowledge and for Love

Tony realized his own inadequacies after he started working, so he went to a technical college as well as an English college, where he studied electrical installation and maintenance and English at the same time. Besides education, Tony wanted to find himself a girlfriend at night school. He was attracted to a few female classmates who looked like TV stars, but it did not work out in the end for various reasons. Tony's wish was finally granted when he went on his graduation trip.

> We went to a Caritas Hong Kong campsite during our graduation trip. In our night school . . . there were only four or five guys and over thirty girls. Those girls didn't do well in school, so they went to work in factories. And they wanted to learn some English, so they went to night school . . . I was quite cheerful and I liked helping people. When someone cooked during an outing or camping, each of us was supposed to serve ourselves. However, I'd get the food for them and go around serving all of them . . . I was trying to be a gentleman. I had to do it. I brought them bowls, chopsticks, and food. I served them all before eating my own food. I ate late, so I finished last. Then one of the girls said, 'You've been working so hard to serve everyone. I'll peel an orange for you when you finish.' That's how I got to know her. There were lots of girls, but none of them ever peeled an orange for me except her. I didn't know her very well. She was from another class.

That was when Tony first got to know that girl. Actually, he had made an impression on her before. When Tony was in Form 5 in the English college, in preparation for his public examination he had to attend a mock examination, and their two classes were put in the same classroom. She sat next to him during the mock exam.

'After I finished answering the questions, I looked at the paper on the desk next to mine. There were lots of mistakes. So, I read it. The first question, the second question . . . The answers were all wrong. There were some blanks that we had to fill, but she made a lot of mistakes.' Tony did not know her name then. He had not even looked at her face clearly.

> I took her paper and gave her mine when the teacher wasn't looking. Then I corrected the mistakes and changed them back again. I was quite bold then. I was only in Form 4. But she was so terrible. She was going to fail for sure.

Tony forgot about it completely afterwards. It was the girl who reminded him when they started dating. 'She told me then. She lived in Ngau Tau Kok and I lived in Choi Hung. We were really close. She seemed fine after we got to know each other better. She looked nice. She was a bit chubby and looked like a singer. It was fine then for people to look plump and round, but not now.'

Tony married her after he graduated in 1980. Like many children from lower-class families, Tony had to work when he was very young to help support his family, but he never complained. He was on good terms with his family. He was spoiled by his father because he was the eldest son in a patriarchal family, but his relationship with his mother was rather complicated.

> I used to hold a grudge against her. I was the eldest. She chased me and beat me with a feather duster whenever I did something wrong. I remember one time I was beaten like crazy. She was really mad. So, I tried to run when she beat me. But she tied me up with a rope and lashed me with her duster. She was angry, but she also wanted to make an example of me, because my younger brothers and sisters were watching. 'That's what you get when you do something wrong.' My relationship with her wasn't too good . . . But in the end, now I know that she was changed because of something that happened, because my father had another woman.

Tony's father's first love was a nurse, but she had to get married after she got pregnant at her clinic by a doctor. Tony's father was disappointed and eventually married Tommy's mother. When Tony's mother found out about it, she started picking fights with her husband all the time, and she took it out on Tony. Tony heard about his father's love story during the 1980s. He was not angry at his father, but his relationship with his mother gradually improved. When his father passed away in 1995, together with his siblings, he bought a subsidized-sale flat for his mother, so that she could have a better place to live with her unmarried children.

Attracted to the Bodies of Older Men Deep Down Inside

Dating women, getting married and having children, Tony seems to be quite 'straight'. So how did he start realizing his same-sex desire?

> Actually, I . . . felt it deep down inside. But I didn't know anything about it, and I knew nothing about homosexuality. I liked watching foreign films. I got excited when I saw a man and a woman doing it on screen. I was more turned on by female bodies then, because censorship was very strict then. You couldn't even see their boobs. Censorship gradually relaxed after the 1970s. It wasn't like that before. There were black bars whenever you saw their boobs. I liked women then, but I liked men too when I saw them. I liked mature and masculine men, especially hunks with lots of hair like Sean Connery. When I watched James Bond, once he showed up, he became my idol. But I didn't think that I might be gay. I just admired his body, which looked great. His hair looked great and he was tall. I liked him a lot . . . But I didn't know it myself. I went to a boys' school and of course there were one or two sissies. When they sang, they did it with girl's voices like sopranos. There was no denying what they were. Besides, their behaviour was very obvious. We even discriminated against them and made fun of them. We called them 'sisters'. We didn't use the word 'sissies' . . . We were just kidding around, but we didn't bully them. They knew it themselves. And I know that I was wrong. I think I was kind of masculine. I know some gay people are rather feminine. I saw them in movies later on, but I felt sick.

Turned on by an Older Man in a Public Toilet

Tony knew that he was attracted to men, but he did not think much about it, so he never explored his sexuality when he was in school or in his adolescence. But he stumbled across a gay cruising spot after he had got married and had children.

Tony's son entered kindergarten in 1984. He usually picked his son up if he got off work early. Sometimes he got there before the class finished, so he had to stroll around. There was a construction site nearby. He accidentally found out that people were cruising in a public toilet near the construction site, but he did not feel anything then.

> I knew that the man stood there to peek at me when I peed, but it was fine. I didn't mind and I just ignored him.

But one day he met an old man after work at a hotel with his colleagues.

> I saw an old man when I went to wash my hands in the toilet. He was wearing a trench coat and standing in the corner taking a piss. I was washing my hands with my colleagues. Our hands were quite dirty so it took a long time, at least five or ten minutes. There were several of us, but there were only one or two sinks. I was the last one. That old man stood there and peed. My colleagues were all finished and gone, so I was wondering why he was still peeing. Why did it take so long? I didn't pay him any attention. I just

wanted to pee and leave. That old man took a look at me and said, 'Do you have a minute, young man? Can I talk to you?' I said, 'I don't know you. What do you want to talk about?' Then he asked me what I was afraid of. He was really old. He couldn't fight me and he couldn't outrun me. So, I asked him what he wanted to talk about. There was a garden outside the toilet. I said 'fine' and we talked outside. He asked me about my sex life. I didn't mind answering his questions and he didn't hesitate to ask. So, we chatted like it was perfectly normal. We talked about jerking off at the end and it was fine. Then he took me to the Mariners' Club. He was probably a sailor . . . We went to the toilet in the attic and we jerked off. We did it together. I had never done that before. It felt okay. We jerked off together and we came. My cum was white and translucent. His cum was clean, but it looked brown. I got scared. Damn it. Did he have an STD? Luckily, we didn't do anything. We only jerked off . . . I left while he was still cleaning up. When he finished, he asked me to stay and wait for him. He wanted to buy me dinner. I said 'fine' but I left once I got out. After I went home, I used Dettol when I took showers for a whole week. I was a bit scared. People told me later that maybe he had a prostate problem, or perhaps he drank too much coffee.

Looking Everywhere in Hong Kong for Gay Men

The sexual encounter with the old sailor was Tony's first same-sex experience. It made him aware that public toilets were cruising spots for gay men, so he started exploring public toilets everywhere in Hong Kong.

> After finding out about public toilets . . . I started looking. When I got off work, I cruised wherever I went. I went all over Hong Kong. I was so crazy that I went all the way from Hung Hom to Kwun Tong. I looked into toilet after toilet on my days off.

According to Tony, public toilets were not just cruising spots, but also hangouts for gay men.

> People just talked . . . They didn't usually have sex, because to be honest, people who cruised in toilets were usually unattractive and ugly, or old. Attractive people didn't have to cruise. They could find themselves some sugar daddies . . . People talked to each other if they got along. They exchanged news. If they fancied each other, they might exchange numbers.

Tony was very careful cruising in toilets, because there was a risk of getting arrested. There were showers in some old toilets, so he brought soap and a towel with him in case he ran into the police.

> The doors of the toilet stalls used to be shorter. You could see over the top and under the bottom, so the cops could see each stall clearly when they passed by. People might get caught because they made noise. That's why we didn't usually have sex there. The drains smelled really bad anyway. Besides, it was too risky. I knew some people in one of the toilets, so they could look out for me. I could do it inside if they happened to be there. Otherwise we just talked. We usually talked instead of having sex.

When Tony met the right guys in toilets, he mostly jerked them off. He seldom had sex with them.

> Sometimes they had anal sex, but it didn't happen very often for me, because we didn't have condoms. It might get you in trouble if you were caught with condoms by the police.

Tony went to saunas too. He got infected with pubic lice and then he passed them on to his wife.

> I was doomed. It was really private and it was sexually transmitted, when your hair rubbed against someone else's. My wife was very respectable, so it had to be me that gave it to her . . . I went to a government doctor, because private doctors were too expensive, and government clinics were free. I was told to bring my spouse with me. After you passed them to someone else, they might pass them back to you. Even after you cleaned them all off, you could get them again if your partner hadn't got rid of them, too. That would be a nightmare, so I had to bring my wife with me. [He got away with it in the end.] Fortunately, I had gone camping earlier and I had only been back for two or three weeks before I contracted them. So, I told her I probably got them from the towels and sheets at that camp. I was so lucky that time.

A Devoted Catholic Who Kept His Nose Clean

After being infected with pubic lice, Tony became more careful and more disciplined.

> I'm a top, so I looked more carefully before I had sex with others. I didn't want to get STDs. I'd be damned if I gave my wife anything again, so I had to be careful.

Moreover, Tony is a Catholic, so he has doctrines to follow since he was young.

> I was in Primary 6, but I wasn't serious, and I wasn't initiated. I was told that I could skip classes on Saturday if I listened to bible teachings, so I went. I had to stay in a self-study class if I didn't go. So, I became a Catholic. That's why I had to behave. I had to follow the doctrines, so I wasn't promiscuous.

He really followed the rules by making his wife his only woman. He has never had sex with anyone else of the opposite sex to this day.

> I did it once before I got married. I saved a lot of money and took a vacation for the first time, to the Philippines . . . I shared my room with another guy. He said he wanted a massage and I had never tried it. It was a proper massage parlour in a hotel. But when the masseuse finished, she asked me if I wanted to get off. She might get an extra tip for it. I thought I had never done it before over all those years, so I might as well try it. It felt really good. I only did it once. I went back to my hotel after getting off, and I became so restless that night. I got a hard-on all night and it didn't go away. I didn't know what to do. I couldn't help it. I was so aroused. It was too exciting, because no woman had ever done it to me. I had to soak myself in cold water to calm down.

Being Kind to Women, Being Casual with Men

Tony has never had another woman other than his wife because of his Catholic belief that he has to be faithful to her. Besides, Tony values his family a lot. He did not want to repeat his father's mistake of having an affair that led to family disputes.

> I'm very old-fashioned and I value my family a lot. I didn't want to have another woman and get her pregnant, so that she might come and fight for my estate one day. I didn't have that much money, but I didn't want my family to fight all the time. Having seen my father and mother fight like that, I didn't want that for myself. After marrying my wife, I had to be with her for the rest of my life.
>
> I never screwed around with women, but I can't say the same about men. There are so many people who do the same nowadays, especially rich married men. A lot of their wives tell them that they can have as much fun as they want, but they shouldn't have illegitimate children to fight for their estate. Their wives don't mind them screwing men, because it's less likely for them to have problems afterwards.

That is why Tony played around with men rather than women.

There were many memorable men in Tony's same-sex love affairs, including the First Lover, the God-brother, the Monk, the God-father, the Security Guard, and the Second Man. Some of his love stories are selected and described in the following sections.

> My god-brother wasn't married. He was a Chinese Vietnamese with some money. He taught me a lot . . . He wanted me to be his husband when he first met me, but I said, 'I can't. I have to be faithful to my wife.' I didn't want to do it, because if it got too serious, my family would be ruined . . . I couldn't be his husband, so we became god-brothers. My god-brother took good care of me. He was a few years older and we shared a lot of common interests. He liked watching movies, listening to music, and collecting CDs, especially of some old singers. He had many vinyl records, so many of them. I liked them as well and I collected a lot of them myself. So, I borrowed from him if there was anything I didn't have.

The God-brother passed away a few years ago.

A Jealous Boyfriend Who Nearly Ruined His Family

Tony met the Monk afterwards. He was studying theology then. He lived in a monastery and taught in a school. 'He liked me a lot. He was chubby. I liked huge and chubby guys.' The Monk had a problem because he was really possessive. He wanted Tony to divorce his wife and leave his family so that they could live together.

I said it wasn't possible. I liked my family. He moved somewhere near my son's kindergarten in my neighbourhood to get close to me. He hoped that I'd be with him one day. He wanted to buy a piano and some appliances as soon as he moved, but he wanted everything new. I didn't have that much money. I only paid the down payment, but not the instalments.

The Monk even made a scene at Tony's place, almost exposing Tony's sexuality. It started when Tony asked the Monk out one day, but stood the Monk up and went to his sister-in-law's home to have dinner. The Monk became really jealous and called Tony at home to argue with him.

He called me and claimed that my wife called him at his office, saying she was from the AIDS Foundation. She asked him to go and have a check-up because his blood test was positive. But I thought my wife wouldn't have said that even if she really called him. It was impossible. He probably made it all up, but I got scared. He asked my mum and my little brother to be there, and said he'd hire someone to beat my wife up. Why was he so overbearing? Because his younger brother worked for a gang, that's why. I was young and naive, so I got scared. I was intimidated by him. He came to my place at 1 a.m. He asked my mum and my little brother to come. I was almost 'outed' by him. So, I ended up cutting all ties with him, because I couldn't go on like that.

Besides, Tony received a call from the bank asking about the Monk's accounts, which led to questions about the Monk's finances, so Tony gave up on him eventually.

The Seven-year Itch with the Security Guard

After breaking up with the Monk, Tony sensed that his wife might be suspicious, so he was on his best behaviour for about seven years, though he went toilet cruising occasionally during that time. He finally had a fresh start when he met the Security Guard.

He was the first who asked me to go bareback [having sex without a condom]. We both wore condoms in the beginning, but he said he didn't want to wear them after a while, because he was kind of allergic to latex. So, after having a check-up and a blood test, we started to do it since we were both safe. We were together for over three years . . . We worked well with each other in bed, because he could take it really hard from me. The best thing about him was his faithfulness in his relationships. He only had one man at a time. I went to saunas with him. He looked quite good. He looked like a cop when he kept his hair short. Many people fancied him, but he wasn't with anyone else when he was with me.

Why did I like him? I took pity on him a bit. His apartment was literally empty. He had nothing but a tatami mat, a tiny television, and a microwave. He cooked with a butane camp stove. He had a small fridge, but no cabinets or anything like that. He kept his clothes in a red-white-and-blue

> nylon canvas bag. Of course, he had two folding chairs and a folding table but that was it. I pitied him when I saw that. So, I went to his place to prepare soup and some nice food for him on my days off. He brought his lunchbox to work, so I always prepared more food for him.

Tony knew the Security Guard had had a male Indonesian flatmate all along. He had dinner with the Security Guard and the Indonesian during the holidays. The Security Guard called Tony his uncle. Tony later found out that the Indonesian was actually the Security Guard's boyfriend, so he was the other man. The three of them got along fine in the beginning. They sometimes had drinks together.

> In the end, the Indonesian guy probably got older and became possessive. He didn't have anyone else in Hong Kong. He wanted my 'friend' to take care of him till he died, so he was afraid that I'd steal his boyfriend and he'd be all alone in his later years. They fought every night at home. My 'friend' said his flatmate was almost abusive because he got paranoid all the time. I had no choice and I didn't want them to fight, so I left.

His relationship with the Security Guard ended after three years.

Becoming the Other Man and Finding Himself the Third Man

After breaking up with the Security Guard, Tony did not find another man for a while. He met the Second Man, who was in his thirties, four years ago.

> I'm the eldest son, so I didn't go on vacations during Chinese New Year. I had to stay home to host visiting relatives. I had to be there every day like I was in jail and I couldn't go out. So, before my holiday ended, I sneaked out and went to a gay sauna the day before I went back to work. That's how I ran into the Second Man and had fun with him.

When Tony met someone he liked in a sauna, he used to leave his number with that man, hoping to turn their hook-up into something else. However, he never heard from anyone.

> None of them ever called, so I thought, 'This one is great. I like him, but anyway, I shouldn't bother leaving my number with him.' I took a shower after having fun with him, then I went upstairs to the karaoke room.'

To Tony's surprise, the man looked for Tony floor after floor when he did not see Tony get out of the shower, and he gave Tony his number very deliberately.

> It wasn't something I had planned. He was such a catch and he was so young. I thought there was no way for him to be into me, but he did have the hots for me ... We hooked up again two weeks later ... I found out that he lived alone. His parents were divorced, so he was all alone. He lived in a public housing apartment. He lived alone and he wasn't married. I went there to prepare soup and food for him when I had time. I helped him all the time at first, but he actually only wanted to hook up with me. He didn't want to be

> serious. However, he was touched by my sincerity in the end, so he finally accepted me after three years. He brought lunch to work, too, So, when I made soup, I prepared more for him. I liked taking care of people.

This new guy had two godfathers and a man he had been in a relationship with for over ten years. Tony moved him sincerely. After his godfathers passed away four years later, Tony became the second man.

The new guy married a few months after getting to know Tony, but they have continued seeing each other.

Tony is a bear (gay slang for a chubby and hairy man) and also likes bear. He met a chubby guy, the Third Man, in a gym at about the same time, and they started seeing each other as well. As a two-timer, Tony naturally had time management issues, so the Second Man and the Third Man got jealous and started fighting.

> I went to the Third Man's flat one day, but then the Second Man asked me to see him out of the blue. The Second Man probably sensed something was up, then he confirmed it by looking at my phone. After getting caught, I told him I had not wanted to do it in the first place, but he was the one who asked me to find a partner. So, I became attached to the Third Man. The Second Man didn't like it at first and he got furious. The Third Man didn't like it either, because I was supposed to spend the nights at his place, but I had to go whenever the Second Man called.

Tony had to allocate his time carefully after that, so that he could satisfy his two lovers. The Second Man moved to the New Territories later on, so Tony did not see him as often as before, but they tried to spend as much time together as possible.

> For example, when he worked night shifts, he'd have dinner with me. Sometimes he came and hung out with me on his days off, about four times a month.... Then I went to the Third Man's place. He didn't mind me sleeping over every night, but I couldn't, because I had to go back home. It was fine for the Third Man eventually. He came with me to play *mahjong* with some old folks, because his mother was put in a nursing home. She liked me a lot. She held my hand all the time and she didn't want to let go.

A Pseudo Marriage with a Closeted Husband

Seeing two men at the same time, this 60-year-old has a wonderful sex life with men. So, naturally, he has lost his sex drive with his wife.

> I haven't touched her in six years. I think I haven't done it in almost ten years, but we went on vacation sometimes so I was forced to do it. It was fine in the beginning, but then I don't know why . . . It got out of hand last year. It was totally ridiculous. She was already in her fifties, so she was at her sexual peak. She climbed on top of me and tried to fuck me. It was pathetic. In the

end, I said, 'I'm too old. I have problems in my prostate or something.' I had to make an excuse so that she'd give it up for good. I have the Second Man and the Third Man, so I have enough fun.

Since Tony does not use condoms when he has sex with them, he's worried that he might be infected, so he goes to gay saunas which provide HIV rapid tests to have his blood tested from time to time. Fortunately, he has not been infected so far.

Tony has not told his family, co-workers, or schoolmates about his same-sex relationships.

> I wanted to come out to my schoolmates so badly, but I would never tell them, no matter how close we are. You don't know what they'd think after all. Some of them might have a problem with homosexuality. Besides . . . they might tell others behind my back. So even though we might be friends, if someone finds out that I'm gay, but he doesn't like it, we might become estranged and I'd lose a friend. That's why I don't usually tell others.

A Self-confessed Traditionalist Who Prefers a Big Family

Tony's son is now in his thirties and is working in telecommunications. Tony was probably too harsh on his son, so they are not too close.

> Because I was quite strict with him, he doesn't like me very much. I pushed him too hard. I had a friend, who was my schoolmate, and he tutored my son for free. He didn't charge me and he didn't even let me pay for his transportation. I must have pushed him too hard.

Having lived the larger part of his life, Tony has his regrets, because he did not see his father on his deathbed. His father, who had moved to Canada, had planned to return to Hong Kong in 1995.

> He was hospitalized a week before his flight. He probably had problems with his intestines . . . But he insisted he was fine and he was then discharged. He was supposed to get on the plane on that Friday but before his flight, he didn't feel well, so he went back to the hospital on Thursday. His attending doctor had a day off, and my father couldn't find another doctor to see him. He missed the flight . . . the doctors were terrible over there. They didn't work during weekends . . . Nobody followed up on his case . . . He passed away the next Monday morning. He couldn't come back. I had to fly there with my son to get him back. He was cremated and we carried his ashes in an urn.

Other than that, Tony said with a cheerful and optimistic personality, he always takes things as they come. He volunteers and helps people whenever he has time, so he is living quite happily and he is quite satisfied with his life. Looking to the future, he hopes that he can see his son getting married.

Tony might have lived a wonderful gay life, but he thinks he is very traditional and prefers a big family.

I'm actually very conservative and stubborn. I like big families. Have you watched those Chinese family drama series? I like seeing those families where every member lives under the same roof and they have dinner together. But it's impossible in real life. There's always a spiteful daughter-in-law and people always scheme against each other. I can only hope that there's a patriarch keeping people in order. I like this kind of family relationship, because I'm such an old-fashioned man.

Tony is the only one who is still living with his wife. He broke up with the Second Man and the Third Man a few years ago and remained single for two to three years but recently he has been jiggling again with two other men. He is a perfect example of a traditional Chinese man and he is almost the same as his own father. The only difference is that he is having affairs with men. He has his own interpretation of loyalty to his wife, which is not something that everybody would agree with. It seems very common for Asians to pursue heterosexual marriage and homosexual relationships at the same time. It happens even more frequently in mainland China (e.g., Kong 2011, 145–73; Fu 2012, 139–66; Wei and Cai 2012). I was referred once by a friend to participate in a karaoke gathering exclusively for married gay men in Seoul, South Korea. Some gay men believe this kind of abnormality created by heterosexual hegemony is the best way for them to stay in the closet. The tragedy of **Brokeback Mountain** *in America in the 1960s is now rewritten with a somewhat happy ending in Asia. For these two-timers, they might enjoy dealing with different partners at the same time. But their 'homowives' may be victims who have been kept in the dark all along.*

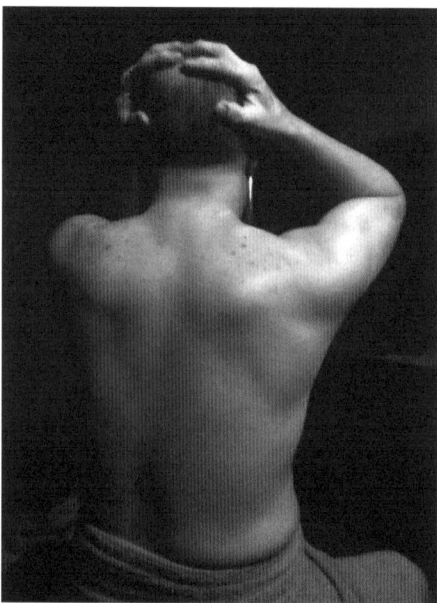

A recent picture of Tony. Source: Author.

13
Nigel Collett

A History Boy, a Military Man, a Writer, and an Activist (1952–)

Born into a working-class family in 1952, Nigel was from an industrial town 80 miles west of London. His family worked in the same railway factory for three generations. He was the first to go through grammar school and escape to university. With a passion for history, he went to St. Peter's College, Oxford, to study modern history. After attending university for three years, he joined the army. He was brought to Asia and finally settled down in Hong Kong.

'I Absolutely Did Not Want to Be Gay'

Nigel grew up in a period of 'complete, utter ignorance about anything gay' and he can't recall anything except 'smutty school boy's jokes'. There were no out gay men where he grew up. It was a time when, 'if you wanted to do anything in life, you wouldn't come across gay people.' Besides, 'I absolutely did not want to be gay. I wanted to be what I knew was normal. I wanted to have a family, to have a career. I wanted to be the same as everybody else.'

The only person he knew who could have been gay was the drag queen Danny La Rue.

> He of course always denied it. But there he was, a beautiful long leggy thing on the stage, wearing sequins and feathers. I didn't want to wear sequins or feathers, so I thought, I don't want that, I don't want to look like that . . . I had no desire to be gay. Only realized I was gay in maybe fifth or sixth form. I realized that fabled time, when ordinary boys who like messing around turn into straight boys, hadn't happened to me yet. And I was waiting for the switch to be flicked and it didn't flick. And I went to university still thinking maybe it might, but it never did.

He felt his first attraction to men at about nine years old, when he watched an American Western series called *Laramie*.

> In this series, there was a ranch [boy] called Jess. In one episode, he got tied up and beaten. . . That was the first time I can ever remember feeling vastly

attracted to the guy who got beaten. And around about that time, there were a couple of other things that happened. Some of the kids and friends at school, where I started feeling something more than liking.

Nigel was kind of a nerd. Typically, he could not do anything physical like football, or anything with any kind of ball. He was the cleverest student in school, but no one ever messed around with him. He didn't have any sexual experience with anyone until he was 13 years old, when he masturbated with a classmate.

> We were together for about two years . . . And then after that, there was a huge gap. And I felt I was really missing the fun. At university, I was totally celibate, having no contact with anybody . . . So, from the age of 15 onwards, I didn't have sex with anybody until I was 30.

Nigel tried going out with girls when he was young, but he never had sex with women.

> When I was . . . at school, I had lots of girlfriends . . . They were just friends of mine and I was closest to some of the girls at school. We were at a mixed school. I hung out with the girls more than the boys . . . At the university, I had no friends, no female friends at all. Oxford in those days, it was 95 per cent masculine . . . And then the army; I had to start taking people out. In the army, you always had to have a guest, at a party or a ball, or dinner. So, I would take people's sisters or I would try to find somebody. Somehow met a nurse or school teacher at the garrison or something else. I met some really nice girls, but none of them I felt any sexual attraction to . . . So, I never get closer than the second date.

The Stupidest Job for a Gay Man

Nigel was happy at Oxford and thought he would spend his life studying history. In the end, he realized he was not good enough and he was not able to carry on at Oxford. At the same time, he began to realize how small his world was and how closeted everything was about him, not only his sexuality.

> The rest of it was more important to me. The reason that happened to me is because I started to get involved in journalism. I was brought in by a friend of mine who ran the *Cherwell*, which was an Oxford University student newspaper. And he wanted someone to do advertisements because it was a commercial newspaper, not subsidized, so [it] had to pay for itself. So, he brought me inside and I started to write. And I started to [meet] huge numbers of people. I saw what journalism was . . . and I had an amazing amount of fun. I stopped working hard and I realized the world was a big place. And, actually, I was persuading myself in the end I needed to go out and become a bigger person. And this wasn't sex, this was everything. I had been half a person up to then. That's when the army came in. I went to it. I had no background for it. I was totally unsuited to it. Really, I just wanted to be stretched, pulled, and shoved and reformed and bent into a different kind of shape. And it did that.

He did not join the army because he fancied men. He went to the army because it seemed exciting, exotic, and connected to politics.

> I went to visit a unit and I ended up in the army . . . which of course was then probably the most macho, heterosexual kind of society you can get. And it would not have been possible at all to be flamboyant or to be in any way out about anything.
>
> . . . It was probably the stupidest job you could ever go into if you're a gay man without thinking about it . . . I was . . . completely unaware of the whole world . . . I didn't even know that, in 1967, homosexuality had been legalized. It didn't even strike me . . . And, in the army, it wasn't legalized until 2001. So, the army was separate. It was a criminal offence to be found out or proved to be taking part in anything with the same sex . . . So, I could have, literally, could have gone to jail if I were found to be having sex with anybody. If I had been suspected, I could have been investigated. Police would have followed up all my contacts and my friends. It would have been a witch hunt that would have spread through all my contacts.

Nigel believes the army was not tolerant of gays. It was not socially acceptable by society and an offence in the army then. 'I think in my generation, it still isn't very acceptable in England to be gay . . . It was a very stuffy, old-fashioned society in my generation. And that generation would not have put up with people who were gay. You could be tolerated but that was as far as it went. And I didn't want to live in that kind of world. That's why I left the army, basically trying to find myself. So, it was a very long process.'

For almost ten years he was absolutely celibate:

> I did ten years in the army, from 1974 to 1983, completely shoving my sexuality into one corner of my mind. Not even bothering with it really, thought

On loan service with the Western Frontier Regiment of the Sultan of Oman's Armed Forces in Thumrait, Dhofar, 1982. Source: interviewee.

I could go on with my career for the rest of my life and that would be it. Then I got pushed into Asia. In 1982 . . . I was now thirty. [I] fell in love with a guy, a man from Pakistan, Balochistan of all places. My soldiers were all Baloch from Balochistan . . . And that shattered all of my illusions. My closet collapsed. And I spent the next ten years . . . working with Gurkha soldiers, Nepalese who served in the British army . . . in Hong Kong mostly.

Ever since falling in love with a Pakistani man, Nigel has only dated Asians:

The first guy I fell in love with was from Pakistan. I never fell in love with anyone in India, but then, anywhere sort of East of India. Yeah, anything up to Japan and Korea . . . It's not like I don't fancy anybody in the West, but it's always kind of not very interesting. Asia's been very different. And therefore, I think there was a sexual component to it. Maybe much more than . . . 'I had to do this'. In England, I might not have had to.

However, he could not really explain his attraction to Asian men.

But with me . . . the partners happened to be Asians. I don't understand why this is, but . . . I had an attraction to Asian men. I would like to have someone investigate how this happens. I have never seen an explanation.

A Long-time Coming Out

Nigel had to be totally closeted when he was in the army. He would not have conceived himself using the word 'gay' until he came to Hong Kong, so it took a long time for him to come out.

The army was a strange world. You can hide yourself away and not be part of society in a way you would find extraordinary outside . . . And the kind of conversations people were having in London, in the army I never had. And so, things like HIV . . . pretty much passed me by in the army.

Moreover, he thinks that society did not really change in the 1960s.

They began to. TV, pop figures . . . kind of changed in the 1960s, but real change didn't come through till the 1980s. So, in the 1970s, it was beginning to spread through the rest of the country. My time was in the provinces . . . Not even conservative, completely ignorant about it. Nobody talked about being out. The word gay wasn't used . . . it was 'queer' or 'pansy.' 'Homosexual' was too long to use.

Besides, it was easier for Nigel to come out when he was away from home in Hong Kong.

I think the social scene in Hong Kong is quite easy for an expat to come out, because you haven't got any pressure at all from anybody. But I think I just happened to be here at the time. I would have had to come out over there if I had found somebody.

When Nigel looks back, he thinks he was just half alive before he finally came out.

> In 1998, I met somebody. I . . . had a relationship at that point, forced myself to come out. And I came out in a splurge, in about three months' time, my family and friends in one go, which was quite dramatic at the time . . . My mother was surprised . . . My father wasn't surprised; I think he suspected.

He has a good relationship with his family now. He can talk to them openly.

> Now it's my mother that is happy talking about it. My father is not very happy talking about the whole thing. My mother would come up with amazing remarks, like, she and myself were just sitting there, 'Are you going to Brighton Pride next week?' . . . whereas my father wouldn't talk about it like that. He's okay around the subject . . . it's just not chatted about . . . My brother wasn't surprised. He's two years younger than me. There were two of us . . . but he was fine. He just married a girl who already has a family, and her daughter was a lesbian. So, the family has been good.

Nigel said he changed from being completely closeted to being totally out about it. 'At the end of that, I felt so released, so liberated that my life completely, utterly changed.' And coming out so late became one of his regrets in life. 'I missed so much. It was an empty life before. This gives me a great contrast, partly why I feel so liberated and happy, because I remember all the days when I didn't feel anything at all. That's my regret.'

But it was not courage that drove him to make that drastic change.

> I can't think I was brave about it, think of how long it took. So, when I talk to young guys about coming out or not coming out, I would never blame anybody for not coming out. And your circumstances are different, and I wouldn't push or force anybody out. I don't feel proud of how long it took me. I think that's partly why I think being able to have something to give back now is good. Because all of the people I was brought up with . . . many in some cases no longer with us . . . did it first in the West. I didn't do anything about it at all, I just benefited from it. So now, I'm doing something.

Paradise in Hong Kong

Nigel was 30 when he got posted to Asia in the army in 1982. Then he went to Africa. He came to Hong Kong in 1984 and stayed here until 1992. It was a time of enlightenment for him.

> [I] came here in 84, and [I] was with them until I retired in 94. And all of that 10 years I struggled with . . . really realizing I had to do something about myself, otherwise I would just . . . I was living in an empty space. Mentally, I was dead. Physically, emotionally I was dead. And eventually [I] forced myself to resign in 1994, in order to go and find myself . . . It was far too late for finding myself, but I was intent on doing it. So, I came out from the army in 94 early. And to my great sadness, because I loved the job. And I was, at that stage, coming back to the Far East.

He spent the next three years building a security business, placing Nepalese as security guards on cruise liners. After setting up first in Nepal, he came back to Hong Kong in 1995 to run it.

It took another three years for him to pluck up his courage to go to a gay bar. He eventually went to his first bar, Zip, in 1997 when he was 45 years old.

> [It] was like paradise, but I was so scared I ran in and out of the door three times and went home without talking to anybody . . . I went from the front entrance. I went straight to the bar then the garden. I went to the loo, I came out, I went to the front door. I came back in again. I did that three times that night. I didn't buy a drink. I didn't speak to anybody, and then I ran home.

Nigel forced himself to go back three times but he failed, because he was petrified.

> Internally, I was still scared of myself, scared of the whole thing, scared that people would find out. It's that scare that people would know . . . to understand that I was gay. I was so frightened of people knowing, of my parents knowing, of my army friends knowing. Even when I left the army behind, I was still frightened by all of that . . . When I think back, I was frightened of myself being open, being clear to myself. Because I'd been building this shell for all these years, I was scared of going out.

He eventually went back a fourth time and became happy with the bars to meet men and never went to saunas or parks.

> To me, I want to meet people, not just bodies. The bars always produce enough people for me. I didn't even need to go to saunas to have sex. I could always find someone in a bar. Even on Tuesday night, on the quiet side. So, I never needed to go to saunas . . . I never found myself beautiful to look at. To think about my sagging stomach standing in a sauna wasn't very attractive, whereas when you're leaning on a wall in Works or Propaganda, in the dark, no one would quite see.

A Relationship Started in a Bar

He met his partner, who is a Singaporean Chinese, in a bar in Singapore. They met at the end of 1999. The two of them worked in the same company for a while and have been together since then. They don't go out as often as they used to now.

He has met only one of his partner's siblings but not his mother, since she doesn't know any of it. However, his partner has seen his family.

> He's stayed with them. I took him to England in 2000 to meet them. They've taken him in. They all sit in a corner and talk about me now, so it's fine. And, they've been very nice about it all. They're very good to him, they like him very much. He's okay with them. Every time when we go back to England, which is once every one or two years, not staying with them, not staying together any longer, because they're a bit old. But [we] can see them. So, the relationship with my family is good. That works very well.

A Writer-turned-activist

Nigel started writing in 2000. As a published author, he eventually got involved in activism after he came back to Hong Kong in 2004.

> In 2005, I published a military biography . . . historical biography, as a result of my being in Buckingham, and I had nothing to do. I did a biography. So, I did go back to academia for a few years there. Did the M.A., published the biography that came out of my dissertation . . . And it was called *The Butcher of Amritsar*. It's about a massacre in India in 1919, a biography of the man who did it. And as a result of that, I became slightly known as a writer. In Hong Kong, it was not too difficult to become known as a writer, because there were not many writers around. So, I got involved in the literary festival and was moderating some of their sessions for three years. In the fourth year, I said, 'We don't have any gay stuff. Why don't we do some gay sessions?' And they were quite excited. They gave me an opportunity for two sessions on a Saturday afternoon at the Fringe Club, to talk about gay literature worldwide and about Hong Kong gay writing. So, I got as many people as we could identify as Hong Kong gay writers to gather in one room, about ten people. One woman and the rest were men. And we talked about gay stuff in Hong Kong. Decided it was quite interesting. We formed a literary group.

The Tongzhi Literary Group was formed after the session and Nigel started getting involved in activism from then on.

> I went on from 2008 till now, still going strong. And with me was Reggie Ho, who got me involved because of journalism. Reggie wanted to resurrect the Tongzhi Committee Joint Meeting. He wanted me to be the administrator, so he asked me to go with him. And I did, I became the English Secretary. I've been doing that ever since. So, my activism only began in 2008. And I've been doing that ever since. And it takes us to where we are now.

It has been a long time since he started exploring the gay circle and he loves it a lot.

> I've made so many friends in it. And before I started with Reggie on the activism thing, I did establish a lot of very close friends. We know a lot of couples, mixed couples usually, we've built a big number of friends through the scene. So, to me, it's a great way, not just in the earlier days when I was single, it was great when I just picked up boys obviously, but after that, the scene becomes a place to make friends, and to get to know people, to enjoy and meet them on a Friday night. The people you know already and have a drink with. I loved that and I still love that. When I go out to the bar, I still enjoy it.

Though the bar scene has not changed much through the years, Nigel thinks that the *tongzhi* community has changed enormously.

> The LGBT world, I think, has developed a lot. So, when I first started getting to know all about this, probably in the early years of the century . . . people were still scared to come out. It was hardly anybody who would talk publicly.

Faces were very rare when I first began to talk to people for my pieces on *Fridae.asia*; I've been writing for *Fridae* since about the same time. Most of the people I wrote about didn't want me to say they were gay. They would say they're a playwright, a playwright writing gay plays. A story about coming out in New York or something, but they wouldn't let me say they were gay.

However, people are more comfortable now with being out.

People are talking about gay things in a way, whereas I remember in the early days, no one was talking much about it. There was very little in the public domain. Now it's very common, it's debated, argued about, open. The feeling of shame has reduced . . . I'm not saying this is all marvellous yet . . . but [it] has changed to some degree, and for the better . . . There's a snowball effect in the public domain. People who are known in the public domain, celebrities, who are being open about themselves, and navigate themselves in light of the times, of changing things. That makes a lot of difference.

Home Is Where the Heart Is

Now in his sixties, Nigel has not thought about ageing seriously.

You slowly realize it's important to think about it. I don't think I have honestly thought about it properly. Internally, I don't feel differently than when I was 50. So, ten years have gone, and I don't feel different. I don't believe I behave very differently. I think . . . the only thing I've come to realize now already, is I'm going to slowly decline, inevitably physically, or eventually mentally, because I've seen my parents. I've seen their generation go. I watched it and I thought 'Oh, okay, it's going to happen to me'. And I think you've got to watch it first to see it, to understand it, to feel it a bit.

He is not scared of dying.

I'm scared of all the things that come, though, like strokes, heart disease, you know, on and on you go . . . I'm sure I will hit some form of a brick wall at some point in my future. And it could be when I'm 65, could be when I'm 70, and that would be the point where I suddenly realize I really am old, and I have to stop doing the things I do now. I haven't stopped anything yet.

Nigel is still running his security guard company in Hong Kong. At the same time, he also writes regularly.

My work offshore is steady, but not increasing, so I don't have the opportunity to do a great deal of additional work. I can keep it running at a reasonable level. I work in Hong Kong in security guarding, that probably takes me half a day . . . The remaining half of the day I write. I'm still writing books. I write on *Fridae*. It's that period I use for the activism. I'm lucky to have time in my hands. And the Hong Kong company can run itself without me getting involved every minute . . . So, I'm in a fortunate position to be able to do that, to enjoy myself as well as doing something useful. The writing takes up a lot of time because I discovered when I did the first book, I really love writing. I find . . . just like putting one word after another. I write anything really, I mean on *Fridae*, I write about anything, from football to drag queens.

As for retirement, he has thought about it but he has not made any plans yet.

> I can't see myself stopping working for maybe ten years, maybe longer. I will never stop doing something. I would probably stop doing what I'm doing with the guarding company and with the ships' manning, but not probably for a decade. After that I just want to write. I see that writing is the final resting place for old educated people, because you can write without needing anything, as long as you can research or do what you want to. I'm not a creative writer. I don't write novels or poetry. I never had that kind of flair, but non-fiction is what I write. So, I need to get sources of information, which means libraries, people. And as long as I can get to a library, I'll be able to write.

His long-term plan depends on his partner. He will go with him wherever he goes. 'If his career takes him somewhere else, I'll go too.' He is very happy with their relationship. They recently married. However, he has made Hong Kong his home and will probably stay here for the rest of his life. 'If he goes, I have to go too. But it is my home.'

Being Gay and Being Free

When asked about what gay means to him right now, Nigel said 'Everything. Almost all of my life is gay . . . in some form. The only part of my life that's not gay is the half a day's work I do at work. Every day, almost everything else, my reading, my writing, my activism, my social life is gay.'

The word 'gay' to him means 'freedom', and he believes his life would be very different if he were straight.

> That would be bloody boring . . . I would join the army. I would have a wife, have some kids. I would have . . . a Volvo, and would have a house . . . And I would have kept going to the same cocktail parties for the whole of my life, talking about the same boring things, holidays, kids in schools, and the university. I'm so pleased . . . People said, 'Are you happy being gay?' Now the answer is 'I'm glad I'm gay', because I have seen so much more of life than I would have ever dreamt of. I think straight people only see some of the world. We see much, much more . . . And we have so much more fun.

Being gay brings him joy.

> I think it's what create[s] life. Artistically, it's full of creativity. I know many more artistic friends than I would have ever dreamt of before. I love the literary side of it, and that always fascinated me. I read for pleasure now. Anything connected with gay. Not only fiction, everything. I really enjoy it. The people are usually much more interesting. And I love the way, although I now work, live as middle class, I have enough contacts through the activism world or whatever, many different kinds and classes of people and background. I love the diversity . . . To me, it's a great joy you can have vast difference, just people who want to have fun. They still think it's good to have fun. Actually, I feel sad for most heterosexual people. Fun does not fit in their

lives at all. Responsibility does. Pleasure, yes, from going out, seeing things at the theatre. But most people have a very ordinary life . . . most of us gay men don't.

Nigel is quite different from my other interviewees. I knew him before, not like others whom I met through this project. He uses his real name whilst others use pseudonyms. But like some of my other interviewees, it took a very long time for him to come out. For a gay man, living in the UK in the 1970s was not easier than living in Hong Kong. The ten years in the army seemed to be the closet of the closet! As he said, this is his regret, as he lived an empty life. That is why I was particularly amused by how he flipped the coin from being a totally closeted person to an out gay man. Nigel is now a public figure and is one of the most outspoken gay men in Hong Kong who is involved heavily with the **tongzhi** *movement. He has just published a book about the notorious suicide case of John MacLennan called* **A Death in Hong Kong** *(2018). We need more people like him. Although being gay often signifies oppression, subordination, pain, and guilt, it also signifies liberation, freedom, pleasure, and joy. I am happy that Nigel is now embracing the positive aspects of being gay. As Foucault (1996) reminds us, being gay is full of possibilities and creativity, as we have to invent, from A to Z, a new way of life!*

Nigel (left) at Human Day Rights Carnival 2009. Source: interviewee.

Conclusion

Transformation of an Academic Project into Participatory Action Research

This project began life in 2009 as an academic project to fill the gap in research on Chinese ageing and sexuality, using the oral history method. It led to various forms of community engagement with a self-help group that finally formed in late 2014, where participants could take control and feel empowered. I did not expect academic research to morph into participatory action research with unintended consequences. In this short conclusion, I will briefly discuss how this research has had three stages, witnessing changes in the level of participation by both the researcher and his subjects, as well as the social transformation of the participants and the production of knowledge on Chinese homosexuality.[1]

The first stage of the research comprised the collection of life stories of older gay men in Hong Kong using the oral history method. Oral history is a very powerful tool to give voice to individuals whose histories are often ignored by orthodox histories (Thompson 1978; Cockcroft 2005; Ames and Diepstra 2010). Through collecting oral testimonials and the 'documents of life' such as diaries, letters, and photographs of these men, I was able to recount their secretive pasts from birth to adulthood against the backdrop of various social, cultural, economic, and political transformations in colonial Hong Kong from the 1930s to the 1980s. We now know a bit more about how they realized same-sex desires; met others; compromised and got married or remained single; manoeuvred between marriage and same-sex romance; formed intimate same-sex relationships; created their own 'scenes', and formed their collective sexual memory through language, culture, fashion, and lifestyle. A queer voice from the past is slowly heard through their stories. Oral history also enabled me to discuss how they negotiate ageing and sexuality in their current lives—the loneliness of being old and gay, the coming out dilemma (not just to their wives or children or grandchildren, but also to their friends in social centres for the elderly), the longing for same-sex intimacy, getting sick and sensing the deterioration of their

---

1. Some of the material in this conclusion appeared in an earlier version in a different form as Kong (2017).

bodies mentally and physically, and the experience of ageism in the youth-oriented gay community.

Since most of them are still closeted, it was the first time that they have ever told their life story (including same-sex intimacy) to a stranger. This was in itself a coming out process. They spoke with laughter, joy, happiness, and pride, as well as tears, anger, remorse, shame, and guilt. These sexual stories (Plummer 1995) were personal and political, powerful and transformative, therapeutic and empowering, revealing narratives that challenged the hegemonic heteronormative script of Chinese masculinity in Hong Kong. It was as a result of these in-depth interviews that I decided to organize tea gatherings with the participants (and asked them to bring friends) as a way of community building in 2012. After *yum cha* at a local restaurant, we visited a volunteer's home for a focus group discussion and loosely focused on one of four themes: work, family, social services, and the gay community. I asked them to bring along objects with special meaning and to share the stories behind them. One man brought the ring his first love had given him; some brought letters from pen-pals and diaries; and several brought old photographs. These gatherings connected these neglected elderly people, and provided a space where they shared their long-buried experiences and opened up their hearts. We gradually formed a small community comprising about five core members and ten who joined us occasionally. I began to look forward to our gatherings and gradually developed a deeper relationship with the participants. It was through this that some 'suppressed' truths (e.g., HIV status) were slowly revealed once trust began to deepen between us.

The emerging small community that grew out of my oral history project clearly had an important story to tell, and together we decided to share it with society. I received a university knowledge exchange award in 2013, which allowed me to publish *Oral History of Older Gay Men in Hong Kong* in 2014. Each person's biography was inspiring. I was fascinated by their dramatic stories and touched by their honesty. I was saddened by their misfortunes and frustrated by their grievances. These are flesh and blood stories, full of laughter and tears. In the course of producing the book, I invited four local and international artists (Bobby K. H. Sham, Wong Kan-tai, Gyorgy Ali Palos, and Chan Ka-kei) to document the men's lives through photographs. Since most of the interviewees are still living in the closet, one of the greatest challenges for the artists was how to photograph these men without showing their faces. The other challenge was to seek ways to show these men's intimate relationships with their specific habitats. They came to our regular monthly gatherings and hung out with some of the participants. The result was four distinctive visual documentations of their lives (see pp. 95–100). The book talk and/or photo exhibition toured various locations in Hong Kong and received tremendously positive feedback from the local community, evidenced by extensive media exposure. I also extended this knowledge

Conclusion

exchange to Macau, Guangdong, and London, and triggered a similar project in Guangdong, China.

The second stage of the research was less about my immersion and participation in the participants' lives, and more about mutual exchange and collaboration between us. The publication of the book and photo exhibition was a collective and collaborative exercise. In contrast with my other academic work in which I hold the authority to represent interviewees' voices, in this project I invited them to participate in the writing process. I wrote the first draft of their life stories and then asked them to read, check, and validate. I am happy that they

Book Launch in Hong Kong. Source: Au Yeung Shing.

Photo exhibition in London. Source: Author.

Set up of Gay & Grey.
Source: K.

Hong Kong Pink Dot 2017.
Source: Pink Dot volunteer.

Hong Kong Pride Parade 2017. Source: Author.

referred to the book as 'our' book, which shows that they assumed ownership of what amounted to a collective project. Publishing the book could thus be seen as a second coming out, which resulted in some new experiences as reported by Shmily and May Wu.

In late 2014, the project has entered the third stage. Building on the momentum created by the book and photo exhibition, I encouraged the original oral history participants and other older gay men who had joined them after the various public events to formally register as a social group called Man Tung Hin (Gay & Grey). The Chinese name means '*tongzhi* in later life supporting each other hand in hand'. Using the concept of 'peer counselling', Gay & Grey is operated by older gay men and offers services and support to other older gay men in Hong Kong. The group has two main purposes. The first is to build a positive older gay community through activities (e.g., monthly teas, karaoke, film screenings, talks, seminars, yoga) and social services (e.g., a helpline to answer queries, delivery of condoms to gay saunas). The group has also established a WhatsApp group that is used for sharing information and sending greetings every day. The ultimate goal is to press for social services catering for elderly *tongzhi* in Hong Kong, such as residential home care or day centres and nursing homes. The second purpose is to raise awareness of the unspoken needs and problems of older gay men amongst both the *tongzhi* community and the general public. Gay & Grey co-organises activities with other *tongzhi* NGOs to enhance mutual understanding and provide public education through school talks, media interviews, and other forms of media exposure.

Participatory action research is an approach to research community that emphasises participation and transformation (Kemmis and McTaggart 2005; Reason and Bradburg 2008). Participation means the change in the participation level between the researcher and the researched, especially focusing on the power issue between the two. Transformation means the transformation of people, such as the researcher, participants, the community concerned, and society at large, and also the transformation of knowledge by producing new and local knowledge for both the academia and the community. Participatory action research thus constitutes an intervention that challenges the boundaries of participation, and thus creates conditions that foster empowerment and social transformation (Dworski-Riggs and Langhout 2010, 226).

From this three-stage process, first, there is a change of the level and scope of participation between researcher and researched. I was initially a researcher (carrying out oral history) and facilitator of a focus group, but then I became an author of the Chinese book, and now I am a friend of Gay & Grey. The participants were initially interviewees in my research project and then became 'co-authors' of the book and the main subjects of the photo exhibition, and now they are Gay & Grey spokespersons. Together, we have come to know one another across the lines of class, age, education, and religion, and have come to appreciate the differences amongst us. It was through this process that a redistribution of power between researcher and researched occurred.

Second, transformation has occurred among these men. It has been an empowering process for them. From the 'first' coming out (talking to me) to the 'second' coming out (publishing the book, participating in the photo exhibition, giving public talks, and being interviewed by the media), most never imagined that anyone would be interested in their lives. They have been living in the shadows for many years. Although many still cannot face the public, most can at least face themselves. Through Gay & Grey, they feel less isolated. They have also found a new social role in being old and gay and in caring for others with similar lived experiences. The group is still in its early stages. It has had difficulty recruiting members of different social and cultural backgrounds (English- and Mandarin-speaking older gay men) and other genders and sexualities (including lesbians and transsexuals). It had also had problems obtaining funding, promoting local networks of older *tongzhi*, and raising awareness amongst service providers and policymakers. Having said that, Gay & Grey exemplifies the idea of building a sexual community through an articulation of identity, development of values and skills, and emergence of a collective identity to challenge the existing order (Weeks 2000, 192).

Third, the transformation that has occurred has not been about the participants alone, but also about theory. The overall research process has produced a new understanding of Chinese homosexuality. Older gay men represent a distinctive generation in Hong Kong *tongzhi* history. They share most of the characteristics of the first generation of Hong Kong people as depicted by Lui (2007). Most experienced the hardships of life in post-war Hong Kong, including extreme poverty, poor living conditions, and unemployment, under the colonial government administration, the close-knit Chinese family network and religion (especially Protestantism and Catholicism). They struggled to live their lives and put their parents or their own family as their top priority. What marks them out amongst the first generation perhaps is their same-sex desire. But unlike the first queer generation in Western countries who were at the forefront of the lesbian and gay movements in the 1960s, they were highly discreet and did not participate in the debates over the decriminalization of homosexuality in the 1980s, and most still do not participate in visible and public *tongzhi* events (e.g., IDAHO, Pride Parade, Pink Dot). They were not keen to find out what was meant by 'homosexuality' or to search for their sexual identity, but were quite anxious to find a suitable social role of being a man (e.g., a hardworking labourer, a filial son, a dutiful husband, or a stern father) under the complex web of family networks. Whether they got married and postponed their search for same-sex desires, secretly sought gay romance, or remained in singlehood, they struggled and created their own selves under familial heteronormativity. The Western coming out model, usually confessional in nature and associated with a confrontational form of identity politics, is less relevant in the Chinese context, especially to the early generation. The real opposition is sometimes less between heterosexuality and homosexuality but more between willingness and refusal to play one's traditional family and gender role. Moreover, the stories collected include men from different social strata as well as British expatriates, thus facilitating an understanding of how class, ethnicity, and material resources affect the undercover lives these men have lived.

It is through these stories that we can have a new understanding of the notion of gayness, coming-out politics and the relationship among (homo)sexuality, space, the family, religion, and the (colonial) state in a non-Western context. This subjugated knowledge thus challenges the universal Western knowledge of homosexuality, which is based on the Western gay experience. I therefore engage with an agenda that not only calls for a need to build connections between empirical investigations in different parts of the world but also on concepts, theories, and methods produced by thinkers working from the colonialized and postcolonial South (Connell 2013). This translated English book is part of this process. By bringing the kaleidoscopic life of these older gay men in the history of Hong Kong to an English-speaking world, I hope to facilitate a critical dialogue that could offer a more nuanced understanding of Chinese homosexual identities, desires, and practices stemming from local experiences but also sensitive to global parameters under the geopolitics of the world system of sexual knowledge.

Glossary

97 Tongzhi Forum	九七同志論壇
A Queer Story	基佬40
Amphetamine	安非他命
Ann Hui	許鞍華
Anson Mak	麥海珊
Anthony Wong Yiu-ming	黃耀明
Big Love Alliance	大愛同盟
Bishônen	美少年之戀
Boat People	投奔怒海
Boy's?	假男假女
Carol 'Do Do' Cheng	鄭裕玲
certificate of good conduct	良民證
Chang Loo	張露
Choi Yuen-wan	蔡元雲
Chor Yuen	楚原
Chou Wah-shan	周華山
City without Baseball	無野之城
Civil Rights for Sexual Diversities	性權會
Cheung Lok	長樂
Denise Ho Wan-see (a.k.a. HOCC)	何韻詩
Derek Chiu	趙崇基
diuyu	釣魚
duanxiu (pinyin)	斷袖
Eddie Peng Yu-Yen	彭于晏
Edward Lam	林奕華
fadan	花旦
fayuen	花園
Family Value Foundation of Hong Kong Limited	維護家庭基金
For My Colours	還我本色
Freeman	逍遙派
Gay Harmony	大同

kei	基
keilo	基佬
gwailo/gweilo	鬼佬
Happy Together	春光乍洩
Hau Wing-Choi	侯永財
Ho Sik-ying	何式凝
Homowives	同妻
Hong Kong Alliance for Family	維護家庭聯盟
Hong Kong Lesbian and Gay Film Festival	香港同志影展
Hong Kong Pride Parade	香港同志遊行
Hong Kong Scholars Alliance for Gender and Sexual Diversity	學人。性。聯盟
Hong Kong Sex Culture Society	香港性文化學會
Hong Kong Ten Percent Club	香港十分一會
Hong Kong Tongzhi Conference	香港同志交流大會
Horizons	啓同服務社
IDAHO (Hong Kong Parade)	國際不再恐同日(香港區遊行)
Isvara	自在社
Jimmy Ngai	魏紹恩
Joint College Queer Union	同窗會
Julian Lee	李志超
Kam Yeh Pao	今夜報
laanzek	爛蓆
Leung Cho-yiu	梁祖堯
Lord Long Yang	龍陽君
Lui Tung Yuen	女同苑
mahjong	麻雀
Man Tung Hin (or Gay & Grey)	晚同牽
Michael Lam (a.k.a. Maike)	邁克
Midnight Blue	午夜藍
Ming Pao	明報
New Creation Association	新造的人協會
Nutong Xueshe	女同學社
Oh! My Three Guys	三個相愛的少年
Oral History of Older Gay Men in Hong Kong	男男正傳：香港年長男同志口述史
Overseas Chinese Daily News	華僑日報
pakpai	白牌
permanent residence	永久居留
Pink Alliance	粉紅同盟
Pink Dot Hong Kong	一點粉紅
pit	撇

Glossary

potong	蒲塘
Q action	大專同志行動
Queer Show	攣到爆
Queer Sisters	姊妹同志
Rainbow Action	彩虹行動
Rainbow of Hong Kong	香港彩虹
Raymond Chan Chi-chuen	陳志全
Samshasha	小明雄
Satsanga	同志健康促進會
Scud	雲翔
Shu Kei	舒琪
Sing Yeh Pao	星夜報
Sun Yat-sen	孫逸仙
szesuk	私塾
Tai Fan	大番
Tai Tat Tei	大笪地
tauto	偷渡
The Blessed Minority Christian Fellowship	基恩之家
The House of 72 Tenants	七十二家房客
The Society of Truth and Light	明光社
tongzhi (pinyin) or *tungzi*	同志
Tongzhi Community Joint Meeting	同志社區聯席會議
Tongzhi New Wave	同志後浪
Women's Coalition of HKSAR	香港女同盟會
Wong Chi-lung	黃智龍
Wong Kar-wai	王家衛
XX Gathering	XX小聚
Yau Ching	游靜
yatkayan	一家人
yaufayuen	遊花園
yi	二
Yip Chi-Wai	葉志偉
Yonfan	楊凡
yuetong	魚塘
Yuk Tak Chee	浴德池
yum cha	飲茶
yutao (pinyin)	餘桃

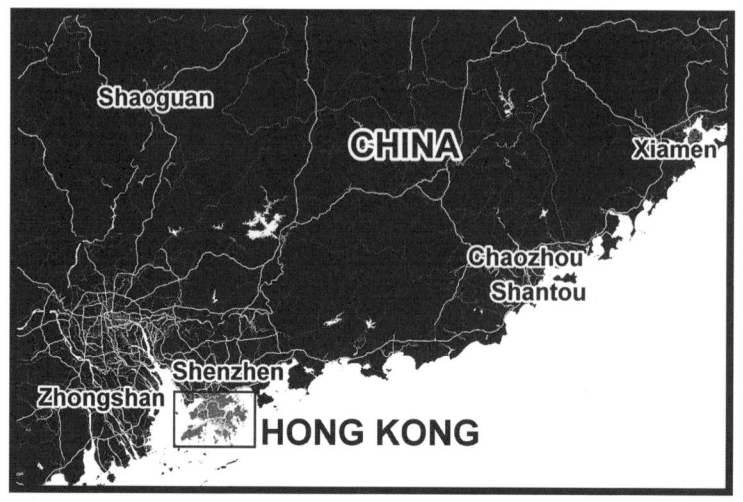

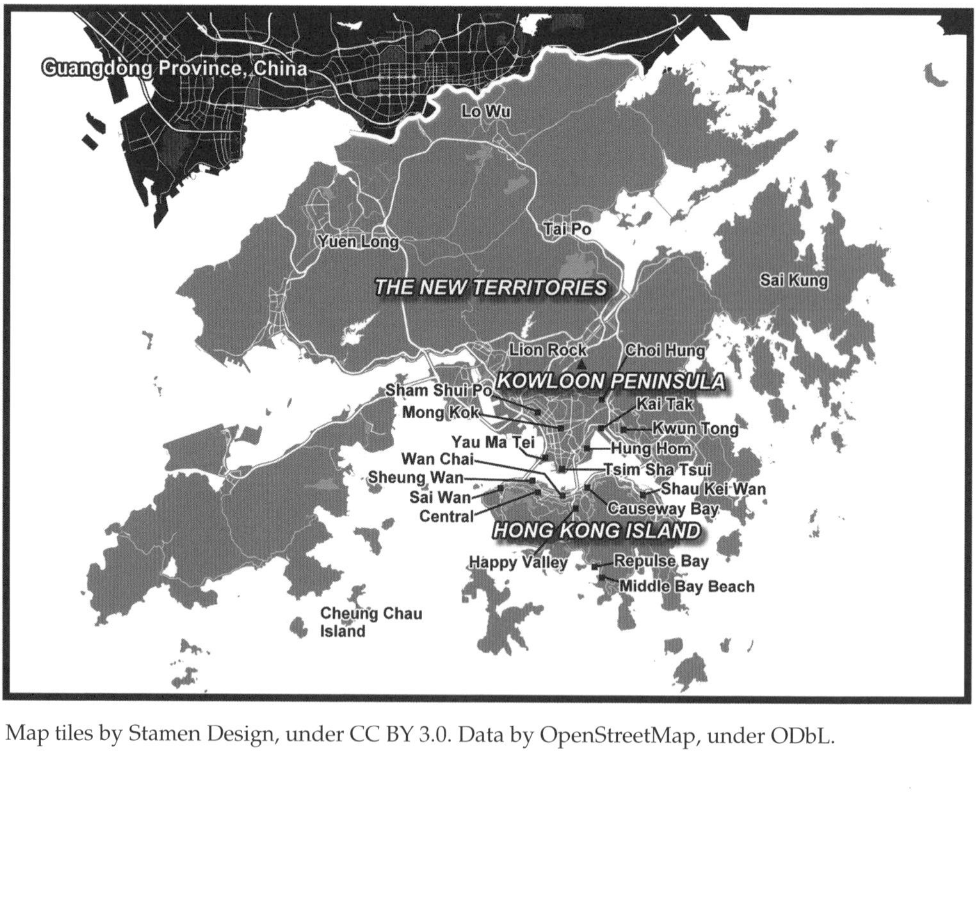

Map tiles by Stamen Design, under CC BY 3.0. Data by OpenStreetMap, under ODbL.

References

Adam, Barry D. 2006. 'Relationship Innovation in Male Couples.' *Sexualities* 9 (1): 5–26.

Altman, Dennis. 1997. 'Global Gaze/Global Gays.' *GLQ: A Journal of Lesbian and Gay Studies* 3 (4): 417–36.

Ames, Natalie, and Stephene Diepstra. 2010. 'Oral History Studies.' In *The Handbook of Social Work Research Methods*, edited by B. Thyer, 397–414. Thousand Oaks, CA: Sage.

Bao, Hongwei. 2018. *Queer Comrades: Gay Identity and Tongzhi Activism in Postsocialist China*. Copenhagen: NIAS Press.

Bell, David. 1995. 'Perverse Dynamics, Sexual Citizenship and the Transformation of Intimacy.' In *Mapping Desire: Geographies of Sexualities* edited by D. Bell and G. Valentine, 304–17. London: Routledge.

Bell, David, and Gill Valentine, eds. 1995. *Mapping Desire: Geographies of Sexualities*. London: Routledge.

Bell, David, and Jon Binnie. 1998. 'Theatres of Cruelty, Rivers of Desire: The Erotics of the Street.' In *Images of the Street: Planning, Identity and Control in Public Space*, edited by N. R. Fyfe, 129–40. London: Routledge.

Berger, Raymond M. 1982. 'The Unseen Minority: Older Gays and Lesbians.' *Social Work* 27 (3): 236–42.

Berlant, Lauren, and Michael Warner. 1998. 'Sex in Public.' *Critical Inquiry* 24 (2): 547–66.

Berry, Chris. 2001. 'Asian Values, Family Values: Film, Video, and Lesbian and Gay Identities.' *Journal of Homosexuality* 40 (3/4): 211–31.

Chan, Phil C. W. 2007. 'Same-Sex Marriage/Constitutionalism and Their Centrality to Equality Rights in Hong Kong: A Comparative-Socio-Legal Appraisal.' *The International Journal of Human Rights* 11 (1): 33–84.

Chauncey, George. 1994. *Gay New York: Gender, Urban Culture, and the Making of the Gay Male World, 1890–1940*. New York: Basic Books.

Cheng, Sheung-Tak, and Alfred C. M. Chan. 2006. 'Filial Piety and Psychological Well-Being in Well Older Chinese.' *The Journal of Gerontology* 61 (5): 262–69.

Chou, Wah-shan 周華山. 1996. *Beijing tongzhi gushi* 北京同志故事 [Stories of *tongzhi* in Beijing]. Hong Kong: Hong Kong Tongzhi Study Press. [Chinese]

Chou, Wah-shan 周華山, Anson Mak 麥海珊, and Kin-bong Kong 江建邦, eds. 1995. *Xianggang tongzhi zhanchulai* 香港同志站出來 [Coming out stories in Hong Kong *tongzhi*]. Hong Kong: Hong Kong Tongzhi Study Press. [Chinese]

Chou, Kee-Lee, Nelson W. S. Chow, and Iris Chi. 2004. 'Leisure and Participation amongst Hong Kong Chinese Older Adults.' *Ageing & Society* 24 (4): 617–29.

Chou, Wah-shan. 2000. *Tongzhi: Politics of Same-Sex Eroticism in Chinese Societies*. New York: Haworth Press.

Chung, Ting-yiu Robert, Ka-lai Karie Pang, and Wing-Yi Winnie Lee. 2012. 'Survey on Hong Kong Public's Attitudes towards Rights of People of Different Sexual Orientations.' Hong Kong: Public Opinion Programme, The University of Hong Kong. Retrieved 5 March 2018. http://hkupop.hku.hk/english/report/LGBT_CydHo/content/resources/report.pdf.

Cockcroff, Tom. 2005. 'Using Oral History to Investigate Police Culture.' *Qualitative Research* 5 (3): 365–84.

Connell, R. W. 1995. *Masculinities*. Cambridge: Polity Press.

Connell, Raewyn. 2013. Review of Saskia Weiringa and Horacio Sivori, ed., *The Sexual History of the Global South*. *Journal of Iberian and Latin American Research* 19 (2): 326–28.

Cronin, Ann, and Andrew King. 2010. 'Power, Inequality and Identification: Exploring Diversity and Intersectionality amongst Older LGB Adults.' *Sociology* 44 (5): 876–92.

Cruz, J. Michael. 2003. *Sociological Analysis of Aging: The Gay Male Perspective*. New York: Routledge.

Cuthbert, Alexander R. 1995. 'The Right to the City: Surveillance, Private Interest and the Public Domain in Hong Kong.' *Cities* 12 (5): 293–310.

de Certeau, Michel. 1984. *The Practice of Everyday Life*. Translated by S. Rendall. Berkeley: University of California Press.

Duggan, Lisa. 2002. 'The New Homonormativity: The Sexual Politics of Neoliberalism.' In *Materializing Democracy: Toward a Revitalized Cultural Politics*, edited by R. Castronovo and Dana D. Nelson, 175–94. Durham, NC: Duke University Press.

Dworski-Riggs, Deanne, and Regina Day Langhout. 2010. 'Elucidating the Power in Empowerment and the Participation in Participatory Action Research: A Story about Research Team and Elementary School Change.' *American Journal of Community Psychology* 45 (3–4): 215–30.

Eng, David L. 2001. *Racial Castration: Managing Masculinity in Asian America*. Durham, NC: Duke University Press.

Faure, David. 1997. *Society: A Documentary History of Hong Kong*. Hong Kong: Hong Kong University Press.

Foucault, Michel. 1986. 'Of Other Spaces.' *Diacritics* 16 (1): 22–27.

Foucault, Michel. 1996 [1989]. 'Friendship as a Way of Life.' In *Foucault Live (Interviews, 1961–1984)*, edited by S. Lotringer, translated by L. Hochroth and J. Johnston, 308–12. New York: Semiotext(e).

Fu, Xiaoxing 富曉星. 2012. *Kongjian • wenhua • biaoyan: Dongbei A shi nantongxinglian qunti de renleixue guancha* 空間•文化•表演：東北A市男同性戀群體的人類學觀察 [Space • culture • performance: Anthropological observations on male homosexual community in a city in Dongbei]. Beijing: Guangming ribao chubanshe. [Chinese]

Gorman-Murray, Andrew. 2007. 'Reconfiguring Domestic Values: Meanings of Home for Gay Men and Lesbians.' *Housing, Theory and Society* 24 (3): 229–46.

Heaphy, Brian. 2007. 'Sexualities, Gender and Ageing: Resources and Social Change.' *Current Sociology* 55 (2): 193–210.

Heaphy, Brian, Andrew K. T. Yip, and Debbie Thompson. 2004. 'Ageing in a Non-heterosexual Context.' *Ageing & Society* 24 (6): 881–902.

References

Hinsch, Bret. 1990. *Passions of the Cut Sleeve: The Male Homosexual Tradition in China*. Berkeley: University of California Press.

Ho, Denny Kwok Leung. 2004. 'Citizenship as a Form of Governance: A Historical Overview.' In *Remaking Citizenship in Hong Kong*, edited by A. S. Ku and N. Pun, 19–36. London: RoutledgeCurzon.

Ho, Petula Sik Ying. 1997. 'Politicizing Identity: Decriminalisation of Homosexuality and the Emergence of Gay Identity in Hong Kong.' Unpublished PhD thesis, University of Essex.

Ho, Petula Sik-Ying, and Adolf Kat-Tat Tsang. 2000. 'Negotiating Anal Intercourse in Interracial Gay Relationships in Hong Kong.' *Sexualities* 3 (3): 299–323.

Ho, Petula Sik-Ying, and Adolf Kat-Tat Tsang. 2004 [2000]. 'Beyond Being Gay: The Proliferation of Political Identities in Colonial Hong Kong.' In *Gendering Hong Kong*, edited by A. K. W. Chan and W. L. Wong, 667–89. Hong Kong: Oxford University Press.

Ho, Petula Sik-Ying, and Adolf Kat-Tat Tsang. 2007. 'Lost in Translation: Sex and Sexuality in Elite Discourse and Everyday Language.' *Sexualities* 10 (5): 623–44.

Hong Kong Government. 1947. *Annual Report on Hong Kong for the Year 1946*. Hong Kong: Hong Kong Government Printer.

Hong Kong Government. 1952. *Hong Kong Annual Report 1951*. Hong Kong: Hong Kong Government Printer.

Ingram, Gordon Brent, Anne-Marie Bouthillette, and Yolanda Retter, eds. 1997. *Queers in Space: Communities/Public Places/Sites of Resistance*. Washington, DC: Bay Press.

Jackson, Peter. A. 2000. '"That's What Rice Queen Study!" White Gay Desire and Representing Asian Homosexualities.' *Journal of Australian Studies* 65 (24): 181–88.

Jones, Julie, and Steve Pugh. 2005. 'Ageing Gay Men: Lessons from the Sociology of Embodiment.' *Men and Masculinities* 7 (3): 248–60.

Kam, Lucetta Yip-lo 金曄路, ed. 2001. *Yueliang de saodong—ta ta de chulian gushi: women de zishu* 月亮的騷動—她她的初戀故事：我們的自述 [Lunar desires: Her same-sex love, in her own words]. Hong Kong: Stepforward Multimedia. [Chinese]

Kemmis, Stephen, and Robin McTaggart. 2005. 'Participatory Action Research: Communicative Action and the Public Sphere'. In *The SAGE Handbook of Qualitative Research*, edited by D. K. Denzin and Y. S. Lincoln, 559–603. Thousand Oaks, CA: Sage.

Kong, Travis Shiu-Ki. 2000. 'The Voices In-Between: The Body Politics of Hong Kong Gay Men.' Unpublished PhD thesis, University of Essex.

Kong, Travis Shiu-Ki. 2002. 'The Seduction of the Golden Boy: The Body Politics of Hong Kong Gay Men.' *Body & Society* 8 (1): 29–48.

Kong, Travis Shiu-Ki. 2004. 'Queer at Your Own Risk: Marginality, Community and Hong Kong Gay Male Bodies.' *Sexualities* 7 (1): 5–30.

Kong, Travis Shiu-Ki. 2005. 'Queering Masculinity in Hong Kong Movies.' In *Masculinities and Hong Kong Cinema*, edited by in L. K. Pang and D. Wong, 57–80. Hong Kong: Hong Kong University Press.

Kong, Travis Shiu-Ki. 2009. 'Where Is My Brokeback Mountain?' *Social Transformations in Chinese Societies* 4: 135–59.

Kong, Travis Shiu-Ki. 2011. *The Chinese Male Homosexualities: Memba, Tongzhi and Golden Boy*. London: Routledge.

Kong, Travis Shiu-Ki. 2012. 'A Fading Tongzhi Heterotopia: Hong Kong Older Gay Men's Use of Spaces.' *Sexualities* 15 (8): 896–916.

Kong, Travis Shiu-Ki 江紹祺. 2014. *Nan nan zheng chuan: Xianggang nianzhang nan tongzhi koushushi* 男男正傳：香港年長男同志口述史 [Oral history of older gay men in Hong Kong]. Hong Kong: Stepforward Multimedia. [Chinese]

Kong, Travis Shiu-Ki, Sky Hoi-Leung Lau, and Eva Cheuk-Yin Li. 2015. 'The Fourth Wave? A Critical Reflection on the *Tongzhi* Movement in Hong Kong'. In *The Routledge Handbook of Sexuality Studies in East Asia*, edited by M. McLelland and V. Mackie, 188–201. London: Routledge.

Kong, Travis Shiu-Ki. 2017. 'Gay & Grey: Participatory Action Research in Hong Kong.' *Qualitative Research* 18 (3): 257–72.

Kong, Travis Shiu-Ki, Sky Hoi-Leung Lau, and Amory Ho-Wang Hui. 2019. 'Tongzhi.' In *Global Encyclopaedia of Lesbian, Gay, Bisexual, Transgender, and Queer (LGBTQ) History*, edited by Howard Chiang. Farmington Hills, MI: Charles Scribner's Sons.

Ku, Agnes S., and Ngai Pun, eds. 2004. *Remaking Citizenship in Hong Kong*. London: RoutledgeCurzon.

Lai, Franco. 2007. 'Lesbian Masculinities: Identity and Body Construction among Tomboys in Hong Kong.' In *Women's Sexualities and Masculinities in a Globalizing Asia*, edited by S. E. Wieringa, E. Blackwood, and A. Bhaiya, 159–79. New York: Palgrave Macmillan.

Lau, Siu Kai. 1982. *Society and Politics in Hong Kong*. Hong Kong: Chinese University Press.

Law, Wing Sang. 1998. 'Managerializing Colonialism.' In *Trajectories: Inter-Asia Cultural Studies*, edited by K. H. Chen, 109–21. London: Routledge.

Leong, Russell, ed. 1996. *Asian American Sexualities: Dimensions of the Gay and Lesbian Experience*. London: Routledge.

Lethbridge, Henry J. 1976. 'The Quare Fellow: Homosexuality and the Law in Hong Kong.' *Hong Kong Law Journal* 6 (3): 292–326.

Leung, Helen Hok-Sze. 2008. *Undercurrents: Queer Culture and Postcolonial Hong Kong*. Hong Kong: Hong Kong University Press.

Levine, Martin P. 1979. 'Gay Ghetto.' *Journal of Homosexuality* 4 (4): 363–77.

Lim, Eng-Beng. 2014. *Brown Boys and Rice Queens: Spellbinding Performance in the Asias*. New York: New York University Press.

Louie, Kam. 2002. *Theorising Chinese Masculinity: Society and Gender in China*. Cambridge: Cambridge University Press.

Louie, Kam. 2003. 'Chinese, Japanese and Global Masculine Identities.' In *Asian Masculinities: The Meaning and Practice of Manhood in China and Japan*, edited by K. Louie and M. Low, 1–15. London: Routledge.

Lui, Tai-Lok 呂大樂, Chun-Hung Ng 吳俊雄, and Kit-Wai Ma 馬傑偉, eds. 2006. *Xianggang, wenhua, yanjiu* 香港•文化•研究 [Hong Kong cultural studies]. Oxford: Oxford University Press. [Chinese]

Lui, Tai-Lok 呂大樂. 2007. *Si dai Xianggangren* 四代香港人 [Hong Kong's four generations]. Hong Kong: Stepforward Multimedia. [Chinese]

Maike 邁克. 2000. *Xingwen ben* 性文本 [Sex text]. Hong Kong: Oxford University Press. [Chinese]

Mak, Anson 麥海珊, and Pui-wai King 金佩瑋. 2000. *Shuangxing qingyu* 雙性情慾 [Bisexual desires]. Hong Kong: Hong Kong Women Christian Council. [Chinese]

Manalansan, Martin F. 2003. *Global Divas: Filipino Gay Men in the Diaspora*. Durham, NC: Duke University Press.

Mathews, Gordon, Eric Kit-Wai Ma, and Tai-Lok Lui. 2008. *Hong Kong, China: Learning to Belong to a Nation*. London: Routledge.

Miller, Neil. 1995. *Out of the Past: Gay and Lesbian History from 1869 to the Present*. New York: Vintage.

Nguyen, Tan Hoang. 2014. *A View from the Bottom: Asian American Masculinity and Sexual Representation*. Durham, NC: Duke University Press.

Ong, Aiwah. 1993. 'On the Edge of Empires: Flexible Citizenship among Chinese in Diaspora.' *positions: east asia culture critiques* 1 (3): 745–78.

Oswin, Natalie. 2008. 'Critical Geographies and the Uses of Sexuality: Deconstructing Queer Space.' *Progress in Human Geography* 32 (1): 89–103.

Parker, Richard. 1999. *Beneath the Equator: Cultures of Desire, Male Homosexuality, and Emerging Gay Communities in Brazil*. London: Routledge.

Phillips, David Rosser, Oi Ling Siu, Anthony G. O. Yeh, and Kevin H. C. Cheng. 2008. 'Informal Social Support and Older Persons' Psychological Well-Being in Hong Kong.' *Journal of Cross-Cultural Gerontology* 23 (1): 39–55.

Plummer, Ken. 1995. *Telling Sexual Stories: Power, Change and Social Worlds*. London: Routledge.

Plummer, Ken. 2010. 'Generational Sexualities, Subterranean Traditions, and the Hauntings of the Sexual World: Some Preliminary Remarks.' *Symbolic Interaction* 33 (2): 163–90.

Pun, Ngai, and Lai-Man Yee, eds. 2003. *Narrating Hong Kong Culture and Identity*. Hong Kong: Oxford University Press.

Reason, Peter, and Hilary Bradbury. 2008. *The SAGE Handbook of Action Research: Participative Inquiry and Practice*. Thousand Oaks, CA: Sage.

Richardson, Diane. 2000. 'Constructing Sexual Citizenship: Theorizing Sexual Rights.' *Critical Social Policy* 20 (1): 105–35.

Rooney, Nuala. 2003. *At Home with Density*. Hong Kong: Hong Kong University Press.

Ruan, Fang-fu, and Yung-mei Tsai. 1987. 'Male Homosexuality in the Traditional Chinese Literature.' *Journal of Homosexuality* 14 (3–4): 21–33.

Salaff, Janet. 1981. *Working Daughters of Hong Kong: Filial Piety or Power in the Family?* Cambridge: Cambridge University Press.

Samshasha 小明雄. 1997[1984]. *Zhongguo tongxingai shilu* 中國同性愛史錄 [History of homosexuality in China]. Hong Kong: Rosa Winkel Press. [Chinese]

Sedgwick, Eve Kosofsky. 1990. *Epistemology of the Closet*. Berkeley, CA: University of California Press.

So, Alvin Y. 2002. 'Conclusion: Crisis and Transformation in the Hong Kong SAR.' In *Crisis and Transformation in China's Hong Kong*, edited by M. K. Chan and A. Y. So, 363–84. Armonk, NY: M.E. Sharpe.

Somerville, Peter. 1992 'Homelessness and the Meaning of Home: Rooflessness or Rootlessness?' *International Journal of Urban and Regional Research* 16 (4): 529–39.

Song, Geng. 2004. *The Fragile Scholar: Power and Masculinity in Chinese Culture*. Hong Kong: Hong Kong University Press.

Suen, Yiu Tung. 2015. 'Lesbian, Gay, Bisexual and Transgender Ageing.' In *Routledge Handbook of Cultural Gerontology*, edited by J. Twigg and W. Martin, 226–33. New York: Routledge.

Suen, Yiu Tung, Wai-ching Angela Wong, Amy Barrow, Miu Yin Wong, Wing-Sze Mak, Po-King Choi, Ching-Man Lam, and Tak-Fai Lau. 2016. 'Study on Legislation against Discrimination on the Grounds of Sexual Orientation, Gender Identity and Intersex Status.' Hong Kong: Gender Research Centre, Hong Kong Institute of Asia-Pacific Studies, The Chinese University of Hong Kong. Retrieved 5 March 2018 http://www.eoc.org.hk/eoc/upload/ResearchReport/20161251750293418312.pdf.

Tam, Tak Chi 譚得志. 2015. *Yesu ye chugui* 耶穌也出櫃 [Jesus Chris is out too]. In *Ren • xing II Shui bu shi ku'er? Bentu ku'er shenxue chutan* 人．性 II 誰不是酷兒？本土酷兒神學初探 [Sexual/beings II: Who is not queer? The exploration on Hong Kong queer theology], edited by R. Wu 胡露茜 and Ming Yi Mak 麥明儀, 43–56. Hong Kong: Hong Kong Christian Institute and Queer Theology Academy. [Chinese]

Tang, Denise Tse-Shang. 2011. *Conditional Spaces: Hong Kong Lesbian Desires and Everyday Life*. Hong Kong: Hong Kong University Press.

Tang, Denise Tse-Shang. 2017. 'All I Get Is an Emoji: Dating on Lesbian Mobile Phone App Butterfly.' *Media, Culture & Society* 39 (6): 816–32.

Thompson, Paul Richard. 1978. *The Voice of the Past*. Oxford: Oxford University Press.

Too, Wing-Tak. 2007. 'A Study of Private/Public Space in Hong Kong.' Unpublished PhD thesis, The University of Hong Kong.

Valentine, Gill. 2000. 'Queer Bodies and the Production of Space.' In *Handbook of Lesbian and Gay Studies*, edited by D. Richardson and S. Seidman, 145–60. London: Sage.

Van Gulik, Robert H. 1961. *Sexual Life in Ancient China: A Preliminary Survey of Chinese Sex and Society from ca. 1500 B.C. till 1644 A.D*. Leiden: E.J. Brill.

Warner, Michael, ed. 1993. *Fear of a Queer Planet: Queer Politics and Social Theory*. Minneapolis, MN: University of Minnesota Press.

Weeks, Jeffrey. 2000. *Making Sexual History*. Cambridge: Polity.

Wei, Wei 魏偉, and Siqing Cai 蔡思慶. 2012. *Tansuo xin de guanxi he shenghuo moshi: Guanyu Chengdu nan tongxinglian banlü guanxi he shenghuo shijian de yanjiu* 探索新的關係和生活模式：關於成都男同性戀伴侶關係和生活實踐的研究 [Exploring a new relationship model and life style: A study of the partnership and family practice among gay couples in Chengdu]. *Chinese Journal of Sociology* 6 (32): 57–85. [Chinese]

Whittle, Stephen. 1994. 'Consuming Differences: The Collaboration of the Gay Body with the Cultural State.' In *The Margins of the City: Gay Men's Urban Lives*, edited by S. Whittle, 27–41. Aldershot: Ashgate.

Wong, Day. 2004. '(Post-)identity Politics and Anti-normalization: (Homo)sexual Rights Movement.' In *Remaking Citizenship in Hong Kong*, edited by A. S. Ku and P. Ngai, 195–214. London: Routledge.

Wong, Day. 2007. 'Rethinking the Coming Home Alternative: Hybridization and Coming Out Politics in Hong Kong's Anti-homophobia Parades.' *Inter-Asia Cultural Studies* 8 (4): 600–616.

Wong, Wai-Ching Angela. 2013. 'The Politics of Sexual Morality and Evangelical Activism in Hong Kong.' *Inter-Asia Cultural Studies* 14 (3): 340–60.

Woodhead, David. 1995. '"Surveillant Gays": HIV, Space and the Constitution of Identities.' In *Mapping Desire: Geographies of Sexualities*, edited by D. Bell and G. Valentine, 231–44. London: Routledge.

Yau, Ching 游靜. 2005. *Xingbie guangying: Xianggang dianying zhong de xing yu xingbie wenhua yanjiu* 性／別光影：香港電影中的性與性別文化研究 [Sexing shadows: Genders and sexualities in Hong Kong cinema]. Hong Kong: Hong Kong Film Critics Society. [Chinese]

Yau, Ching 游靜, ed. 2006. *Xing zhengzhi* 性政治 [Sexual politics]. Hong Kong: Cosmosbooks. [Chinese]

Yau, Ching, ed. 2010. *As Normal as Possible: Negotiating Sexuality and Gender in Mainland China and Hong Kong*. Hong Kong: Hong Kong University Press.

Yeung, Gladys T. Y., and Helene H. Fung. 2007. 'Social Support and Life Satisfaction among Hong Kong Chinese Older Adults: Family First?' *European Journal of Ageing* 4 (4): 219–27.

Yip, Chi-wai 葉志偉. 2003. *Turan dushen* 突然獨身 [Suddenly single]. Hong Kong: Friendmily Business. [Chinese]

Yip, Chi-wai 葉志偉. 2004. *Buneng* 不能 [Almost perfect]. Hong Kong: Kubrick. [Chinese]

Yip, Paul S. F., Iris Chi, Helen Chiu, Chi Wai Kwan, Yeates Conwell, and Eric Cane. 2003. 'A Prevalence Study of Suicide Ideation among Older Adults in Hong Kong SAR.' *International Journal of Geriatric Psychiatry* 18 (11): 1056–62.

Please go to the following link or scan the QR code to complete a short questionnaire to express your opinions about the book. Your comments are highly appreciated. Thank you very much!

https://sociology.hku.hk/travisk.html